R+G.

OFTEN SPLIT SPEECH
AS IF ONE CHARACTER.
TWEEDLEDUM, DEEDLEDEE.
DIFFICULT TO SEPERATE 79
HUMOUROUS.
ADDS VARIETY
CAUGHT UP TO ACTION TO
    BIG FOR THEM.
LACK RUTHLESSNESS. .
EITHER GREEDY / STUPID,
H WARNS THEM AT . 2:2 .
NO CONTROL OVER FATES.
LINK TO OPHELIA → ALLOW THEMSELVES
                TO BE USED BY KING.

3:3 WARN OF FATE .
    NOT ABLE TO REALISE IT.

EXECUTION CAUSES NO GREAT
   SADDNESS.

H E I N E M A N N

S H A K E S P E A R E

Hamlet

edited by Elizabeth Seely and Ken Elliott

with additional notes and activities by
Rick Lee

Series Editor: John Seely

Heinemann Educational Publishers
Halley Court, Jordan Hill, Oxford OX2 8EJ
a division of Reed Educational & Professional Publishing Ltd
MELBOURNE   AUCKLAND
FLORENCE   PRAGUE   MADRID   ATHENS
SINGAPORE   TOKYO   SAO PAULO
PORTSMOUTH NH   MEXICO CITY
IBADAN   GABORONE   JOHANNESBURG
KAMPALA   NAIROBI

Printed in the *Heinemann Advanced Shakespeare* series 1996

2000 99 98 97
10 9 8 7 6 5 4 3 2

A catalogue record for this book is available from the British Library on
request.
ISBN 0 435 19300 7

Cover design Miller Craig and Cocking
Cover photograph from Donald Cooper

Page make-up by Sharon Rudd

Produced by Celia Floyd, Basingstoke

Printed by Clays Ltd, St Ives plc

CONTENTS

How to use this book

This edition of *Hamlet* has been prepared to provide you with several different kinds of information and guidance.

The introduction

Before the text of the play there is:
- a summary of the plot
- an explanation of how *Hamlet* fits in to the literary theme of revenge which was so popular in Shakespeare's day
- a brief explanation of Shakespeare's texts.

The text and commentary

On each right-hand page you will find the text of the play. On the facing left-hand pages there are three types of support material:
- a summary of the action
- detailed explanations of difficult words, phrases and longer sections of text
- suggestions of points you might find it useful to think about as you read the play.

End-of-act activities

After each act there is a set of activities. These can be tackled as you read the play. Many students, however, may want to leave these until they undertake a second reading. They consist of the following.

Keeping track: straightforward questions directing your attention to the action of the act.

Drama: practical drama activities to help you focus on key characters, relationships and situations.

The key elements: a short section listing important elements in the act.

Key scene: a focus on an important scene in the act. This is intended to help you combine an understanding of the characters and broader themes of the play with the ability to comment on the text in detail.

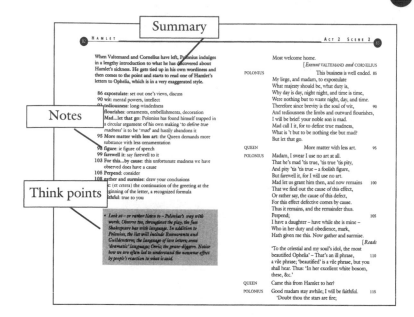

Close study: work on the text of selected extracts from the play, designed to help you tackle Shakespeare's language in detail.

Writing: progressive activities throughout the book help you to develop essay writing skills.

Explorations

At the end of the book there are a variety of different items designed to draw together your thoughts and insights about the play as a whole:

- how to approach thinking about the whole play
- work on character
- work on the themes and issues
- guidance on how to tackle practical drama activities
- advice on preparing for an examination
- advice on essay writing, together with a sample essay written by an A-level student, with comments
- practice essay questions
- glossary of technical terms.

Imagery.

DISEASE, CORRUPTION, DEATH → (47)
ANIMAL → Pg 51/115 MADNESS →
APPEARACE & REALITY → 55
NATURE → 23.
DUAL NATURE OF MAN (139.)
DEGENERATION.
PROSTITUTION (171)
SUPERNATURAL (165)

The plot

Act 1

On the battlements of Elsinore castle at midnight the relief guard, consisting of **Barnardo** and **Marcellus**, takes over from **Francisco**. **Horatio** is to join them. The atmosphere of dark and cold and the midnight hour is deepened by mention of a **Ghost** which has now appeared for two nights in succession. It looks like the late **King Hamlet**, father of **Hamlet, Prince of Denmark**. Horatio, the young Hamlet's fellow-student and friend, whom the sentries have told about the Ghost, has come to see whether it will appear again.

The Ghost, armed from head to foot, does appear and Horatio, visibly shaken, claims that this apparition means there is some threat to the State of Denmark. Although only recently returned from university in Germany, he seems to be very well-informed about the reasons for the preparations for war they have all observed. The Ghost appears again but, although challenged, it will not speak. They decide to tell Prince Hamlet what has happened.

The new king, **Claudius**, brother of the late King Hamlet, has married **Gertrude**, the dead man's widow. To the whole court he explains that **Fortinbras, Prince of Norway** is laying claim to land that his father, **old Fortinbras**, once forfeited to King Hamlet. Claudius is sending ambassadors to try to deal with the matter before it comes to war.

Claudius then grants permission to **Laertes** to leave the court and return to France. Laertes is the son of **Polonius**, counsellor to the king. Hamlet is then reproached by Claudius, his uncle, and by Gertrude, his mother, for what seems to them an excessive period of mourning for his father. Hamlet protests that his grief is very real, agrees not to return to university at Wittenberg and, when he is left alone, gives expression to his depression and his misery.

Horatio tells Hamlet about the appearance of what seems to be his father's ghost and it is decided that Hamlet too will keep watch that night.

Laertes, about to leave for France, says goodbye to his sister **Ophelia**. Their talk has clearly turned on the subject of Hamlet's affection for her. Laertes warns her to keep him at arm's length, as Hamlet will not be allowed a free choice in love because he is still a potential heir to the throne. Polonius, their father, loads Laertes with advice on the way he should behave. Once Laertes has left, Ophelia becomes the object of Polonius's recommendations. He warns her not to believe Hamlet's protestations of love and not to talk to him.

When the Ghost next appears, Hamlet speaks to it as though it is his dead father. Against his friends' advice he follows when it beckons: the Ghost tells him that he is his father's spirit, at present suffering the torments of purgatory. He was murdered, he claims, by Claudius and is grieved that Gertrude, his widow, so swiftly gave her affections to his murderer. The Ghost knows that his son will seek to avenge his murder, but tells him to leave Gertrude to the torments of her conscience, and above all to remember him. This Hamlet swears to do. He also swears his friends to secrecy.

Act 2

Polonius sends an acquaintance to spy on his son Laertes in Paris and to report back to him. Ophelia has been carrying out her father's instructions to ignore Hamlet and in some distress tells Polonius of Hamlet's apparently crazed behaviour in her presence. The King and Queen have become increasingly concerned at the changes in Hamlet and call upon old school friends of his, **Rosencrantz** and **Guildenstern**, to try to find out the cause of his strange moods.

The ambassadors sent to Norway return with news of the success of their mission – young Fortinbras is to be prevented by his uncle from raising an army to fight with Denmark. Polonius tells Claudius and Gertrude that he has discovered the reason for Hamlet's madness – he is in love with Ophelia. Hamlet is pointedly rude to Polonius and demonstrates his 'craziness' to him and to Rosencrantz and Guildenstern, deliberately misleading all three. When Hamlet learns that a troupe of actors is about to arrive, he has the idea of trying to prove to himself that Claudius is guilty of the Ghost's accusations. He will ask the players to act out a similar story to the alleged murder of his father by his uncle.

Act 3

Rosencrantz and Guildenstern report back to Claudius and Gertrude. Ophelia is set to walk, reading her prayer book, where Hamlet may meet her, while Claudius and Polonius listen to their conversation. Hamlet contemplates suicide, but is concerned that there may be something worse after death. This hesitation causes indecision, he claims. Ophelia speaks of returning Hamlet's gifts and he maintains he has never loved her. He rejects her quite brutally and tells her to go to a convent where she will not be tempted to give birth to another generation. Ophelia mourns his descent into madness.

Claudius, increasingly alarmed by what he has heard, decides to bring forward the journey to England he has apparently already planned for Hamlet in the care of Rosencrantz and Guildenstern.

Hamlet takes Horatio into his confidence over his plan to trap Claudius into showing his guilt as he watches the murder played out on the stage. The mime which precedes the spoken play shows the affectionate king and queen parting in the garden. When the king is asleep, a man approaches him, shows that he covets the crown and pours poison in the king's ears. Although the queen is distressed at the king's death she soon responds to gifts from the poisoner and accepts his love. Claudius reacts when the spoken play is under way. He rises hastily and leaves. Hamlet and Horatio agree about the guilty reaction they have observed. Gertrude sends for Hamlet by Rosencrantz and Guildenstern. Hamlet shows them that he is suspicious of them. He reminds himself that he must keep himself in check when he talks to his mother.

Claudius has become aware of the danger he runs while Hamlet is at court and speeds up the arrangements for him to go under Rosencrantz and Guildenstern's guard to England. On his way to his mother's room – where, by arrangement with Claudius, Polonius has already hidden to hear what mother and son will say – Hamlet comes across Claudius, apparently at prayer. He is full of remorse for the murder he committed, but is unable to repent or pray properly because he will not give up what his crime has secured for him. Hamlet, assuming that Claudius is confessing his sins to God and receiving forgiveness, will not kill him.

Hamlet speaks aggressively to the Queen, frightening her. She calls for help and Polonius answers. Hamlet draws his sword and kills whoever is hiding behing the arras, possibly thinking it is Claudius. Hamlet goes on to contrast his father with Claudius until Gertrude sees what she has done and begs him to stop. The Ghost enters again, unseen by Gertrude who sees her son apparently talking to the empty air, confirming his madness. He is being rebuked by the Ghost for not turning his energies to vengeance. Hamlet assures her he is not mad and begs her not to tell Claudius this, and to stop sleeping with Claudius.

Act 4

Gertrude reports the death of Polonius to Claudius. He arranges to have the body taken to the chapel and to speed up Hamlet's departure for England. Rosencrantz and Guildenstern have letters to the King of England instructing him to arrange for Hamlet's death. Before Hamlet leaves, he meets some of Fortinbras's troops who are crossing Denmark on their way to fight in Poland. The sight of his resolution makes Hamlet again reproach himself for his own lack of action in avenging his father. Ophelia, deeply distressed by Hamlet's rejection of her, now has to face the fact that he has killed her father. She has been driven mad with grief. Laertes, already angered and hurt by his father's murder and unceremonious burial, is now forced to face his sister's madness.

Horatio learns from a letter, delivered to him by a sailor, that when the ship in which he was travelling with his gaolers was attacked by pirates, Hamlet did a deal with his captors and escaped on the pirate ship, which is shortly to return to Denmark. When Claudius learns this, he plots with Laertes to rid themselves of Hamlet for good. They plan a fencing match between Laertes and Hamlet where Laertes's blade will be sharp, not blunted as for an exhibition bout, and will also have been smeared with a poison to which there is no antidote. In addition, Claudius will poison a goblet of wine to be offered to Hamlet as refreshment. No sooner has all this been agreed, than Gertrude brings news of Ophelia's death by drowning.

Act 5

While two grave-diggers prepare Ophelia's grave, Horatio and Hamlet look on. Before Hamlet realizes whose funeral is about to take place he is made to consider the reality of death and the fact that human flesh and blood return to earth. The funeral procession arrives and Laertes and Hamlet fight over the grave, competing in their love for the dead girl. Horatio is given charge of Hamlet and then learns that while at sea Hamlet discovered Claudius's death plot against him and managed to substitute a letter instructing the English king to execute Rosencrantz and Guildenstern.

Bets are laid on the planned fight between Hamlet and Laertes. Hamlet scores the first two hits and, before Claudius can stop her, Gertrude celebrates with a drink from the poisoned goblet. As Laertes wounds Hamlet with the poisoned foil, they exchange rapiers in the scuffle and Laertes is wounded with his own foil. As Gertrude dies she tells Hamlet that it is the drink which has poisoned her and Hamlet orders the door to be locked, crying 'treachery'. Laertes falls, admitting to Hamlet that the blade which has wounded them both was poisoned, and that there is no hope for either of them. He puts the blame on Claudius. Hamlet wounds the king with the poisoned rapier and then forces him to drink from the poisoned cup. He dies. Laertes and Hamlet forgive each other. Hamlet dissuades Horatio from committing suicide, placing on him the duty of explaining all the recent events, so that Hamlet will not appear to be an unprincipled murderer and traitor.

The sound of Fortinbras's army returning from Poland is heard in time for Hamlet to give him his dying vote as future King. Fortinbras, promising to listen to Horatio's account, has the bodies removed and Hamlet's corpse raised up. Hamlet shall have the funeral rites due to a soldier and a prince.

Hamlet and the tradition of revenge

Revenge tragedy was already popular with Elizabethan and Jacobean audiences, so Shakespeare was working within an established dramatic genre which had its own conventions.

Elizabethan writers plundered the work of the Roman dramatist, Seneca, and the revenge tragedy often featured sex, violence, bloody carnage and intrigue. It is certainly not difficult for us to understand the appeal of such drama. It is exciting, even sensational, and it employs ghosts and bloodthirsty revengers whose pursuit of private revenge in the name of family honour often ends in a bloodbath. Plays such as Kyd's *Spanish Tragedy* or even Shakespeare's *Titus Andronicus* do not shrink from the horrors of human savagery and the fashion continued well into the seventeenth century with the plays of Webster, Tourneur and Middleton. You might find it interesting to look at plays such as *The Duchess of Malfi* or *The Changeling*.

In *Hamlet*, Shakespeare follows the convention of using a ghost to incite revenge. He sets his play in a courtly context and his central character is a melancholy young man who embarks on a quest for bloody revenge in the name of duty and family honour. The conclusion of the play is violent and exciting and the bodies pile up in the conventional manner. However, what is most interesting is what Shakespeare does with a form of drama which, in the hands of others, is often crude, confusing and melodramatic. The conventional revenger focuses, at whatever cost to himself or others, on the pursuit of 'blood for blood' and his problems, if indeed he has any, are mostly to do with means and opportunity as he schemes his way towards violent retribution.

Shakespeare's *Hamlet* is radically different and much more complex. The play is more ambitious than most revenge tragedies in its exploration of revenge as a process and its recognition that such behaviour is neither normal nor easy, particularly for a human being who is capable of 'thought' and 'conscience'. For most of the play, *Hamlet* grapples with complicated issues which are not necessarily resolved by the simple certainties of 'blood for blood'. Although *Hamlet* has been famously described as 'an artistic failure' and it is probably true that its most fervent admirer would have to admit that it is a sprawling play with numerous loose ends, the play has a depth and scope which make it richer and more challenging than most revenge tragedies.

However, much of the impact of the play comes from the fact that the impulse to revenge oneself, and the emotional, moral and practical difficulties which surround that impulse, are only too familiar to any audience. It is interesting to consider how the play forces us to examine our own attitudes to revenge. Both legally and morally, revenge is regarded as dubious, and yet almost every audience, or group of students, wants Hamlet to respond to murder by becoming a murderer. Few people have any difficulty in identifying with Hamlet's surge of violent passion when he learns the 'truth' about his father's death, but it seems that the play is constantly asking us to reflect on the ethics of revenge. It is possible to argue that the form of revenge tragedy was not the ideal vehicle for all of Shakespeare's concerns in this play, but there is no doubt about the appeal and fascination it continues to hold. In the end, 'the play's the thing'.

LAERTES.
TAKES PLACE OF OPHELIA + POLONIUS.
CONTRAST WITH HAMLET.
THEIR FIRST APPEARANCE.
DESCRIBED BY HORATIO "UNIMPROVED -- FULL"
LACKS PRINCES EDUCATION.
COMPARES HIMSELF "LIKE RENDERING PELICAN"
PELICANS WERE CREDITED WITH GIVING OWN BLOOD TO
    NOURISH YOUNG.
MORE CONCERNED WITH APPEARANCE.
DESCRIPTION OF FATHER 'NOBLE' UNDERLINES THIS.
UPSET BY FATHERS "OBSCURE FUNERAL" NOT DEATH.
4:7 C. HATTERS L. IN ORDER FOR HIM TO BECOME PART
    OF PLAN.
GRAVEYARD SC → H. SIMPLICITY "I LOVED OPHELIA"
CONTRASTED HER BROTHERS MELODRAMATIC
LANGUAGE (5:1)
AGAIN, FUNERAL NOT DEATH.
INSTRUMENT OF C. TREACHERY.
"THE KING IS TO BLAME" ENERGISES H. VENGANCE.

The text of Shakespeare's plays

Shakespeare's work is generally treated with such immense respect that it may seem strange to admit that we cannot be certain exactly what he wrote. The reasons for this mystery lie in the circumstances of the theatre and publishing in the sixteenth and seventeenth centuries.

Shakespeare was a professional actor and shareholder in a company of actors, the Lord Chamberlain's Men, for whom he wrote his plays. Since copyright and performing rights did not exist before the eighteenth century there was the risk that, if a play was successful, other companies would perform it and reap the financial rewards. To avoid this, acting companies guarded the handwritten copy of a completed work. It was their most valuable resource and was kept by the prompter: each actor was given only his own lines and cues. None of these manuscripts survives to the present day. The lack of printed texts may seem strange but, like the work of other playwrights of his time, Shakespeare's plays existed essentially as oral, not written, texts. His concern was with what they looked and sounded like on stage.

However, there was money to be made from printed plays and during his lifetime nearly half of Shakespeare's plays were printed in what are known as quartos: paperback editions of single plays. Some of these, called 'bad' quartos, are pirated editions based on the memories of actors and audience. Others are much more accurate and may have been authorised by Shakespeare or the shareholders in his company, perhaps to capitalize on a popular success which was about to go out of repertory or to forestall a pirate edition. None, however, seems to have been supervised by the playwright and all differ, often considerably, from the key text of Shakespeare's plays, the *First Folio*.

The *First Folio*, published in 1623, is a collected edition of all Shakespeare's plays (with the exception of *Pericles*). It was edited by John Hemming and Henry Condell, two shareholders in the Lord Chamberlain's Men, using 'good' quartos, prompt copies and other company papers to provide an accurate text as a fitting memorial to their partner. They did not start the editing process until after Shakespeare died and apparently based their editorial decisions on what had happened in the theatre. We cannot be certain how far they represent what Shakespeare's ultimate intentions might have been. Even if Shakespeare had approved the text which went to the printer, it was the custom of writers to leave much of the detail of spelling and punctuation to the printer or to a scribe who made a fair copy from the playwright's rough drafts. The scribe and the printer thus introduced their own interpretations and inaccuracies into the text. The *First Folio* was reprinted three times in the seventeenth century and each edition corrected some inaccuracies and introduced new errors. A modern editor tries to provide a text which is easy to read and close to Shakespeare's presumed intentions. To do this the editor may modernize spelling and change punctuation, add stage directions and scene divisions, and make important decisions about which of several readings in quarto and folio editions is most acceptable. If you are able to compare this edition of the play with other editions, you are likely to find many minor variations between them as well as occasional major differences which could change your view of a character or situation.

The text of *Hamlet*

The earliest published text of Shakespeare's *Hamlet*, as opposed to versions of the story which appeared in the late 1580s, is dated 1603. We cannot be certain when Shakespeare wrote this play but it seems highly unlikely that it was any earlier than the beginning of the seventeenth century. This is also suggested by the internal evidence of references to *Julius Caesar*, which was being performed in 1599. Only two copies have survived of this first 'quarto' (Q1) and most critics regard it as an unreliable and unauthorized version of the play.

The second version of the play is another quarto (Q2) which is dated either 1604 or 1605. This publication is widely accepted as being based on Shakespeare's own manuscript.

The third version is to be found in the first folio (F) which was published in 1623 after Shakespeare's death. This version omits passages which were in the second quarto but it contains new passages and some 'variant' readings. For example, Hamlet's first soliloquy in Act 1 scene 2 includes the best known of these variant readings as the first folio gives us *'solid flesh'* while the quartos give us *'sallied flesh'*.

What all this means is that we have no definitive version of the play: no original manuscript has survived.

Soliloquy

1:2 → 129 (26)   3:1 → 56 (122)
1:2 → 253   3:2 → 386 (158-161)
1:5 → 92 (55)   3:3 → 73 (168)
2:2 → 553 (111)

Cinvoius → 3:3 36

HAMLET,
PRINCE OF DENMARK

CHARACTERS

HAMLET, Prince of Denmark, son of the dead King Hamlet
CLAUDIUS, King of Denmark, Hamlet's uncle
GERTRUDE, Queen of Denmark, formerly wife of King Hamlet,
  mother of Hamlet
GHOST of King Hamlet
POLONIUS, chief councillor to Claudius
LAERTES, son of Polonius
OPHELIA, daughter of Polonius
REYNALDO, servant of Polonius
HORATIO, friend and fellow-student of Hamlet
MARCELLUS ⎫
BARNARDO ⎬ officers of the watch
FRANCISCO ⎭
VALTEMAND ⎫ ambassadors to Norway
CORNELIUS ⎭
ROSENCRANTZ ⎫ former schoolfellows of Hamlet
GUILDENSTERN ⎭
OSRIC ⎫ courtiers
GENTLEMAN ⎭
FORTINBRAS, Prince of Norway
CAPTAIN in the Norwegian army
PLAYERS
First CLOWN, the sexton and gravedigger
Second CLOWN, his mate
PRIEST
English AMBASSADORS

Lords, Ladies, Officers, Soldiers, Sailors, Messengers, and
Attendants

SCENE *The Danish royal castle at Elsinore*

At the castle of Elsinore, at midnight, the guard is being changed. It is a bitterly cold night. Barnardo takes over from Francisco. Horatio and Marcellus join him for the watch.

2 **Nay, answer me**: the newcomer should prove who he is
　unfold yourself: declare who you are, identify yourself
3 **Long live the King!**: Francisco recognizes Barnardo's voice
6 **carefully upon your hour**: punctually
8 **relief**: Barnardo is relieving him of his guard duty
9 **sick at heart**: in low spirits
13 **rivals of my watch**: my opposite numbers on guard duty
15 **ground**: country
　liegemen to the Dane: loyal subjects of the King of Denmark

> • *What is the atmosphere of this opening scene and how is it created on the page?*

A 1 5 2 1 12 9 (- HAMLET)

BROKEN RHYTHM
GENERATES AN
ATMOSPHERE OF
UNEASE,
APPREHENSION +
CONFUSION

Act one

[handwritten: mood of anxiety + dread.]

Scene 1

[handwritten: political situation given dramatically.]

Elsinore

Enter BARNARDO *and* FRANCISCO, *two sentinels*

BARNARDO	Who's there? *[handwritten: tone	tension	insecurity]*
FRANCISCO	Nay, answer me. Stand and unfold yourself.
BARNARDO	Long live the King!
FRANCISCO	Barnardo?
BARNARDO	He. 5
FRANCISCO	You come most carefully upon your hour.
BARNARDO	'Tis now struck twelve, get thee to bed Francisco.
FRANCISCO	For this relief much thanks, 'tis bitter cold,
	And I am sick at heart. *[handwritten: sickness	disease]*
BARNARDO	Have you had quiet guard? *[handwritten: state of many a country]*
FRANCISCO	Not a mouse stirring. 10
BARNARDO	Well, good night.
	If you do meet Horatio and Marcellus,
	The rivals of my watch, bid them make haste.

Enter HORATIO *and* MARCELLUS

[handwritten: (technique)]

FRANCISCO	I think I hear them. Stand ho, who is there?
HORATIO	Friends to this ground. *[handwritten: shared lines emphasise tone etc.]*
MARCELLUS	And liegemen to the Dane. 15
FRANCISCO	Give you good night.
MARCELLUS	O, farewell honest soldier.
	Who hath relieved you?
FRANCISCO	Barnardo has my place.
	Give you good night. [*Exit*

[handwritten: short lines show tension.]

Horatio has been asked to join the watch because, having
been told that Barnardo and Marcellus have seen a ghost, he
insists it is their imagination. They tell him they have seen it
for two nights. As they start to give him the details, the
Ghost appears. It looks like the dead king. They ask Horatio
to speak to it.

19 **A piece of him**: either he does not feel that all his body is
there, because he is numb with cold, or he is joking that
because it is dark and misty the others can see him only
fitfully, as he can see them. In Shakespeare's day, plays were
performed in daylight, so the language and the acting had to
indicate the time of day and the weather in the scene being
played.

21 **thing**: creature

23 **fantasy**: imagination

24 **will not...seen of us**: (Horatio) cannot persuade himself to
believe in this terrible sight we have now seen twice

25 **dreaded**: terrible

26 **entreated him along**: asked him to come with us

27 **watch...night**: keep watch throughout the night

29 **approve our eyes**: confirm what we have seen

31 **assail your ears**: tell you. The words '*assail*' (attack) and
'*fortified*' (defended) suggest that Horatio is strongly resisting
their story.

36 **pole**: the pole star. The star to the west of this has been held
to be the bright star Capella.

37 **t'illume**: to light up

39 **The bell then beating one**: as the clock was striking one

40 **break thee off**: stop speaking

41 **same figure like**: same form as

42 **scholar**: Horatio has been a student and so would not only
be quick-witted and clever enough to talk to the Ghost, but if
it seemed to be evil, he might know the religious form of
words in Latin to exorcize it

BROUGHT HORATIO TO WITNESS THE GHOST

MARCELLUS   Holla, Barnardo!

BARNARDO   Say,
What, is Horatio there?

HORATIO   A piece of him.

BARNARDO   Welcome Horatio, welcome good Marcellus.   20

HORATIO   What, has this thing appeared again tonight? *FIRST*
                                                          REFERENCE
BARNARDO   I have seen nothing.   *TO GHOST.*

MARCELLUS   Horatio says 'tis but our fantasy,
SUSPENSE   And will not let belief take hold of him
                Touching this dreaded sight twice seen of us.   25
NOT   Therefore I have entreated him along,   *WHAT IS*
TELLING US   With us to watch the minutes of this night,   *IT?*
IT IS A   That if again this apparition come,
GHOST   He may approve our eyes and speak to it.

HORATIO   Tush, tush, 'twill not appear. *HORATIO IS SCEPTICAL*
                                                OF A GHOST
BARNARDO   Sit down awhile,   30
                                                  EXISTENCE
                And let us once again assail your ears,
                That are so fortified against our story,
HONOURABLE   What we have two nights seen. *× MILITARY IMAGES*
HORATIO   Well, sit we down, *IDEA OF ATTACK -*
TRUSTWORTHY   And let us hear Barnardo speak of this. *DANGER*
HONEST   *THEY FEEL*
                                                          THE COUNTRY IS
BARNARDO   Last night of all,   *IN.*   35
                When yond same star that's westward from the
                    pole
                Had made his course t'illume that part of
                    heaven
                Where now it burns, Marcellus and myself,
                The bell then beating one –

                Enter GHOST

MARCELLUS   Peace, break thee off. Look where it comes
                    again!   40
BARNARDO   In the same figure like the King that's dead. *CAREFUL*
                                                              ALLUDO TO
MARCELLUS   Thou art a scholar, speak to it Horatio. *WHO IT IS*
                                                          ON - IT IS.
                EDUCATED - HOPE HE
                    COULD COMMUNI...   *THE*
                COMMUNICATE WITH   *KING.*
WANT HORATIO   *WITH*
VALIDATE THEIR   *THE GHOST*
        STORY

Horatio speaks to the Ghost, but it turns away and goes
without a word. Horatio is shaken by what he has seen. He
agrees the apparition is the image of the dead king and
suggests that he is warning them of some calamity to come.

43 'a: he. The word is scarcely pronounced. The apparition is
usually referred to as 'it'.

44 harrows me: distresses me

45 It would be spoke to: it wants me to speak to it

46 What art thou that usurp'st: what are you, you who are
trespassing on

47 Together with: also assuming, taking on

48 the majesty of buried Denmark: the late King of Denmark

49 sometimes: in former times, previously

50 stalks away: walks haughtily away

51 I charge thee: I order you

57 Without...eyes: without the knowledge that my eyes saw this
and are my guarantee for what happened

61 Norway: King of Norway
combated: fought

62 parle: talk, conversation, or more specifically 'a meeting to
discuss terms under a truce'

63 He smote...on the ice: the reading of this line has been
much discussed. The question is whether to accept (a) the Q1
and Q2 version '*sleaded pollax*' or (b) the F version '*sledded
Pollax*' (see Introduction page xv for an explanation of these
terms). In (a) the weapon 'poleaxe' seems to be meant, with
which King Hamlet struck the ice; (b) suggests that he fought
with the Poles (Polacks) who had come in sledges.

65 jump: precisely

66 martial stalk: a slow and stately walk, like a soldier

67 In what...opinion: in detail I do not know what to think,
but as far as my general opinion goes

69 bodes...to our state: threatens our state with some disastrous
outbreak

70 Good now sit down: do please sit down now

> • *What early indications do we gain of Horatio's
> character and the role he will play?*

BARNARDO	Looks 'a not like the King? Mark it Horatio.
HORATIO	Most like. It harrows me with fear and wonder.
BARNARDO	It would be spoke to.
MARCELLUS	Question it Horatio.
HORATIO	What are thou that usurp'st this time of night,
	Together with that fair and warlike form
	In which the majesty of buried Denmark
	Did sometimes march? By heaven I charge thee
	speak.
MARCELLUS	It is offended.
BARNARDO	See it stalks away.
HORATIO	Stay, speak, speak, I charge thee speak.

[*Exit* GHOST

MARCELLUS	'Tis gone and will not answer.
BARNARDO	How now Horatio, you tremble and look pale.
	Is not this something more than fantasy?
	What think you on 't?
HORATIO	Before my God I might not this believe,
	Without the sensible and true avouch
	Of mine own eyes.
MARCELLUS	Is it not like the King?
HORATIO	As thou art to thyself.
	Such was the very armour he had on
	When he the ambitious Norway combated;
	So frowned he once, when in an angry parle
	He smote the sledded Polacks on the ice.
	'Tis strange.
MARCELLUS	Thus twice before, and jump at this dead hour,
	With martial stalk hath he gone by our watch.
HORATIO	In what particular thought to work I know not,
	But in the gross and scope of my opinion,
	This bodes some strange eruption to our state.
MARCELLUS	Good now sit down, and tell me he that knows,

Line numbers: 45, 50, 55, 60, 65, 70

Handwritten annotations: "THE IMAGE HAS CUT INTO HIM - FEAR + WONDER", "HORATIO", "AMAZED.", "BATTLE THAT WILL FOLLOW", "A COMMAND.", "REFERENCE TO FEAR.", "ARMOUR PAST BATTLES", "COLDNESS OF ATMOSPHERE"

Marcellus asks about the state of alert. Horatio tells of a challenge to battle between the King of Norway and of Denmark, with land as the prize. King Hamlet won, killing Fortinbras. Now his son wants to reclaim the land, fairly won.

71 **Why...land**: why the subjects of this nation have the burden of this present strict and careful watch imposed upon them

73 **daily cast...war**: brass cannons are being produced every day and arms deals are made abroad

75 **impress of shipwrights**: conscription of shipbuilders
whose sore task...the week: whose heavy work goes on day and night, seven days a week

77 **toward**: (stress on first syllable) about to happen

78 **Doth...the day**: the work goes on at night as well

80 **whisper**: rumour

81 **even but now**: just a few moments ago

82 **by Fortinbras...the combat**: challenged by Fortinbras – who was led on by a most ambitious pride – to do battle

83 **Thereto pricked on**: incited to it

85 **For...him**: this was the western world's opinion of him

86 **sealed compact**: formal agreement

87 **ratified**: confirmed
heraldry: a code of chivalrous behaviour between monarchs

89 **stood seized of**: possessed

90 **moiety competent**: similar amount

91 **gaged**: pledged
had: would have

93 **cov'nant...designed**: contract and understanding of these terms

96 **unimproved mettle**: undisciplined spirit

97 **skirts**: border territories

98 **Sharked up**: hastily assembled a random crowd (as a shark might gobble up a shoal of fish) of lawless men, committed to action. The soldiers will only get their keep, so 'stomach' puns on 'food' and 'stomach' for the fight.

- *The Fortinbras story begins – a framework device completed in the final scene of the play. Note where he reappears.*

(POLITICAL)

INTENSE
ACTIVITY
TAKING
PLACE.

Why this same strict and most observant watch

GUARDS

So nightly toils the subject of the land,

And why such daily cast of brazen cannon,
And foreign mart for implements of war,

ALL ARMOURE
PREPARING

NOT EVEN
REST.

Why such impress of shipwrights, whose sore
    task

FOR
WAR
75

Does not divide the Sunday from the week,
What might be toward that this sweaty haste
Doth make the night joint-labourer with the day,
Who is't that can inform me?

HORATIO   ELABORATE SPEACH   That can I.

DANGER
OF
INVASION
BY FORTINBRAS

HEARD OF.

At least the whisper goes so; our last King,   80
Whose image even but now appeared to us,
Was as you know by Fortinbras of Norway,
Thereto pricked on by a most emulate pride,
Dared to the combat; in which our valiant
    Hamlet –

REVENGE

OLD
HAMLET
KILLED
OLd FORTIN-
BRAS

For so this side of our known world esteemed
    him –   85
Did slay this Fortinbras, who by a sealed compact,
Well ratified by law and heraldry,

HAMLET
GAINED
THE
LAND

Did forfeit, with his life, all those his lands
Which he stood seized of to the conqueror.
Against the which a moiety competent   90
Was gaged by our King, which had returned
To the inheritance of Fortinbras,
Had he been vanquisher; as by the same
    cov'nant
And carriage of the article designed,

FULL OF
PASSION/
EMOTION.

His fell to Hamlet. Now sir, young Fortinbras, 95
Of unimproved mettle hot and full,
Hath in the skirts of Norway here and there
Sharked up a list of lawless resolutes
For food and diet to some enterprise
That hath a stomach in't; which is no other,   100
As it doth well appear unto our state,
But to recover of us, by strong hand

NOT COMPLIMENTARY IN THE LIST OF
MEN FORTINBRAS HAS.

Horatio considers that the possibility of invasion by young Fortinbras may be the reason for putting the state on a warlike footing. Barnardo agrees. Horatio goes on to explain that there were natural warnings of disaster in Rome before Julius Caesar was murdered. As Horatio finishes, the ghost appears again, and Horatio tries to find out why it has appeared.

103 **terms compulsatory**: compelling means
106 **head**: origin, cause
107 **post-haste and rummage**: hasty preparation and commotion
109 **Well may it sort**: that may well be the reason
portentous: ominous, warning of some calamity
112 **mote**: speck of dust
113 **palmy**: triumphant
115 **tenantless**: empty
116 **gibber**: jabber, babble
117–118 some words appear to have been left out here. The sense should either continue the idea of line 116 or introduce that of line 117.
117 **stars...fire**: comets
118 **Disasters**: an unfavourable aspect of a star or planet. Sunspots may be meant here.
the moist star...empire stands: the moon which influences the tides. Neptune is the god of the sea.
121 **And even the like...countrymen**: just such warnings of terrible happenings have been given to our people in this country
121 **precurse**: heralding
122 **harbingers**: forerunners, messengers
123 **omen coming on**: the approaching disaster
125 **climatures**: regions
127 **cross it**: cross its path
133 **If thou art privy to**: if you have some secret knowledge of
134 **happily**: possibly

And terms compulsatory, those foresaid lands
So by his father lost; and this I take it
Is the main motive of our preparations,   105
The source of this our watch, and the chief head
Of this post-haste and rummage in the land.

BARNARDO   I think it be no other but e'en so.
            Well may it sort that this portentous figure
            Comes armed through our watch so like the
                King   110
            That was and is the question of these wars.

HORATIO   A mote it is to trouble the mind's eye.
            In the most high and palmy state of Rome,
            A little ere the mightiest Julius fell,
            The graves stood tenantless, and the sheeted
                dead   115
            Did squeak and gibber in the Roman streets;
            As stars with trains of fire and dews of blood,
            Disasters in the sun; and the moist star,
            Upon whose influence Neptune's empire stands,
            Was sick almost to doomsday with eclipse.   120
            And even the like precurse of feared events,
            As harbingers preceding still the fates,
            And prologue to the omen coming on,
            Have heaven and earth together demonstrated
            Unto our climatures and countrymen.   125

Enter GHOST

            But soft, behold, lo where it comes again.
            I'll cross it, though it blast me. Stay illusion,
            If thou hast any sound or use of voice,
                                    [*It spreads its arms*
            Speak to me.
            If there be any good thing to be done   130
            That may to thee do ease and grace to me,
            Speak to me.
            If thou art privy to thy country's fate
            Which happily foreknowing may avoid,

As Horatio puts his third point to the Ghost, the cock crows. They move to prevent the Ghost leaving, but at the sound, and just as it appeared about to speak, the Ghost goes away. Horatio explains that at cockcrow spirits have to return to their place. Marcellus explains that some people believe that towards Christmas the cock crows all day and people are safe from spirits.

136 uphoarded: hoarded up, saved up

137 Extorted: taken by force, or some other unfair means

140 partisan: a long-handled spear with short, sharp blades projecting from the end of it

143 being so majestical: since it seems so like a king

145 it is...invulnerable: like empty air it cannot be hit or injured by us

148 started: took fright

149 fearful: terrible

150 trumpet: (here) trumpeter, announcing the arrival of an important person

152 the god of day: Phoebus Apollo
at his warning...confine: there was a belief that at cockcrow all ghosts and spirits had to return to their place, on pain of punishment

154 extravagant...hies to his confine: the spirit, straying beyond its limits, returns to its own territory; The word '*confine*' also carries the play on words of 'imprisoned'.

156 probation: proof

158 'gainst: (against) just before

162 no planets strike: no evil influence of planets has power to harm

163 takes: strikes (with misfortune or disease)

164 So hallowed and so gracious: so blessed

| | O speak. | 135 |

(margin note: NO RESPONSE)

Or if thou hast uphoarded in thy life
Extorted treasure in the womb of earth,
For which they say you spirits oft walk in
death,

(margin note: BREAK OF DAY = / GHOST LEAVES)

[*The cock crows*

Speak of it; stay and speak. Stop it Marcellus.

MARCELLUS	Shall I strike at it with my partisan?	140
HORATIO	Do, if it will not stand.	
BARNARDO	'Tis here.	
HORATIO	'Tis here.	
MARCELLUS	'Tis gone. [*Exit* GHOST	

We do it wrong, being so majestical,
To offer it the show of violence;
For it is as the air invulnerable,   145
And our vain blows malicious mockery.

(margin note: TO CONFRONTATIONAL TO THE GHOST ∴ NO RESPONSE)

| BARNARDO | It was about to speak when the cock crew. | |
| HORATIO | And then it started like a guilty thing | |

Upon a fearful summons. I have heard
The cock, that is the trumpet to the morn,   150
Doth with his lofty and shrill-sounding throat
Awake the god of day, and at his warning,
Whether in sea or fire, in earth or air,
The extravagant and erring spirit hies
To his confine; and of the truth herein   155
This present object made probation.

(margin note: GHOSTS RETURN TO GRAVES AT SOUND OF COCK.)

| MARCELLUS | It faded on the crowing of the cock. | |

Some say that ever 'gainst that season comes
Wherein our Saviour's birth is celebrated,
The bird of dawning singeth all night long,   160
And then they say no spirit dare stir abroad;
The nights are wholesome, then no planets strike,
No fairy takes, nor witch hath power to charm,
So hallowed and so gracious is that time.

(margin note: COCK PREVENTS SPIRITS WANDERING IF IT CROWS DURING NIGHT.)

| HORATIO | So have I heard and do in part believe it. | 165 |

Dawn is breaking. Hamlet's friends will tell him what they
have seen. They are sure the Ghost will speak to him.

166 **russet**: the name given to a coarse woollen homespun cloth,
worn by country people. The colour was reddish-brown
(today's meaning) grey or neutral. (Compare modern
French 'roux, rousse' which, among other uses, describes
auburn hair.)
169 **impart**: tell
173 **As needful...fitting our duty?**: it is appropriate because we
love him as a friend and owe him duty as crown prince

Claudius is holding court beside his queen, Hamlet's
mother. He comments on the mixture of joy and grief that
has accompanied the funeral and his marriage.

Flourish: Fanfare of trumpets
2 **green**: fresh
it us befitted: it was right for us
4 **To be...woe**: the whole country is united in one sorrowing
expression
5 **discretion**: rational judgement
6 **wisest sorrow...ourselves**: our sorrow is tempered with
wisdom and we have also thought of ourselves
8 **sometime**: former
9 **imperial jointress**: a jointress held property in common with
her husband and had a right to it after his death. Gertrude's
status as Queen has not changed.
11 **With...eye**: one eye shining with happiness, the other with
tears
12 **mirth...marriage**: merriness at the funeral and mournfulness
in marriage
13 **dole**: misery, grief
14 **barred**: refused to consider
15 **Your better wisdoms**: your best counsels

> • *How would you describe the language of Claudius's
> first speech? What are his political and personal aims
> here?*

[handwritten annotations in margins]
MOON IS ESTABLISHED

DESCRIPTION ALLOWS AUDIENCE TO KNOW THE DIFFERENCE BETWEEN NIGHT + DAY

But look the morn in russet mantle clad
Walks o'er the dew of yon high eastward hill.
Break we our watch up, and by my advice
Let us impart what we have seen tonight
Unto young Hamlet; for upon my life,   170
This spirit dumb to us will speak to him.
Do you consent we shall acquaint him with it,
As needful in our loves, fitting our duty?

MARCELLUS   Let's do't I pray, and I this morning know
Where we shall find him most convenient.   175

[*Exeunt*

[handwritten] NEED TO TELL HAMLET.
BEWILDERED MEN CREAT TENTION = POTENTIAL TRAGEDY.

Scene 2

[handwritten] OLD HAMLET WAS WELL LIKED · RESPECTED

HEAD ON TO THE DIFFICULTIES IE DEATH + MARRIAGE
↓
A NEW

Flourish. Enter CLAUDIUS *King of Denmark,*
GERTRUDE *the* QUEEN, COUNCILLORS, POLONIUS
and his son LAERTES, VALTEMAND, CORNELIUS,
HAMLET, *and others*   *[handwritten]* BUSINESS OF STATE.

KING

[handwritten] HAS TO HANDLE THE MARRIAGE CAREFULLY

Though yet of Hamlet our dear brother's death
The memory be green, and that it us befitted
To bear our hearts in grief, and our whole
      kingdom
To be contracted in one brow of woe,
Yet so far hath discretion fought with nature,   5
That we with wisest sorrow think on him,
Together with remembrance of ourselves.
Therefore our sometime sister, now our Queen,
Th' imperial jointress to this warlike state,
Have we as 'twere with a defeated joy,   10
With an auspicious and a dropping eye,
With mirth in funeral and with dirge in marriage,
In equal scale weighing delight and dole,
Taken to wife; nor have we herein barred
Your better wisdoms, which have freely gone   15
With this affair along – for all, our thanks.

[handwritten] IMPORTANT NOT TO AVOID THIS TO HIDE THE GUILT OR HIS INVOLVEMENT.

[handwritten] 10 } PARADOX

[handwritten] LESSEN THE GUILT OF THE SPEEDY MARRIAGE.

[handwritten] TONE → USES 'WE' = FORMALITY OFFICIAL BUSINESS LIKE

Claudius is sending two ambassadors to the present King of Norway, the aged and bedridden uncle of young Fortinbras, asking him to put a stop to his nephew's warlike activities. His reasoning is that the King may not know what is going on, and that it is his subjects who are being formed into an army. Claudius turns to Laertes, son of Polonius, who has a request.

17 **that you know**: what you already know
18 **weak supposal**: poor opinion
20 **disjoint and out of frame**: disrupted and disordered
21 **Colleagued...advantage**: his ally only this impression that he can make gains
23 **Importing**: concerning
24 **bonds of law**: legal agreements
29 **impotent**: powerless
31 **gait**: progress
   in that...full proportions: pointing out that the raising of troops, enlisting of men, in quantities necessary for this enterprise
33 **his subject**: his subjects
36 **Giving to you...allow**: the ambassadors are not empowered to negotiate with the King of Norway. The spelling of '*delated*' is an alternative one for 'dilated' – 'fully detailed'.
43 **suit**: request
44 **You cannot...voice**: any reasonable request will be granted by the Danish king
47 **native**: (here) closely allied
48 **instrumental**: of service

> • *What place do Laertes and his father seem to hold in the estimation of Claudius?*

CONTRASTS WITH SCENE 1. LIGHT.

LANGUAGE = ELABORATE IMAGES TO COVER UP WHAT'S BEEN DONE.

= PARADOX
(TWO OPPOSITES TO SHOW CONTRASTS)

Now follows that you know, young Fortinbras,
Holding a weak supposal of our worth, ↑ TAKE OVER
Or thinking by our late dear brother's death AS COUNTRY IS
Our state to be disjoint and out of frame, 20 WEAK
Colleagued with this dream of his advantage, + HAS
He hath not failed to pester us with message UNDERESTIM-
Importing the surrender of those lands ATED CLAUDIUS
Lost by his father, with all bonds of law,
To our most valiant brother. So much for him. 25
Now for ourself, and for this time of meeting,
Thus much the business is: we have here writ

TELLING THE PEOPLE THIS IS WHY HE MUST TAKE CONTROL.

To Norway, uncle of young Fortinbras,
Who, impotent and bed-rid, scarcely hears
Of this his nephew's purpose, to suppress 30
His further gait herein, in that the levies,
The lists, and full proportions, are all made
Out of his subject; and we here dispatch
You good Cornelius, and you Valtemand,
For bearers of this greeting to old Norway; 35
Giving to you no further personal power
To business with the King, more than the scope
Of these <u>delated articles</u> allow. WRITTEN TO NORWAY
Farewell, and let your haste commend your duty. SAYING YOUNG FORTIN-
BRAS WILL NOT TAKE
OVER.

CORNELIUS }
VALTEMAND } In that and all things will we show our duty. 40

KING We doubt it nothing: heartily farewell.

[*Exeunt* VALTEMAND *and* CORNELIUS

TONE BECOMES PERSONAL NOT 'WE' BUT 'YOU'

And now Laertes what's the news <u>with you</u>?
You told us of some suit; what is't Laertes?
You cannot speak of reason to the Dane,
And lose your voice. What wouldst <u>thou</u> beg,
Laertes, 45
That shall not be my offer, not thy asking?
The head is not more native to the heart,
The hand more instrumental to the mouth,
Than is the throne of Denmark to thy father.

ADOPTS A MORE FRIENDLY TONE; BUT WHAT IS THE PURPOSE OF IT

Laertes asks permission to leave court and return to France.
Polonius, though reluctant to see him go, has agreed.
Claudius grants his request, and turns to Hamlet. Both
Claudius and Hamlet's mother, Gertrude, gently reproach
Hamlet for persisting in his grief, asking why, when death is
a fate common to all, his father's death should seem unique.

50 dread: revered

58 slow leave: eventual permission

59 laboursome petition: repeated requests

60 Upon...hard consent: consenting to his desire, I gave my
grudging agreement

62 Take thy fair hour: choose when you wish to go

63 thy best graces...at thy will: spend your time usefully

65 A little more...kind: Hamlet's first words are an *aside* (see
GLOSSARY page 326). Though Claudius and Hamlet are
relations – uncle and nephew – (which is more than the vague
'*kin*') they are not men of the same kind, and, in a play on
words, there is no affection between them.
kind: nature, quality inherited at birth

67 I am too much in the sun: he is too much the centre of
attention, and too much 'the son' – which he must resent (see
Pun, GLOSSARY page 328)

68 nighted colour: sombre clothes and sombre mood

70 vailed lids: lowered eyelids

75 particular with thee: unique to you

- *Are there any differences to be observed in the
  language used to, and by, Laertes and Hamlet?*
- *Hamlet has recently returned from university for the
  funeral of his father and his mother's wedding. There
  he has studied and discussed, words and wit will have
  been important - 'on the one hand this - on the other
  that, but then again...'. His friends have been young,
  lively and clever. Start to look at what and who
  surround him at court, and draw your conclusions.*

What wouldst thou have, Laertes?

LAERTES   My dread lord, 50
[*WANTS TO RETURN*]
Your leave and favour to return to France;
From whence though willingly I came to Denmark
To show my duty in your coronation,
Yet now I must confess, that duty done,
My thoughts and wishes bend again toward
    France,   55
And bow them to your gracious leave and   [*suggest wordy + pompus*]
    pardon.

KING   Have you your father's leave? What says Polonius?

POLONIUS   He hath, my lord, wrung from me my slow leave
By laboursome petition, and at last
Upon his will I sealed my hard consent.   60
I do beseech you give him leave to go.   [*King uncle? farther?*]

KING   Take thy fair hour Laertes, time be thine,
And thy best graces spend it at thy will.   [*bitterness antagonism*]
But now my cousin Hamlet, and my son.

HAMLET   [*Aside*] A little more than kin, and less than kind. 65

KING   How is it that the clouds still hang on you?   [*won't accept their relationship*]

HAMLET   Not so, my lord; I am too much in the sun.

QUEEN   Good Hamlet, cast thy nighted colour off,
And let thine eye look like a friend on Denmark.
[*upset depressed sober mood*]
Do not for ever with thy vailed lids   70
Seek for thy noble father in the dust.   [*ironic response*]
Thou know'st 'tis common, all that lives must   [*running on sun*]
    die, (*fact*)   [*dimming it. (depressed)*]
Passing through nature to eternity.

HAMLET   Ay madam, it is common. (- *vulgar*)

QUEEN   If it be,
Why seems it so particular with thee?   [*shocked*]   75

HAMLET   Seems madam? Nay it is; I know not 'seems'.
'Tis not alone my inky cloak, good mother,
Nor customary suits of solemn black,

[*Hamlet first expression of how he feels towards his mother + uncle.*]

Hamlet's grief is deep and real, not an act put on for show. Claudius briefly commends his mourning then attacks it as excessive. He urges Hamlet to regard him as a father and assures him he is next in line for the throne.

79 **windy...breath**: heavy sighs forced out
80 **fruitful river in the eye**: the eye teeming with tears
81 **the dejected...visage**: sad expression (on the face)
82 **shapes**: outward forms
84 **they are...might play**: these are all outward signs of grief which could be acted. It is worth noting Hamlet's deep interest in the craft of acting, here and elsewhere in the play.
85 **passes show**: is deeper than mere appearance
87 **commendable**: the stress falls on the first syllable
90 **That...lost his**: that dead father's own father had died
91 **filial obligation**: the duty of sons and daughters to parents
92 **obsequious sorrow**: the sorrow proper at a funeral
   but to persever...condolement: to insist obstinately on going on grieving ('persever' stress on second syllable)
94 **impious**: lacking in reverence
95 **incorrect**: uncorrected, not submissive
96 **unfortified**: without inner strength
98 **For...heart?**: Why do we take something so to heart which we know has to happen? Why should we obstinately oppose and reject something which is as usual as any of the things commonly observed by our senses?
101 **a fault**: an offence
103 **whose common...fathers**: fathers are dying all the time
105 **the first corse**: an unintentional *irony* (see GLOSSARY page 327) on Claudius's part since the reference is to Abel, killed by his brother Cain
106 **throw to earth**: throw away (in his father's grave)
107 **unprevailing**: pointless
112 **impart toward**: offer this to you

> • *Examine the subject matter of Claudius's reply to Hamlet. Compare the style of Claudius's speech which opens the scene, and this one. What effect do the lists have in this second speech? (lines 87–106)*

CONTRAST BETWEEN THE APPEARANCE OF GRIEF
+ THE REALITY

FOCUS ON
THE
STRENGTH
OF HIS
GRIEF.

PUTTING IT ON
(CLOTHES)

KING
/
HE KNOWS
THAT HAMLET
HAS THE
POWER TO BUILD
OPPOSITION
HE MUST BE
CAREFUL
WHAT HE
SAYS

IS HE
ACCUSING
OTHERS
FOR
PUTTING
ON A
SHOW
OF
GRIEF?

HIS GRIEF
COMES
FROM
WITHIN

PLAYING
A
PART

UNDERSTAND-
ABLE
TO GRIEVE
BUT DEATH
IS A
FACT

IT IS WEAK
+ UNMANLY

Nor windy suspiration of forced breath,
No, nor the fruitful river in the eye,   80
Nor the dejected haviour of the visage,
Together with all forms, moods, shapes of grief,
That can denote me truly. These indeed seem,
For they are actions that a man might play;
But I have that within which passes show –   85
These but the trappings and the suits of woe.
'Tis sweet and commendable in your nature,
    Hamlet,
To give these mourning duties to your father.
But you must know, your father lost a father;
That father lost, lost his; and the survivor
    bound   90
In filial obligation for some term
To do obsequious sorrow; but to persever
In obstinate condolement is a course
Of impious stubbornness, 'tis unmanly grief;
It shows a will most incorrect to heaven,   95
A heart unfortified, a mind impatient,
An understanding simple and unschooled.
For what we know must be, and is as common
As any the most vulgar thing to sense,
Why should we in our peevish opposition   100
Take it to heart? Fie, 'tis a fault to heaven,
A fault against the dead, a fault to nature,
To reason most absurd, whose common theme
Is death of fathers, and who still hath cried,
From the first corse till he that died today,   105
'This must be so'. We pray you throw to earth

SHOW OF
EMOTIONS
TO THE
COURT

HE'S
TAKING ON
BOARD
THE
OPPOSITION
HAMLET
MAY
GIVE.

This unprevailing woe, and think of us
As of a father, for let the world take note
You are the most immediate to our throne;
And with no less nobility of love   110
Than that which dearest father bears his son,
Do I impart toward you. For your intent
In going back to school in Wittenberg,

Gertrude joins Claudius in asking Hamlet to stay at court and he agrees. Claudius welcomes this decision and expresses his pleasure. He will celebrate by marking each round of drinking with gunfire. Hamlet, left alone, shows that his private mood is very low indeed and talks of suicide. He contrasts his father and Claudius, much to the latter's disfavour, and strongly disapproves of the speedy marriage.

114 **most retrograde...desire**: very much against our wishes

115 **bend you**: submit yourself, consent (to remain)

122 **Be as ourself**: enjoy the same standing as myself

125 **No jocund health...clouds shall tell**: every happy toast drunk today by the King of Denmark shall be announced to the skies by the great cannon

127 **rouse...again**: (cf carouse) round of drinking shall echo from heaven again

129 **solid**: '*sallied*' is the Q2 reading, taken to mean 'sullied' or 'unclean'. The church had long maintained that the body was unclean. '*Solid*' suggests a body that is too stubbornly alive to be disposed of easily.

132 **Or that...self-slaughter**: the sixth commandment 'Thou shalt do no murder' is taken to refer to self-murder also
   canon: set of rules, commandments

133 **How...world**: Hamlet is still grieving, but these are also like the sentiments of someone in a state of depression

136 **rank and gross**: luxuriant and thick

137 **merely**: completely

140 **Hyperion to a satyr**: Hyperion is identified by Shakespeare with the sun god, Apollo, the personification of divine beauty. Satyrs were woodland gods, half man half goat in form, attending on Bacchus. They had a reputation for lechery.

141 **beteem**: allow *HIS FATHER IS OPPOSITE ENDS OF THE SPECTRUM TO*

- *What do we learn about Hamlet's mood in this first soliloquy? How far is it possible to say what exactly has caused it?*

(✱ IMAGE OF DEATH, DECAY)

CLAUDIUS

Handwritten note (top): CLAUDIUS WANTS HAMLET TO STAY SO CLAUDIUS CAN KEEP AN EYE ON HIM

Handwritten (left): MORE IN CONTROL WITH HAMLET CLOSE.

It is most retrograde to our desire;
And we beseech you, bend you to remain   115
Here in the cheer and comfort of our eye,
Our chiefest courtier, cousin, and our son.

QUEEN Let not thy mother lose her prayers Hamlet.
I pray thee stay with us; go not to Wittenberg.

HAMLET I shall in all my best obey you madam.   120

KING Why 'tis a loving and a fair reply.
Be as ourself in Denmark. Madam come.
This gentle and unforced accord of Hamlet
Sits smiling to my heart; in grace whereof,
No jocund health that Denmark drinks today,   125
But the great cannon to the clouds shall tell,
And the King's rouse the heavens shall bruit
    again,
Re-speaking earthly thunder. Come away.
[*Flourish. Exeunt all but* HAMLET

Handwritten (left): HAPPY HAMLET IS SMILING

Handwritten (right): DELIBERATLY CLAUDIUS SAYING HE'LL OBEY CLAUDIUS. CELEBRATION. SHAKESPEAR IS PAINTING A REALISTIC PICTURE OF HOW THEY WOULD CELEBRATE

HAMLET O that this too too solid flesh would melt,
Thaw and resolve itself into a dew,   130
Or that the Everlasting had not fixed
His canon 'gainst self-slaughter. O God, God,
How weary, stale, flat and unprofitable
Seem to me all the uses of this world!
Fie on 't, ah fie, 'tis an unweeded garden   135
That grows to seed, things rank and gross in
    nature
Possess it merely. That it should come to this –
But two months dead, nay not so much,
    not two –
So excellent a king, that was to this
Hyperion to a satyr, so loving to my mother   140
That he might not beteem the winds of heaven
Visit her face too roughly. Heaven and earth,
Must I remember? Why she would hang on him
As if increase of appetite had grown
By what it fed on, and yet within a month –   145

Handwritten (right): CONTEMPLATING SUICIDE / WANTS TO FADE AWAY AS HE KNOWS IT'S A MORTAL SIN TO COMMIT SUICIDE / HUMAN/GOAT SEX ETC / COMPARES OLD HAMLET TO CLAUDIUS; USING CLASSICAL IMAGES

Handwritten (left): HAMLET SOLILOQUY / HOW HE SEES THE WORLD IMAGE OF UNWEEDED GARDEN --- DISTORTION/ DECAY IMAGE OF WORTHLESS-NESS / OLD HAMLET FATHER OF SON.

The suddenness with which his mother's wedding followed
the funeral of his father, whom he had plainly both loved
and admired, distresses Hamlet. He cannot understand the
lack of taste she displayed in choosing Claudius, who, he
feels, cannot compare with his father. He is hurt and
miserable, and has to keep silent. He greets Horatio and
Marcellus.

146 frailty...woman: *personification* of an abstract noun, so
that '*frailty*' is held to equal '*woman*' (see GLOSSARY page 328)

147 or e'er those shoes were old: she had new shoes for the
funeral and they were still quite new at the time of her
wedding

149 Niobe: according to Greek fable Niobe boasted of her
twelve children to the mother of Apollo and Diana. They
avenged the insult by killing them all. Niobe wept herself to
death and was changed into a stone from which water
flowed.

150 wants discourse of reason: lacks the ability to reason

153 I to Hercules: Hercules was the strong and ingenious man
of Greek myth, succeeding in accomplishing twelve
apparently impossible labours. Hamlet is putting himself at
the other end of this scale. By using these classical references
Hamlet is pointing to extremes which Shakespeare's
audience will readily understand and at the same time
ensuring we feel the universal nature of Hamlet's present
experience.

154 unrighteous: hypocritical

155 flushing in her galled eyes: redness in her sore eyes

156 post With such dexterity: hurry so smartly

157 incestuous: marriage to one's husband's brother is one of
many liaisons expressly forbidden in the *Book of Common
Prayer's* 'A Table of Kindred and Affinity'

163 I'll change that name with you: I'll exchange that name –
'*good friend*' – with you

168 what...Wittenberg?: what does bring you from Wittenberg?

169 a truant disposition: a desire in my nature to play truant, a
tendency to laziness

171 Nor...yourself: nor will I allow you to offend my ears by
trying to make me believe what you are accusing yourself of

Handwritten note at top: FROM SUICIDE TO COMPARISONS OF FATHER + UNCLE. THEN THE MAST OF MARRIAGE

Handwritten margin notes:
RESENTFUL TONE.

BITTER
DEPRESSED
RESENTFUL

↑ =
SENSE OF
FORBODING =
(DOOM)

Let me not think on 't – frailty, thy name is
woman. ALL WOMEN – WEAK WILLED *(OPTIONAL)*
A little month or e'er those shoes were old
With which she followed my poor father's body,
Like Niobe all tears, why she, even she –
O God, a beast that wants discourse of reason   150
Would have mourned longer – married with my
uncle, ANIMAL WOULD MOURN LONGER.
My father's brother, but no more like my father
Than I to Hercules; within a month –
Ere yet the salt of most unrighteous tears   PRIVATE WAY
Had left the flushing in her galled eyes,   155 HE CONDEMNS HIS
She married. O most wicked speed, to post MOTHER –
With such dexterity to incestuous sheets. NONE DOES
It is not, nor it cannot come to good: THIS IN
But break, my heart, for I must hold my tongue. PUBLIC

Enter HORATIO, MARCELLUS, *and* BARNARDO

(HORATIO WORTH)
LOYALTY + TRUST

HORATIO	Hail to your lordship.
HAMLET	I am glad to see you well 160 Horatio – or I do forget myself.
HORATIO	The same my lord, and your poor servant ever.
HAMLET	Sir, my good friend, I'll change that name with you. And what make you from Wittenberg Horatio? Marcellus. 165
MARCELLUS	My good lord.
HAMLET	I am very glad to see you. Good even sir. But what in faith make you from Wittenberg?
HORATIO	A truant disposition good my lord.
HAMLET	I would not hear your enemy say so, 170 Nor shall you do mine ear that violence To make it truster of your own report Against yourself. I know you are no truant. But what is your affair in Elsinore?

In talking to his friends Hamlet makes plain his attitude to his father's death and his mother's hasty marriage. Hamlet's references to his father lead Horatio into his subject – the visitation by his father's ghost. He goes on to describe what the three of them have seen.

177 **I prithee**: please, I beg you

179 **hard**: closely

180 **Thrift**: economy
The funeral...tables: the meat pies left over from the funeral feasting were served cold at the marriage feast

182 **dearest foe**: worst enemy – in the sense of 'the man I most love to hate'. Hamlet would expect this man to be in hell. Compare later (Act 3 scene 3) his reason for not killing Claudius at prayer.

183 **Or ever**: before

192 **Season your admiration**: keep your amazement in check

193 **With an attent ear**: and listen well

198 **waste**: desolate period. Some suggest a pun heard in waste/waist/middle for the dead period in the middle of the night.

200 **at point, exactly, cap-a-pie**: correctly in every detail, from head to foot

203 **fear-surprised**: overcome by fear

204 **Within his truncheon's length**: as close to them as the length of his baton (indicating his military rank)
distilled: dissolved

Pg 23 → SOLILOQUY.

HAMLET SHARE WITH AUDIENCE WHAT HE CAN'T VOICE IN PUBLIC. WORDS "WEARY, STALE, FLAT + UNPROFITABLE (133) SHOW HIS WEARINESS. SPEECH CONTRASTS DRAMATICALLY WITH CLAUDIUS' FLOWING LINES. THE DISJOINTED RHYTHM + DISLOCATED PROGRESS OF HAMLET'S THOUGHTS CONVEY HIS INNER TURMOIL.

SHOW HOW HE THOUGHT OF HIS FATHER NOT JUST EXCELLENT BUT SUPERHUMAN, OPPOSITE END OF THE SPECTRUM TO CLAUDIUS (140) HOW LOVING MUM + DADS RELATIONSHIP WAS (144) WHICH CONJURES UP PROTECTIVE IMAGE. HIS DISGUST IS PRESENT THROUGH IMAGES + SOUNDS OF WORDS. HE FEELS BOUND TO SUFFER IN SILENCE.

	We'll teach you to drink deep ere you depart. 175
HORATIO	My lord, I came to see your father's funeral.
HAMLET	I prithee do not mock me, fellow-student, I think it was to see my mother's wedding.
HORATIO	Indeed my lord it followed hard upon.
HAMLET	Thrift, thrift, Horatio. The funeral baked meats 180 Did coldly furnish forth the marriage tables. Would I had met my dearest foe in heaven Or ever I had seen that day Horatio. My father – methinks I see my father.
HORATIO	Where my lord?
HAMLET	In my mind's eye Horatio. 185
HORATIO	I saw him once, 'a was a goodly king.
HAMLET	'A was a man, take him for all in all, I shall not look upon his like again.
HORATIO	My lord, I think I saw him yesternight.
HAMLET	Saw? Who?
HORATIO	My lord, the King your father. 190
HAMLET	The King my father?
HORATIO	Season your admiration for a while With an attent ear, till I may deliver Upon the witness of these gentlemen This marvel to you.
HAMLET	For God's love let me hear. 195
HORATIO	Two nights together had these gentlemen, Marcellus and Barnardo, on their watch, In the dead waste and middle of the night, Been thus encountered – a figure like your father, Armed at point, exactly, cap-a-pie, 200 Appears before them, and with solemn march Goes slow and stately by them; thrice he walked By their oppressed and fear-surprised eyes, Within his truncheon's length, whilst they distilled

[Handwritten margin notes: "IRONIC", "HAVE SEEN HIS FATHER", "RATHER HAVE DIED THAN SEE THIS 2ND MARRIAGE", "DREAMS / MEMORY"]

Horatio speaks of the fear felt by the men who first saw the Ghost, and confirms that it is the image of Hamlet's father. Horatio explains, in answer to Hamlet's question, why he thinks it did not speak. Hamlet admits he is troubled, learns that they will keep watch that night and that the Ghost was in full armour.

205 act: action, effect
207 dreadful: full of dread, awe-struck
209 delivered: reported
216 it: a form of the possessive before 'its'
   address Itself to motion: was about to make a movement
222 writ...duty: part of the duty we owe you – just as if it had been some written condition of their service

Almost to jelly with the act of fear,   205
Stand dumb, and speak not to him. This to me
In dreadful secrecy impart they did,
And I with them the third night kept the watch,
Where, as they had delivered, both in time,
Form of the thing, each word made true and
     good,   210
The apparition comes. I knew your father;
These hands are not more like.

HAMLET   But where was this?

MARCELLUS   My lord, upon the platform where we watch.

HAMLET   Did you not speak to it?

HORATIO   My lord, I did,
But answer made it none: yet once
     methought   215
It lifted up it head, and did address
Itself to motion like as it would speak;
But even then the morning cock crew loud,
And at the sound it shrunk in haste away,
And vanished from our sight.

HAMLET   'Tis very strange. 220

HORATIO   As I do live, my honoured lord, 'tis true;
And we did think it writ down in our duty
To let you know of it.

HAMLET   Indeed, indeed sirs, but this troubles me.
Hold you the watch tonight?

MARCELLUS ⎫
                    ⎬   We do my lord.   225
BARNARDO ⎭

HAMLET   Armed say you?

MARCELLUS ⎫
                    ⎬   Armed my lord.
BARNARDO ⎭

HAMLET   From top to toe?

MARCELLUS ⎫
                    ⎬   My lord, from head to foot.
BARNARDO ⎭

AGITATED - SHORT - SHARP QUESTIONS

Hamlet questions the three men closely about the appearance of his father as ghost. He includes what looks like a trick question about the colour of his beard. Hamlet then decides to be present that night with the aim of speaking to the apparition. He asks for their continued silence and arranges the rendezvous.

229 beaver: visor, face-piece of helmet which was hinged and could be raised
235 amazed: bewildered
240 grizzled: grey
242 sable silvered: black flecked with white. The word '*sable*' is still the word for black in heraldry.
243 Perchance: perhaps
   I warr'nt: I'm sure, I guarantee
244 assume: take on
245 hell itself should gape: the mouth of hell should open wide
246 bid...peace: these remarks made by Hamlet point up the doubt that always exists when ghosts appear – do they come to bring evil, and possible death and damnation, or are they good spirits? Hamlet is not sure whether (line 244) a spirit has 'taken on' his father's appearance or whether (line 255) it truly is '*My father's spirit*'.
247 If...silence still: if you haven't yet mentioned what you have seen, please continue to keep quiet about it
249 hap: happen
251 requite your loves: repay your affection

HAMLET IS EUPHORIC WHILST HORATIO IS DISTINCTLY COOL.

HAMLET	Then saw you not his face.	
HORATIO	O yes my lord, he wore his beaver up.	
HAMLET	What, looked he frowningly?	230
HORATIO	A countenance more in sorrow than in anger.	
HAMLET	Pale, or red?	
HORATIO	Nay very pale.	
HAMLET	And fixed his eyes upon you?	
HORATIO	Most constantly.	
HAMLET	I would I had been there.	
HORATIO	It would have much amazed you.	235
HAMLET	Very like, very like – stayed it long?	
HORATIO	While one with moderate haste might tell a hundred.	
MARCELLUS BARNARDO	} Longer, longer.	
HORATIO	Not when I saw't.	
HAMLET	His beard was grizzled – no?	240
HORATIO	It was as I have seen it in his life, A sable silvered.	
HAMLET	I will watch tonight, Perchance 'twill walk again.	
HORATIO	I warr'nt it will.	
HAMLET	If it assume my noble father's person, I'll speak to it though hell itself should gape And bid me hold my peace. I pray you all, If you have hitherto concealed this sight, Let it be tenable in your silence still; And whatsoever else shall hap tonight, Give it an understanding but no tongue. I will requite your loves. So fare you well. Upon the platform 'twixt eleven and twelve I'll visit you.	245 250

TIES IN WITH LAST LINES

Having said goodbye to his friends, Hamlet again expresses his unease, and his impatience for the night to come. He anticipates that some crime will be disclosed.

256 doubt: suspect
258 Though...o'erwhelm them: however deeply buried they may be

Laertes, about to leave for France, says goodbye to his sister, Ophelia, and hopes she will write to him. The question of Hamlet's affection for her is raised. Laertes warns it may be short-lived and being a prince he may not be free to marry where he chooses.

1 **My necessaries are embarked**: my belongings are on the ship
2 **give benefit...assistant**: are favourable and ships are available
5 **trifling of his favour**: his pretended affection
6 **Hold it...primy nature**: think of it as a whim, a bit of nonsense as short-lived as a violet in the springtime of life
8 **Forward**: precocious, before its proper time
9 **The perfume...of a minute**: a sweet scent, filling just one moment
10 **No more but so?**: no more than that?
11 **For nature...withal**: growing up is not merely a question of physical size and strength, but as the body grows, so do the mental and spiritual sides, inwardly, at the same time
12 **thews**: muscles
   temple: body
15 **no soil...of his will**: no stain or deceit spoils his honest intentions
17 **His greatness weighed**: when you consider his position

- *What do these exchanges tell us about the relationship between Laertes and Ophelia?*
- *What seems to be Laertes's opinion of Hamlet at this stage?*

ALL	Our duty to your honour.
HAMLET	Your loves, as mine to you. Farewell.

[*Exeunt*

My father's spirit – in arms – all is not well.   255
I doubt some foul play. Would the night
   were come.
Till then sit still my soul. Foul deeds will rise,
Though all the earth o'erwhelm them, to
   men's eyes.   [*Exit*

Scene 3

Enter LAERTES *and* OPHELIA *his sister*

LAERTES	My necessaries are embarked. Farewell.
	And sister, as the winds give benefit,
	And convoy is assistant, do not sleep,
	But let me hear from you.
OPHELIA	Do you doubt that?
LAERTES	For Hamlet, and the trifling of his favour, 5
	Hold it a fashion, and a toy in blood;
	A violet in the youth of primy nature,
	Forward, not permanent, sweet, not lasting,
	The perfume and suppliance of a minute,
	No more.
OPHELIA	No more but so?
LAERTES	Think it no more. 10
	For nature crescent, does not grow alone
	In thews and bulk, but as this temple waxes,
	The inward service of the mind and soul
	Grows wide withal. Perhaps he loves you now,
	And now no soil nor cautel doth besmirch 15
	The virtue of his will; but you must fear,
	His greatness weighed, his will is not his own,
	For he himself is subject to his birth.

Laertes says Hamlet may be speaking the truth when he declares his love, but since he might become King his wife will have to be officially approved. Ophelia should not risk her reputation by encouraging him. She agrees to follow his advice if he will live by it too.

20 **Carve for himself**: serve his own wishes
21 **safety**: some peope prefer the reading '*sanity*', others '*sanctity*' which adds a spiritual dimension to the concept of the state
22 **circumscribed**: limited
23 **voice...that body**: vote and consent of that state
26 **in his particular act and place**: with his sphere of activities and in his position. F's alternative reading '*his peculiar sect and force*' is glossed as 'the special circumstances of his class and power'.
27 **May give his saying deed**: may act on what he has been saying
28 **main**: general
30 **credent**: trustful
31 **or your chaste...importunity**: or give in to his demands, which are difficult to resist, and let him sleep with you
34 **And keep...desire**: a military metaphor. Ophelia's affections are the front-line troops; she should stay safely out of the battle.
36 **The chariest maid...enough**: the most careful girl is generous enough if she does no more than reveal her beauty to the moon
38 **'scapes not...strokes**: cannot escape being attacked by slander
39 **canker**: disease of roses or a pest, the canker-worm. Shakespeare often uses *metaphor* and *simile* (see GLOSSARY pages 328–329) from his knowledge of gardening and the countryside.
   the infants of the spring: tender young shoots appearing early in the year
40 **buttons be disclosed**: buds open
42 **Contagious blastments**: attacks of blight which spread
44 **Youth...near**: youth would rebel, even if there were no one around to watch
49 **puffed...libertine**: boastful and reckless seducer
50 **primrose path of dalliance**: easy route to flirtation (and worse!)
51 **recks not...rede**: does not pay attention to his own advice

> • *It is easy to think of Ophelia mainly as a victim, but note the spirited reply she gives to her brother here.*

He shows genuine concern

He may not, as unvalued persons do,
Carve for himself, for on his choice depends   20
The safety and health of this whole state,
And therefore must his choice be circumscribed
Unto the voice and yielding of that body
Whereof he is the head. Then if he says he
    loves you,
It fits your wisdom so far to believe it   25
As he in his particular act and place
May give his saying deed, which is no further
Than the main voice of Denmark goes withal.
Then weigh what loss your honour may
    sustain,
If with too credent ear you list his songs,   30
Or lose your heart, or your chaste treasure open
To his unmastered importunity.
Fear it Ophelia, fear it my dear sister,
And keep you in the rear of your affection,
Out of the shot and danger of desire.   35
The chariest maid is prodigal enough,
If she unmask her beauty to the moon;
Virtue itself 'scapes not calumnious strokes.
The canker galls the infants of the spring
Too oft before their buttons be disclosed,   40
And in the morn and liquid dew of youth
Contagious blastments are most imminent.
Be wary then, best safety lies in fear.
Youth to itself rebels, though none else near.

OPHELIA   I shall the effect of this good lesson keep   45
As watchman to my heart. But good my brother,
Do not as some ungracious pastors do,
Show me the steep and thorny way to heaven,
Whiles like a puffed and reckless libertine
Himself the primrose path of dalliance treads,   50
And recks not his own rede.

LAERTES   O fear me not.
I stay too long – but here my father comes.

His position will control what he choses.

Warning of the dangers of such an attachment

Again springtime tinted with corruption disease + decay

He should follow his own advice

Nice relationship will be forced to change.

She's not completely convinced with what Laertes is saying.

Polonius comes upon his son and daughter and is surprised that Laertes has not yet left. However, he now takes the opportunity to deliver a lecture to Laertes, composed of wise sayings about friends, clothes, quarrelling, expressing opinions, buying clothes, borrowing or lending money and integrity. Laertes says goodbye to his father again.

54 Occasion smiles...leave: it is good fortune to have a second chance to say goodbye

56 The wind...for: the wind is filling your sails and the others are waiting for you

58 precepts: instructions

58 these few...character: (stress on second syllable) set down or memorize these few instructions

59 Give...act: do not express your thoughts and do not act on any unruly thought

61 Be thou...familiar: be friendly, but not with everyone

62 their adoption tried: when their friendship has been tried and tested

63 Grapple them: hold them

64 But do...courage: Polonius tells him not to be too eager to give his hand to any untried person he's only just met
courage: some people prefer the reading 'comrade'. The word '*courage*' meant both 'heart' and 'spirit', and 'person'.

67 Bear't that: manage things so that

69 censure: judgement

70 habit: clothing

72 For...chief in that: people are often judged by their dress and Frenchmen of rank and position or of superior degree or nobility are the most gifted at choosing the right clothes. (Laertes, of course, is returning to France.)

77 borrowing...husbandry: borrowing damages the whole business of managing your money

81 my blessing...thee: may my blessing make this advice bear fruit

83 The time invites you: it is time you were on your way

> • *What does Polonius reveal about himself in this homily to his son, his first speech of any length in the play?*

Enter POLONIUS

A double blessing is a double grace;
Occasion smiles upon a second leave.

POLONIUS   Yet here Laertes? Aboard, aboard, for shame;   55
The wind sits in the shoulder of your sail,
And you are stayed for. There – my blessing
    with thee.
And these few precepts in thy memory
Look thou character. Give thy thoughts no tongue,
Nor any unproportioned thought his act.   60
Be thou familiar, but by no means vulgar.
Those friends thou hast, and their adoption tried,
Grapple them unto thy soul with hoops of steel;
But do not dull thy palm with entertainment
Of each new-hatched, unfledged courage.
    Beware   65
Of entrance to a quarrel, but being in,
Bear't that th' opposed may beware of thee.
Give every man thy ear, but few thy voice;
Take each man's censure, but reserve thy
    judgement.
Costly thy habit as thy purse can buy,   70
But not expressed in fancy; rich, not gaudy,
For the apparel oft proclaims the man;
And they in France of the best rank and station
Or of a most select and generous, chief in that.
Neither a borrower nor a lender be,   75
For loan oft loses both itself and friend,
And borrowing dulleth edge of husbandry.
This above all, to thine own self be true,
And it must follow, as the night the day,
Thou canst not then be false to any man.   80
Farewell, my blessing season this in thee.

LAERTES   Most humbly do I take my leave my lord.

POLONIUS   The time invites you; go, your servants tend.

LAERTES   Farewell Ophelia, and remember well

Handwritten annotations:
FORMAL TONE
KEEP THINGS TO HIMSELF
BE FRIENDLY NOT TOO FRIENDLY
IMAGERY — STRENGTH OF BOND BETWEEN FRIENDS
DON'T DO THINGS ILL ADVISED
"COMRADE"
AVOID CONFRONTATION
KEEP IT IF YOU ARE
CONSIDER OTHERS OPINIONS; KEEP YOURS TO YOURSELF
REFLECT IN YOUR CLOTHING IN THE IMPRESSION YOU ARE MAKING
YOUR NOT MANAGING YOUR MONEY EFFECTIVELY
MAKING DON'T BE SHOWY
BE HONEST + OPEN WITH YOURSELF
DON'T BE INVOLVED IN THOSE THINGS WHICH ARE WRONG

Laertes, before leaving, reminds Ophelia to remember what he has said to her. Polonius asks what this was, and she mentions Hamlet. This triggers an interrogation on the part of Polonius who has already heard that Hamlet has been visiting her. Ophelia clearly thinks Hamlet's expressions of love are genuine. Polonius warns her of her youth and inexperience.

89 touching: concerning

90 Marry well bethought: to be sure, well remembered

93 bounteous: generous

95 caution: warning

97 behoves: befits

99 tenders: offers, declarations

101 green girl Unsifted: inexperienced and untried girl

106 ta'en: taken

  tenders: (here) offers of money

107 sterling: genuine. Originally a pound sterling was a pound weight of silver pennies, whereas some currencies already used base metals for their coinage, as we do today.

  Tender yourself: take more care of yourself with the double meaning of: Offer yourself at a higher rate (see *Pun*, GLOSSARY page 328).

108 not to...thus: a metaphor taken from horsemanship. A horse ridden long and fast to a state of exhaustion would not be able to breathe properly.

109 tender me a fool: present me as a fool, make me look a fool

110 importuned...love: (stress on second syllable) expressed his love

111 fashion: his way of behaving, just a whim

112 go to: go on! (ie how can she believe this?)

113 hath...to his speech: has backed up what he has said

• *What is your intuitive reaction to where the truth lies when you read this whole conversation?*

What I have said to you.

OPHELIA   'Tis in my memory locked,   85
And you yourself shall keep the key of it.

LAERTES   Farewell.   [*Exit Laertes*

POLONIUS   What is't Ophelia he hath said to you?

OPHELIA   So please you, something touching the Lord
Hamlet.

WARNING OPHELIA OF HAMLET

POLONIUS   Marry well bethought.   90
'Tis told me he hath very oft of late
Given private time to you, and you yourself
Have of your audience been most free and
bounteous.
If it be so, as so 'tis put on me,
And that in way of caution, I must tell you,   95
You do not understand yourself so clearly
As it behoves my daughter, and your honour.
What is between you? Give me up the truth.

SHE IS NOT IN A POSITION TO BE A SUIT-ABLE PARTNER OF HAMLET

OPHELIA   He hath my lord of late made many tenders
Of his affection to me.   100

POLONIUS   Affection? Pooh, you speak like a green girl
Unsifted in such perilous circumstance.
Do you believe his tenders as you call them?

DUBIOUS ABOUT HAMLETS FEELINGS

OPHELIA   I do not know my lord what I should think.

POLONIUS   Marry I'll teach you; think yourself a baby,   105
That you have ta'en these tenders for true pay
Which are not sterling. Tender yourself more
dearly;
Or – not to crack the wind of the poor phrase
Running it thus – you'll tender me a fool.

SHE'S MISINTERRETED DESIRE FOR REAL LOVE

LOOKING AT HIP POSITION ALSO

OPHELIA   My lord he hath importuned me with love   110
In honourable fashion.

POLONIUS   Ay, fashion you may call it; go to, go to.

SHE FEELS HAMLET IS GENUINE

OPHELIA   And hath given countenance to his speech, my
lord,
With almost all the holy vows of heaven.

Polonius insists that Hamlet's words are fired with his present feelings of love for her, but Ophelia must not believe him. He is young, and his position allows him more scope than she can permit herself. He may want her, but not to marry her. She is not to speak to him again. Ophelia promises to obey her father.

115 **springes...woodcocks**: snares to catch woodcocks (a game-bird, something like a snipe and considered rather stupid.)

116 **prodigal**: generously, lavishly

118 **extinct in both**: with both light and heat extinguished

121 **Be somewhat scanter**: limit

122 **Set...parley**: set more store on your negotiating position than to accept his demand to discuss terms for surrender. The *metaphor* (see GLOSSARY page 328) is that of a castle – her virginity – under siege.

125 **larger tether**: a longer tethering rope. Hamlet is allowed more licence than Ophelia.

126 **In few**: in short

127 **for they are brokers...beguile**: for they are marriage-brokers, go-betweens, who are not offering what they say they are, but making you listen to dishonourable entreaties, promising blessed and holy marriage, all the better to charm you. There are punning references: broker is marriage broker, shady financier, dealer in secondhand clothes; investments are financial dealings, clothes; bonds are both financial and marriage bonds.

133 **slander any moment leisure**: debase any free moment

● *Assess Polonius's attitude to relationships.*

Hamlet, Horatio and Marcellus are on the castle battlements just after midnight. It is very cold.

1 **shrewdly**: keenly

2 **eager**: sharp

3 **lacks of twelve**: not yet midnight

A TRAP TO CATCH FOOLS

POLONIUS	Ay, springes to catch woodcocks. I do know, 115
	When the blood burns, how prodigal the soul
Images	Lends the tongue vows. These blazes daughter,
FIRE AND	Giving more light than heat, extinct in both,
PASSION	Even in their promise, as it is a-making,
IT WILL	You must not take for fire. From this time 120
BURN OUT	Be somewhat scanter of your maiden presence.
NO DEPTH	Set your entreatments at a higher rate
MORE LIGHT	Than a command to parley. For Lord Hamlet,
THAN HEAT =	Believe so much in him that he is young,
WON'T	And with a larger tether may he walk 125
LAST .	Than may be given you. In few Ophelia,
	Do not believe his vows, for they are brokers, *WARNING HER OFF.*
	Not of that dye which their investments show,
	But mere implorators of unholy suits,
	Breathing like sanctified and pious bonds 130
	The better to beguile. This is for all: *APPEARANCE/*
	I would not in plain terms from this time forth *REALITY*
	Have you so slander any moment leisure *(MAY LOOK*
	As to give words or talk with the Lord *GOOD BUT*
	Hamlet. *COMMAND . BENEATH THE*
	Look to 't I charge you; come your ways. 135 *SURFACE*
	THEY
OPHELIA	I shall obey, my lord. [*Exeunt* *ARE*
	JUST 'UNHOLY

IMPLICIT MEANING TO LOOKING *SUITS"*
FOR MARRIAGE,T - FOR HAMLET
THERE IS A LESS MORAL
MEANING(IE DESIRE)

Scene 4

Enter HAMLET, HORATIO, *and* MARCELLUS

HAMLET	The air bites shrewdly, it is very cold.
HORATIO	It is a nipping and an eager air.
HAMLET	What hour now?
HORATIO	I think it lacks of twelve.
MARCELLUS	No, it is struck.
HORATIO	Indeed? I heard it not; it then draws near the
	season 5

From inside the three hear trumpets and cannon-fire when a toast is drunk. Hamlet dislikes this practice and resents the impression it gives to other nations. He sees how one defect in a man can seem to colour the whole personality and affect others' opinion of him.

6 **held his wont**: was accustomed
8 **doth wake...reels**: holding his celebrations tonight, with toasts, drinking and wild dances
10 **Rhenish**: wine from the Rhine
12 **triumph**: celebration of his toast
15 **it is a custom...observance**: a custom much better left out
17 **east and west**: in all directions, the world over
18 **traduced and taxed**: slandered and accused
19 **clepe**: call
with swinish...addition: put a stain on any distinction we may have by calling us pigs
22 **pith and marrow...attribute**: the essential, innermost nature of our qualities
24 **mole of nature**: some birthmark
27 **By the...complexion**: some excess in their physical make-up. (A person's constitution was thought to be composed of the four humours: blood, phlegm, choler and melancholy which needed to be kept in proper balance. From this belief we have the descriptions of people as being 'sanguine', 'phlegmatic', 'choleric' or 'melancholy', depending on which humour was seen to predominate.)
28 **pales**: fences
29 **o'er-leavens...manners**: just as too much yeast will cause dough to be sour, or not rise properly, so will some habit, carried to excess, ruin otherwise acceptable manners
32 **nature's livery**: a uniform showing that nature is your master
fortune's star: a mark made by chance
33 **his virtues...fault**: however pure, however varied a man's merits may be, he will be subject to blame for that one fault

- *Note any indications of what Hamlet might have been like as king.*

CELEBRATION IN THE CASTLE – SHOWS HAMLETS
BITTERNESS.

        Wherein the spirit held his wont to walk.
          [*A flourish of trumpets, and cannon fire within*
        What does this mean my lord?

HAMLET   The King doth wake tonight and takes his rouse,
        Keeps wassail, and the swaggering up-spring
          reels;
        And as he drains his draughts of Rhenish down, 10
        The kettle-drum and trumpet thus bray out
        The triumph of his pledge.

HORATIO   Is it a custom?

HAMLET   Ay marry is't,
        But to my mind, though I am native here,
THE
REPUTATION   And to the manner born, it is a custom   15
THEY HAVE   More honoured in the breach than the
FOR EXCESS   observance.
DRINKING   This heavy-headed revel east and west
UNDERMINES Makes us traduced and taxed of other nations.
THE GOOD   They clepe us drunkards, and with swinish phrase
THINGS THEY Soil our addition; and indeed it takes   20
PERFORM.   From our achievements, though performed at
          height,
        The pith and marrow of our attribute.

REPEATING   So, oft it chances in particular men,
THE   That for some vicious mole of nature in them,
ARGUMENT As in their birth, wherein they are not guilty – 25
ONE FAULT Since nature cannot choose his origin –
RUINS   By the o'ergrowth of some complexion,
ALL   Oft breaking down the pales and forts of reason,
GOOD   Or by some habit, that too much o'er-leavens
– QUALITIES The form of plausive manners – that these men, 30
        Carrying, I say, the stamp of one defect,
        Being nature's livery, or fortune's star,
        His virtues else be they as pure as grace,
        As infinite as man may undergo,
        Shall in the general censure take corruption 35

The Ghost appears. Hamlet immediately addresses it, still doubting whether it is a good or evil spirit, but giving it all the names his father would have had. He then specifically asks why this spirit has had to leave his tomb and revisit the earth. The Ghost beckons him away as though it wants to speak to him alone. Hamlet's friends warn him not to go.

36 **The dram of eale...scandal**: it is not possible to know the correct reading of this line, but the sense appears to be that the smallest drop of evil poisons the whole, the least doubt brings the whole noble enterprise into question

39 **ministers of grace**: messengers of God

40 **spirit of health...damned**: a good spirit or an evil demon

41 **airs**: gentle breezes

43 **questionable shape**: shape that I must put questions to

47 **canonized**: buried in accordance with the rites of the church
hearsed: coffined

48 **cerements**: burial clothes, waxed cloth to wrap a dead body in (modern French *cire* means wax)
sepulchre: tomb

52 **in complete steel**: (stress on first syllable of '*complete*' in full armour

53 **glimpses**: fitful gleams

54 **hideous**: terrifying
fools of nature: ignorant human beings

55 **horridly...disposition**: shaking ourselves so violently

59 **As if it...desire**: as if there were something it wanted to communicate

61 **more removed ground**: somewhere further off

• *Can you find any clues about whether the Ghost is a 'spirit of health' or 'goblin damned'?*

From that particular fault. The dram of eale
Doth all the noble substance of a doubt
To his own scandal.

Enter GHOST

HORATIO   Look my lord, it comes.

THOU, THEE, THY – FAMILIARITY BETWEEN HIM + HIS FATHER

HAMLET   Angels and ministers of grace defend us.

Be thou a spirit of health or goblin damned,   40

ARE YOU GOOD OR EVIL

Bring with thee airs from heaven, or blasts
    from hell,

WHY HAS HE APPEARED + IN FULL ARMOUR. SUGGEST A BATTLE

Be thy intents wicked, or charitable,
Thou com'st in such a questionable shape,
That I will speak to thee. I'll call thee Hamlet,
King, father, royal Dane. O answer me.   45
Let me not burst in ignorance, but tell

HE HAD A CHRISTIAN BURIAL – SO WHY DOES HE WALK.

Why thy canonized bones, hearsed in death,
Have burst their cerements; why the sepulchre,
Wherein we saw thee quietly interred,
Hath oped his ponderous and marble jaws,   50
To cast thee up again. What may this mean,
That thou, dead corse, again in complete steel
Revisits thus the glimpses of the moon,
Making night hideous, and we fools of nature

SERIES OF QUESTIONS

So horridly to shake our disposition   55
With thoughts beyond the reaches of our souls?
Say, why is this? Wherefore? What should we do?

                         [GHOST *beckons*

HORATIO   It beckons you to go away with it,
As if it some impartment did desire
To you alone.

CONCERN FOR HAMLET.

MARCELLUS   Look with what courteous action   60
It waves you to a more removed ground.
But do not go with it.

HORATIO   No, by no means.

HAMLET   It will not speak; then I will follow it.

HORATIO   Do not my lord.

Hamlet dismisses his friends' fear for him, saying he does not value his life, and that his soul, being immortal like the Ghost, cannot be corrupted. Horatio is concerned that the spirit may draw Hamlet to his death in the sea at the foot of the cliff. Hamlet is desperate to follow the Ghost and forces them to let him go. Horatio and Marcellus decide to follow, at a distance.

65 set...pin's fee: value my life at the cost of a pin
69 the flood: the sea
71 beetles: overhangs (like beetle brows – scowling eyebrows)
73 deprive...reason: deprive you of the rule of reason
75 toys of desperation: desperate fancies
78 It waves me still: it is still beckoning me on
81 fate: destiny, future
83 Nemean lion's nerve: the first of the twelve labours of Hercules was to kill the Nemean lion, which had been terrifying people. Its skin was so tough that his club made no impression, so he squeezed it to death and ever after wore its skin. It is interesting to compare Hamlet's reference here to the Hercules story, to his reference in Act 1 scene 2 line 153.
nerve: sinew
85 lets: hinders, prevents
87 waxes: grows
89 Have after: let's go after him

> • *There are further pointers here to Horatio's personality and his role in the play.*

[handwritten: IT ONLY PRESENTS A SPIRITUAL/PSYCHOLOGICAL DANGER]

[handwritten: PROFOUNDLY IRONIC AS THE GHOST IS NOT LIFE THREATENING]

HAMLET	Why, what should be the fear?
	I do not set my life at a pin's fee, *[STARTS]* 65
	And for my soul, what can it do to that *[LITTLE IMPORTANCE IN]*
	Being a thing immortal as itself? *[HIS OWN LIFE? HAS LITTLE TO]*
	It waves me forth again. I'll follow it. *[LOSE]*
HORATIO	What if it tempt you toward the flood my lord,
	Or to the dreadful summit of the cliff 70
	That beetles o'er his base into the sea,
	And there assume some other horrible form,
	Which might deprive your sovereignty of reason
	And draw you into madness? Think of it. *[IRONIC]*
	The very place puts toys of desperation, 75 *[SIGNIFICANT OF]*
	Without more motive, into every brain *[MADNESS IN]*
	That looks so many fathoms to the sea, *[THE PLAYS AS]*
	And hears it roar beneath. *[A WHOLE]*
HAMLET *[CONSIDERED]*	It waves me still. *[HAMLET]*
	Go on, I'll follow thee. *[THREISON MADNESS TO]*
MARCELLUS	You shall not go my lord. *[WATCH OTHERS]*
HAMLET	Hold off your hands. 80
HORATIO	Be ruled, you shall not go.
HAMLET	My fate cries out,
	And makes each petty artery in this body
	As hardy as the Nemean lion's nerve.
	Still am I called. Unhand me gentlemen.
	By heaven I'll make a ghost of him that
	lets me. 85
	I say, away! Go on, I'll follow thee.

[Exeunt GHOST and HAMLET

HORATIO	He waxes desperate with imagination. *[IMAGE OF]*
MARCELLUS	Let's follow, 'tis not fit thus to obey him. *[DISEASE]*
HORATIO	Have after. To what issue will this come? *[+ CORRUPTION]*
MARCELLUS	Something is rotten in the state of Denmark. 90
HORATIO	Heaven will direct it.
MARCELLUS	Nay, let's follow him.

[handwritten left margin: IRONIC IDEA OF SUICIDE WHICH WE KNOW HI HAS PREVIOUSLY 14 CONSIDERED]

[Exeunt

[handwritten: RELATION WITH WHAT DID HAMLET COMES TO SAY]

When Hamlet asks the Ghost to speak, saying he will not follow him any further, the Ghost says Hamlet will feel bound to seek revenge, when he hears his story. He confirms that he is his father's spirit, and that he will be in Purgatory until the sins he was unable to confess have been purged away. He is not allowed to tell the terrible secrets of Purgatory.

  6 **bound**: obliged

11 **fast in fires**: he is in Purgatory. The Church held that souls which were destined for Heaven had nevertheless to be purged of their sins until they were fit to meet God.

13 **But that**: except for the fact that

16 **harrow up**: tear apart

17 **Make...spheres**: make both your eyes burst out from your head, like stars leaving their proper course

18 **knotted and combined**: tangled and wound together

19 **particular**: individual

    an end: on end; 'an' is an obsolete form

20 **fretful porpentine**: bad-tempered porcupine

21 **eternal blazon**: proclamation of what goes on in the immortal world

> • *Hamlet, and the audience, are given the confirmation that Purgatory has unspeakable horrors in store. This adds weight to all the later emphasis on confession and absolution as a prelude to a good death.*

Scene 5

Enter GHOST *and* HAMLET

HAMLET   Where wilt thou lead me? Speak, I'll go no further.

GHOST   Mark me.

HAMLET   I will.

GHOST   My hour is almost come

When I to sulphurous and tormenting flames

Must render up myself.

HAMLET   Alas poor ghost!

GHOST   Pity me not, but lend thy serious hearing   5

To what I shall unfold.

HAMLET   Speak, I am bound to hear.

GHOST   So art thou to revenge, when thou shalt hear.

HAMLET   What?

GHOST   I am thy father's spirit,

Doomed for a certain term to walk the night,   10

And for the day confined to fast in fires,

Till the foul crimes done in my days of nature

Are burnt and purged away. But that I am forbid

To tell the secrets of my prison-house,

I could a tale unfold whose lightest word   15

Would harrow up thy soul, freeze thy young

    blood,

Make thy two eyes like stars start from their

    spheres,

Thy knotted and combined locks to part,

And each particular hair to stand an end,

Like quills upon the fretful porpentine.   20

But this eternal blazon must not be

To ears of flesh and blood. List, list, o list!

If thou didst ever thy dear father love –

HAMLET   O God!

The Ghost reveals that he was murdered by his brother, Claudius, not bitten by a snake. He also alleges, with disgust, that Gertrude whom he loved and honoured in accordance with his marriage vows, had already been seduced before his death by his brother. Lust had led her astray.

25 unnatural: monstrous

27 as in the best it is: as it is even in the most extenuating circumstances

28 strange and unnatural: it was fratricide – murder of a brother. This crime, like other murders of blood relations, is considered more '*unnatural*' than other forms of killing. Also this was a murder of envy, for gain.

31 apt: ready to respond

32 fat...ease: gross weed that grows so luxuriantly

33 Lethe: the river of forgetfulness which, according to Greek myth, flowed through Hades. The souls, waiting to cross, drank from it and so forgot their existence on earth.

37 forged process: invented description

38 Rankly abused: massively deceived

40 prophetic soul: Hamlet has felt all along that things are wrong, but he is not claiming to have suspected this crime

43 wits: mental powers

44 wit: intellect

46 will: desire

49 even with the vow: with that very vow

53 moved: affected

54 lewdness...heaven: lust pays court to it in angelic form

56 sate...bed: become glutted in a heavenly bed

> • *Notice the context of the first mention of words such as 'unnatural' and 'incestuous'.*

[handwritten annotation: FAR MORE SIGNIFICANCE IN ELIZABETHAN TIMES (GOING AGAINST NATURAL ORDER)]

GHOST	Revenge his foul and most unnatural murder. 25
HAMLET	Murder?
GHOST	Murder most foul, as in the best it is,
	But this most foul, strange and unnatural.

[handwritten annotation: MURDER IS FOUL ANYWAY BUT THIS IS WORSE AS IT WAS HIS BROTHER]

HAMLET	Haste me to know 't, that I with wings as swift
	As meditation or the thoughts of love, 30
	May sweep to my revenge.

[handwritten annotation: ONLY TIME WHEN HE WANTS THINGS TO GO QUICK]

GHOST	I find thee apt,
	And duller shouldst thou be than the fat weed
	That roots itself in ease on Lethe wharf,
	Wouldst thou not stir in this. Now Hamlet, hear.
	'Tis given out that, sleeping in my orchard, 35
	A serpent stung me; so the whole ear of Denmark
	Is by a forged process of my death
	Rankly abused. But know, thou noble youth,
	The serpent that did sting thy father's life
	Now wears his crown.

[handwritten annotation: GENERAL COMMENTS ON CORRUPT DENMARK]

[handwritten annotation: ANIMAL IMAGERY]

[handwritten annotation: HAMLET HAS ALREADY SUSPECTED THIS]

HAMLET	O my prophetic soul! 40
	My uncle?

[handwritten annotation: ANIMAL IN THE FORM OF INCEST]

GHOST	Ay, that incestuous, that adulterate beast,
	With witchcraft of his wits, with traitorous gifts –
	O wicked wit and gifts that have the power
	So to seduce – won to his shameful lust 45
	The will of my most seeming-virtuous Queen.
	O Hamlet, what a falling-off was there,
	From me whose love was of that dignity
	That it went hand in hand even with the vow
	I made to her in marriage, and to decline 50
	Upon a wretch whose natural gifts were poor
	To those of mine.
	But virtue, as it never will be moved,
	Though lewdness court it in a shape of heaven;
	So lust, though to a radiant angel linked, 55
	Will sate itself in a celestial bed,
	And prey on garbage.
	But soft, methinks I scent the morning air;

[handwritten annotation: GERTUDE HAS BEEN SEDUCED BY CLAUDIUS. CLEVERLY WORKED OUT PLAN]

[handwritten annotation: APPEARANCE VS REALITY]

[handwritten annotation: BOTH HAMLETS' ARE COMPARING THE TWO BROTHER]

[handwritten annotation: SAME AS HAMLETS OBSESSION WITH THE PHYSICAL RELATIONSHIP OF MOTHER + UNCLE]

Hamlet's father claims that while he was resting in his
garden, Claudius crept up and poured poison in his ears. It
took instant effect, clotting his blood and producing scaly
sores all over his body. He was sent unprepared to his death
and now suffers the torments of Purgatory. Although asking
Hamlet for vengeance, he tells him to leave his mother to
God. He senses morning is near, and leaves. Hamlet is
devastated by the news.

59 orchard: orchard or garden

61 secure: (stress on first syllable) when he felt relaxed and safe

62 hebona: a poisonous tree or plant – possibly ebony or
henbane

64 leperous distilment: the liquid obtained from the poisonous
plant, causing a scaly outbreak on the skin

66 quicksilver: mercury

67 gates and alleys: veins and pathways

68 sudden vigour...milk: suddenly taking effect, it clots and
curdles, like acid dropped into milk (eager is French 'aigre' –
'sour', wine vinegar is 'vinaigre' in French – wine that has
gone sour)

71 tetter barked...loathsome crust: skin eruption crusted over
like leprosy, with horrid and revolting sores

75 dispatched: deprived by murder

76 blossoms of my sin: my sins full-blown

77 Unhouseled...unaneled: without the sacrament, without
preparation for death, without extreme unction (anointing
the head of a dying person with holy oil)

85 Taint not thy mind: do not let it affect your mind
contrive: plot

89 matin: morning (cf modern French)

90 'gins to pale...fire: the glow-worm's light seems to become
fainter as daylight grows

93 shall I couple hell?: shall I add hell (to these exclamations)

> • *What is the Ghost actually asking of his son?*

(handwritten margin note: DETAILED ACCOUNT OF MURDER + HOW THE POISON EFFECTED HIM QUICKLY)

Brief let me be. Sleeping within my orchard,
My custom always of the afternoon,   60
Upon my secure hour thy uncle stole,
With juice of cursed hebona in a vial,
And in the porches of my ears did pour

(handwritten margin note: RASHES LIKE LEPROSY.)

The leperous distilment, whose effect
Holds such an enmity with blood of man,   65
That swift as quicksilver it courses through
The natural gates and alleys of the body,
And with a sudden vigour it doth posset
And curd, like eager droppings into milk,
The thin and wholesome blood; so did it mine,   70
And a most instant tetter barked about,
Most lazar-like, with vile and loathsome crust
All my smooth body.
Thus was I sleeping, by a brother's hand
Of life, of crown, of queen, at once dispatched;   75
Cut off even in the blossoms of my sin,

(handwritten margin note: THIS IS WHAT THE GHOST IS SUFFERING – HE IS WANDERING ASTHE WAS UNABLE TO CONFESS HIS SINS BEFORE HIS DEATH)

Unhouseled, disappointed, unaneled,
Not reckoning made, but sent to my account

(handwritten margin note: (LINK WITH OPPURTUNITY FOR HAMLET TO KILL CLAUDIUS LATER))

With all my imperfections on my head –
O horrible! O horrible, most horrible!   80
If thou hast nature in thee, bear it not,
Let not the royal bed of Denmark be

(handwritten margin note: WHAT HAMLET TAKES ON BOARD.)

A couch for luxury and damned incest.
But howsoever thou pursuest this act,
Taint not thy mind, nor let thy soul contrive   85
Against thy mother aught; leave her to heaven,

(handwritten margin note: GOD WILL DECIDE)

And to those thorns that in her bosom lodge
To prick and sting her. Fare thee well at once.

(handwritten margin note: WHILST ASKING HAMLET TO GET REVENGE HE DOES NOT WANT HER MOTHER INVOLVED)

(handwritten margin note: HE GUILT IS BAD ENOUGH)

The glow-worm shows the matin to be near,
And 'gins to pale his uneffectual fire.   90
Adieu, adieu, adieu. Remember me.   [*Exit*

HAMLET   O all you host of heaven! O earth! What else?

(handwritten margin note: ★ SOLILOQUY)

And shall I couple hell? O fie! Hold, hold,
    my heart,
And you my sinews, grow not instant old,

Hamlet vows to follow the spirit's injunction to 'remember him', and to do so will dispose of everything he has ever learnt which is irrelevant to this overriding concern. He curses his mother and Claudius. When Horatio and the others appear, anxious for his safety, he will not tell them what has happened.

95 **bear me stiffly up**: keep me upright
96 **holds a seat...globe**: has a place in this disordered world, with a possible punning reference to the confusion in his head (*Pun*, see GLOSSARY page 328)
98 **table**: writing tablet, notebook
99 **fond**: foolish
100 **saws**: maxims, sayings
forms: shapes, images
pressures: impressions
101 **observation**: duty
110 **my word**: he has not yet made any formal vow to the ghost
111 **'Adieu...me'**: the Ghost's words will serve to remind Hamlet constantly, throughout the play, what is required of him
118 **Come bird, come**: Hamlet answers with a falconer's call

SOLILOQUY.

ACT 1 SCS AS WHAT.
MORE GRAPHIC + DETAILED THAN PREVIOUSLY.
DENMARK SEEN AS PRISON LIKE
SCENE IN GRAVEYARD IS ONLY ONE OUTSIDE THE
CASTLE.
WE SEE HAMLETS CHANGE HERE.
HE HAS DETERMINATION FOR REVENGE.
UNLIKE BEFORE HE SHOWS STRENGTH NOT
WEAKNESS.
METAPHORE OF BOOKS EXPRESSING IS NEW FOCUS,
CONCENTRATION.
HE NO LONGER NEEDS BOOKS FOR LEARNING ALL HE
NEEDS IS TO CONCENTRATE ON REVENGE
ALSO ACKNOWLEDGES APPEARANCE VS REALITY.
HAMLET REALISES, NOTHING IS AS IT SEEMS.
ALSO SHOWS HOW HAMLET FINDS IT DIFFICULT TO
PUT HIS BELIEFS INTO ACTION. IE → HE DISREGARDS
BOOKS THEN STARTS TO WRITE → DOESN'T FOLLOW IT THROUGH

But bear me stiffly up. Remember thee? 95
Ay thou poor ghost, whiles memory holds a seat
In this distracted globe. Remember thee?
Yea, from the table of my memory
I'll wipe away all trivial fond records,
All saws of books, all forms, all pressures past 100
That youth and observation copied there,
And thy commandment all alone shall live
Within the book and volume of my brain,
Unmixed with baser matter – yes, by heaven!
O most pernicious woman! 105
O villain, villain, smiling, damned villain!
My tables – meet it is I set it down,
That one may smile, and smile, and be a villain;
At least I am sure it may be so in Denmark:

                [*Writes*

So uncle, there you are. Now to my word; 110
It is 'Adieu, adieu, remember me'.
I have sworn't.

Enter HORATIO *and* MARCELLUS

MARCELLUS	My lord, my lord!
HORATIO	
MARCELLUS	Lord Hamlet!
HORATIO	Heaven secure him.
HAMLET	So be it.
HORATIO	Hillo, ho, ho, my lord!
HAMLET	Hillo, ho, ho, boy! Come bird, come.
MARCELLUS	How is 't my noble lord?
HORATIO	What news my lord? 120
HAMLET	O wonderful!
HORATIO	Good my lord tell it.
HAMLET	No, you will reveal it.
HORATIO	Not I my lord, by heaven.

(handwritten annotations:)

extended metaphor of books – no more book learning, similar convenient on this revenge

image of appearance & reality.

115

t/ HAMLET HAS CHANGED

APPEARANCE REALITY (not as they seem)

ALTHOUGH DISCARD BOOKS, MEMORIES ETC HE IMMEDIATELY BEGINS TO WRITE. HE WILL FIND IT DIFFICULT TO PUT HIS BELIEFS IN ACTION

MOCK HUMOUR AFTER INTENSITY PREVIOUSLY

KEEP OTHERS AT BAY

(DISGUISE)

KNOWING THE TRUTH HIS MANNER CHANGES. SELF ANALYSIS TO OFF HAND COMMENTS.

Having asked his friends to be discreet, Hamlet then speaks in generalities, and says they should part. Horatio senses that Hamlet is not talking sense, but at the mention of the word *'offence'* Hamlet's mind again turns to what he has been told and he informs his friends quite brusquely that he will not tell them, but swears them to secrecy about what they do know.

128 arrant knave: complete villain

131 circumstance: words

140 by Saint Patrick: the patron saint of Purgatory, but also known for ridding Ireland of snakes. Perhaps Hamlet is thinking not only of Purgatory, where his father's spirit is in torment, but also of *'The serpent that did sting thy father's life...'* (Act 1 scene 5 line 39).

143 For: as for

144 O'ermaster: overcome

- *How would you describe Hamlet's state of mind and mode of speech when the Ghost has gone?*

MARCELLUS	Nor I my lord.
HAMLET	How say you then, would heart of man once think it 125 But you'll be secret?
HORATIO MARCELLUS }	Ay by heaven my lord.
HAMLET	There's never a villain dwelling in all Denmark But he's an arrant knave.
HORATIO	There needs no ghost, my lord, come from the grave To tell us this.
HAMLET	Why right, you are in the right, 130 And so without more circumstance at all I hold it fit that we shake hands and part; You as your business and desire shall point you, For every man has business and desire, Such as it is, and for mine own poor part 135 I will go pray.
HORATIO	These are but wild and whirling words my lord.
HAMLET	I am sorry they offend you, heartily, Yes faith, heartily.
HORATIO	There's no offence my lord.
HAMLET	Yes by Saint Patrick but there is, Horatio, 140 And much offence too. Touching this vision here – It is an honest ghost, that let me tell you – For your desire to know what is between us O'ermaster 't as you may. And now good friends, As you are friends, scholars, and soldiers, 145 Give me one poor request.
HORATIO	What is 't my lord? We will.
HAMLET	Never make known what you have seen tonight.

WARNING THEM .

Hamlet now makes Horatio and Marcellus swear, upon his sword, that they will never speak of what they have seen. The Ghost, back in his own place, repeats the word 'swear', and every time they hear him, they move on. They are struck by the strangeness of the events. Hamlet warns them that he may appear to act strangely.

152 **Upon my sword**: the hilt and blade of the sword form a cross. Oaths were commonly sworn on the Bible or on a cross.

156 **truepenny**: honest fellow

157 **in the cellarage**: down below

162 **hic et ubique**: (Latin) here and everywhere

169 **pioneer**: digger, miner or member of military pioneer or engineer corps for tunnelling or excavating

   remove: move off

171 **And...welcome**: the law of hospitality must make a stranger welcome

173 **in your philosophy**: in philosophy or science (not in Horatio's own philosophy)

HORATIO MARCELLUS	} My lord we will not.
HAMLET	Nay but swear 't.
HORATIO	In faith my lord not I. 150
MARCELLUS	Nor I my lord in faith.
HAMLET	Upon my sword.
MARCELLUS	We have sworn my lord already.
HAMLET	Indeed, upon my sword, indeed.
GHOST	[*Beneath*] Swear. 155
HAMLET	Ha, ha, boy, say'st thou so? Art thou there, true- penny? Come on – you hear this fellow in the cellarage – Consent to swear.
HORATIO	Propose the oath, my lord.
HAMLET	Never to speak of this that you have seen, Swear by my sword. 160
GHOST	[*Beneath*] Swear.
HAMLET	Hic et ubique? Then we'll shift our ground. Come hither gentlemen, And lay your hands again upon my sword, Swear by my sword 165 Never to speak of this that you have heard.
GHOST	[*Beneath*] Swear by his sword.
HAMLET	Well said old mole, canst work i' th' earth so fast? A worthy pioneer. Once more remove, good friends.
HORATIO	O day and night, but this is wondrous strange. 170
HAMLET	And therefore as a stranger give it welcome. There are more things in heaven and earth, Horatio, Than are dreamt of in your philosophy. But come – Here as before, never, so help you mercy, 175

Hamlet insists Horatio and Marcellus are never to hint that they know what is the matter with him, or what may have caused any strangeness in him. The Ghost again reinforces this and they swear. Hamlet expresses his gratitude to, and affection for, them and curses the burden that has been placed on him.

176 How...myself: however oddly I may seem to behave
177 As I perchance...on: as I may later on think it fit to assume strange moods
180 encumbered: folded
183 'If...speak' or 'There be...might': 'if we cared to speak' or 'there are those, who if they were allowed'
184 giving out: hinting
188 perturbed: disturbed
189 commend me: entrust myself, a leave-taking phrase
194 The time...joint: the world has become corrupted
O cursed spite...set it right: that fortune should bear me such malice that I was ever born to put things right

GHOST

* INSTIGATE REVENGE
* INSIGHT TO HAMLET
* DRAMATIC EFFECT
* SOPHISTICATION TO PLAY
* GIVES POLITICAL BACKGROUND
* RELIGION
? SET SCENE = APPEARANCE / REALITY
                DISORDER / DECAY.

How strange or odd some'er I bear myself –
As I perchance hereafter shall think meet
To put an antic disposition on –
That you at such times seeing me never shall,
With arms encumbered thus, or this
   head-shake,   180
Or by pronouncing of some doubtful phrase,
As 'Well, well, we know', or 'We could, an if we
   would',
Or 'If we list to speak', or 'There be, an if they
   might',
Or such ambiguous giving out, to note
That you know aught of me – this do swear   185
So grace and mercy at your most need help you.

GHOST   [*Beneath*] Swear.

HAMLET   Rest, rest, perturbed spirit. [*They swear*] So
   gentlemen,
With all my love I do commend me to you;
And what so poor a man as Hamlet is   190
May do, t' express his love and friending to you,
God willing, shall not lack. Let us go in together,
And still your fingers on your lips I pray.
The time is out of joint. O cursed spite,
That ever I was born to set it right.   195
Nay come, let's go together.   [*Exeunt*

Handwritten annotations:
- HOW HAMLET DESCRIBES HIS BEHAVIOR
- MANY CHARACTERS TRY TO FIND A REASON FOR THIS 'ANTIC DISPOSITION'
- * NEED IN HAMLET TO HAVE THE MEN OUTER REINFORCED BY GHOST SPEAKING.

CTIVITIES

Keeping track

Scene 1

1 What mood and atmosphere are created in the first scene, and how does Shakespeare achieve this effect?
2 How do Horatio and the sentries react to the Ghost? What is their understanding of its nature and intentions?
3 What does Horatio's speech (lines 79–107) reveal about the background to events on stage?
4 What do the references to 'the King' after line 41 tell you about the attitude of Horatio and the two guards towards Hamlet's father?

Scene 2

1 What is Claudius trying to do in his first speech (lines 1–16)?
2 How does he try to do it and is he successful in his intention?
3 In lines 17–39 Claudius explains what he is doing to deal with the military and political crisis which threatens Denmark. What do you think of the way he handles this crisis?
4 How does Claudius behave towards Laertes and Polonius when he deals with Laertes' request to return to France (lines 42–62)? What political skills does he show in this exchange?
5 What arguments do Claudius and Gertrude use to try to persuade Hamlet that he is behaving unreasonably?
6 Hamlet reacts violently to his mother's use of the word 'seems' and he launches into a verbal attack on her. Why does this word (line 76) have such significance for him and what does the strength of Hamlet's attack reveal?
7 Hamlet's first soliloquy reveals a mood of suicidal despair. Why exactly does he feel like this? Is this mood justified by what has happened and what he knows?

Scene 3

1 Laertes and Polonius both offer Ophelia 'good advice'. What does this scene reveal about their attitudes to people and life?
2 What do Polonius and Laertes think of Hamlet?

Scenes 4 and 5

1 In these scenes Hamlet learns the 'truth' about his father's murder and his mother's betrayal. What is Hamlet's initial reaction to the Ghost (Scene 4 lines 39–57)?

2 How does the Ghost persuade Hamlet to take action (Scene 5)? (Look closely at what he says and how he says it.) Why does he succeed so easily?

3 How does Hamlet react to the Ghost's revelations?

4 What exactly has the Ghost persuaded Hamlet to do?

5 What do you think Hamlet should do now? What do you want him to do? What are the alternatives?

6 Does the fact that the 'truth' has been revealed by a ghost make any difference?

7 What do you understand from lines 195–196:
   > '*O cursed spite,*
   > *That ever I was born to set it right*'?
   Is Hamlet having doubts already?

Drama

1 Imagine you are the set designers for a theatre production of *Hamlet*. Produce drawings and designs for the opening scene, which capture or evoke the appropriate atmosphere. You have a free hand to be as inventive as you like. The conventional approach would probably include grey stone battlements, soldiers in long cloaks and a smoke machine. What would it be like, set in a penthouse suite with state of the art security systems or in a police state with Nazi style uniforms or . . .? You decide.

2 Now think about the problem of portraying the Ghost. How would you do this on stage to make it convincing and frightening – remembering that a modern audience would be used to the sophistication of horror movie effects?
   • What are the pros and cons of having an actor or a voice over?
   • Some small companies would double up the Ghost with another character, some might even openly use the same actor to play the Ghost and Claudius. What would be the advantages and disadvantages of this approach?
   Discuss your ideas and try out the best in action.

3 Use FORUM THEATRE (see page 299) to explore the moment when Hamlet says '*But I have that within which passes show –*' (Act 1 scene 2 line 85).
   Look at the soliloquy (Act 1 scene 2 lines 129–159) for ideas. Start with Hamlet and gradually include all the members of the court to find all the nuances of tension and subtext.

4 Improvise modern versions of the exchanges between Ophelia, Polonius and Laertes. The two men both give her advice – does she heed them?

   If status relationships were measured on a scale of 10 to 1, from the most powerful to the lowest status, the conventional reading might place Polonius on 8, Laertes at 5 and Ophelia at 2. Play about with these status rankings, altering the balance and see what difference it makes to the portrayals. Find and alter the subtexts.

5 • The actor playing the part of the Ghost is having trouble making the allusion to hell a convincing speech (Act 1 scene 5 lines 9–23). What advice could you give to help him imagine the horrors to which he refers? Elizabethans had a very vivid picture of hell: ours may be different. In groups, encourage your actor to imagine the horrors which will make him shiver with fear.

   • Look at the Ghost's speech (Act 1 scene 5 lines 42–88). Divide it into sections of about five lines each, using the punctuation as a guideline. Either in groups, or as a whole class, choose different people to deliver the lines, as though the Ghost's voice was coming from a variety of directions, while one student becomes the cowering Hamlet receiving the story as a series of blows.

The key elements

In each Act of the play there are key scenes, speeches or developments which you will need to think about and study in detail. In Act 1 these are:
• the major characters
• the first court scene
• the first soliloquy
• the Ghost and its revelations.

Key scene

Hamlet's first soliloquy: Act 1 scene 2

Keying it in

1 This speech comes after we have seen Claudius and Gertrude attempting to persuade Hamlet to 'look like a friend on Denmark'. Look at Act I scene 2 lines 76–86.
   • What is Hamlet's mood?
   • What unspoken accusations does he make?

2 Look again at lines 65–120.
  • What evidence is there so far of Hamlet's attitude to Claudius?
  • Why does he want to leave Denmark?
  • Why does Claudius try so hard to make him stay?

The speech itself

3 Look at lines 129–137.
   When Hamlet is left alone on stage, his first lines give us an insight into his emotional state. He is experiencing a mood of suicidal despair.
  • How do the language and imagery of the lines convey Hamlet's feelings?
  • Do you think Hamlet's grief goes beyond 'normal' mourning for a loved one?

4 Look at lines 138–146.
   This section reveals Hamlet's view of the relationship between his mother and his father.
  • how had he seen the relationship?
  • how does Hamlet make the contrast between his father and Claudius?
  • why do you think he says '*Must I remember?*' (line 143)
   Hamlet concludes that, '*frailty, thy name is woman.*'
  • is this fair on Gertrude?
  • is this fair on '*woman*' in general?
  • what are the implications for Hamlet's feelings for Ophelia?

5 Look at lines 147–159.
   This section of the soliloquy reveals even more about Hamlet's attitude to his mother and her recent marriage.
  • What does he object to:
       the fact that she remarried at all
       that she married this particular man
       the timing of the marriage?
  • What evidence, if any, can you find to support these possible explanations?
  • How far do you 'understand' his feelings and sympathize with him?

Overview

In this soliloquy the keynote is the mood of profound disillusion. Hamlet expresses a sense of disgust with his mother, with women and with life in general. His revulsion is so powerful and intense that he wishes he were dead.

1 List the reasons for his feelings of disgust.
2 How do the language and structure of the speech convey the intensity of his feelings?

Close study

Scene 5 lines 92–112 ('*O all you host of heaven!*')
The soliloquy comes immediately after the Ghost's revelations.

1 How does the language of the opening two lines convey
   Hamlet's feelings?
2 What is meant by '*And shall I couple hell?*'
3 What are Hamlet's fears about his '*heart*' and '*sinews*'?
4 What does Hamlet mean when he says '*whiles memory holds
   a seat In this distracted globe*'?
5 How does he show his determination to fulfil his duty to
   revenge?
6 What are the '*trivial fond records*' he refers to in line 99?
7 What does he mean by '*baser matter*' in line 104?
8 How does his language in lines 104–105 reveal his attitude to
   Gertrude and Claudius?
9 Do you think it is significant that he mentions Gertrude first?
10 How do the language and structure of this speech as a whole
   suggest Hamlet's mood?

Hamlet and revenge

Act 1 also sets in motion the theme of revenge which is central to
our response to the play. The Ghost places the responsibility of
revenge on Hamlet by appealing to his sense of filial duty and by
playing on his feelings of outrage at murder and disgust at sexual
betrayal.

Hamlet reacts passionately and violently to the Ghost's
revelations and he accepts the burden of revenge instantly and
willingly. His first thoughts are to '*sweep to my revenge*' and he
dedicates himself to the task, promising to erase from his mind '*all
trivial fond records*'.

• Do you find his reaction 'normal' and 'natural'?
• What would you think of Hamlet if he did not respond with
  this surge of 'blood' and violent passion?

It is also worth noting that in this initial mood of violent
passion Hamlet expresses complete confidence in the Ghost. He
says to Horatio '*It is an honest ghost*' (Act 1 scene 5 line 142).

However, there are some hints even at this stage that Hamlet
may not find revenge an entirely straightforward business. When
he says, '*And shall I couple hell?*' (Act 1 scene 5 line 93) perhaps
Hamlet is aware of the enormity of the task and of the awesome
implications of involvement with evil. When he says, '*O cursed
spite That ever I was born to set it right*', he seems to be

experiencing unease and even a sense of reluctance. He appears to be questioning his adequacy as a revenger.

There remains the issue of the 'antic disposition'. Hamlet tells Horatio and the others that he may assume an appearance of madness and swears them to secrecy. He gives no explanation for this decision and it is often taken to be an obviously sensible part of his strategy to achieve revenge.

However:

- why does he suddenly decide to pretend to be mad
- what is his purpose
- what can he gain by this?

By the end of Act 1, Hamlet has accepted that he has a duty to revenge his father's murder and betrayal, but it is possible to detect some unease in him and his plan of action is not entirely clear.

Assignments

1 In Act 1 we are introduced to six major characters. They are:

    Hamlet   Claudius   Gertrude
    Ophelia   Laertes   Polonius

In note form, record your first impressions of each of them.
Identify key quotations to use as evidence to support your views.

Essays

2 Imagine you are an ambassador from England, newly arrived in Denmark. You have to write a report to the English king informing him of recent developments and the political situation in Denmark.
    Write your report.

3 Look closely at Hamlet's first encounter with the Ghost in Act 1.
How does the Ghost persuade Hamlet to accept the role of revenger?

Polonius is employing Reynaldo to deliver money and letters to Laertes in France. Reynaldo is also being asked by Polonius to find Danish acquaintances of his son. He is to claim some small knowledge of Laertes, and to suggest to people who might know Laertes that the young man is leading a rather wild existence.

1 **notes**: letters
7 **Danskers**: Danes
8 **what means...keep**: what means they have and where they lodge
10 **encompassment...question**: by this roundabout means and general drift of enquiry
11 **come you...touch it**: you will come nearer the point of your questions than by any direct approach
13 **Take you...him**: pretend to be slightly acquainted with him
20 **forgeries**: inventions
   rank: offensive
22 **wanton**: wilful
24 **gaming**: gambling

- *What further revelations are there here about Polonius's character? How does he perceive his role as father?*

Act two

Scene 1

Enter POLONIUS *and* REYNALDO

POLONIUS   Give him this money, and these notes, Reynaldo.

REYNALDO   I will my lord.

POLONIUS   You shall do marvellous wisely, good Reynaldo,
Before you visit him, to make inquire
Of his behaviour.

REYNALDO   My lord, I did intend it.   5

POLONIUS   Marry well said, very well said. Look you sir,
Inquire me first what Danskers are in Paris,
And how, and who, what means, and where
          they keep,
What company, at what expense; and finding
By this encompassment and drift of question,   10
That they do know my son, come you more
          nearer
Than your particular demands will touch it.
Take you as 'twere some distant knowledge of him,
As thus, 'I know his father and his friends,
And in part him' – do you mark this Reynaldo?   15

REYNALDO   Ay, very well my lord.

POLONIUS   'And in part him – but', you may say, 'not well:
But, if't be he I mean, he's very wild;
Addicted so and so'; and there put on him
What forgeries you please, marry none so rank   20
As may dishonour him, take heed of that;
But sir, such wanton, wild, and usual slips
As are companions noted and most known
To youth and liberty.

REYNALDO   As gaming my lord?

Reynaldo is taken aback at some of the suggestions he is expected to make about Laertes. He says that to suggest he goes with prostitutes would dishonour him. Without saying so explicitly, Polonius makes it clear that Reynaldo's task is to spy on his son and to find out what kind of life he is leading far from home, in a foreign country. Polonius forgets what he was saying.

26 Drabbing: associating with prostitutes

30 That...incontinency: not that he is promiscuous

31 breathe...quaintly: hint at his faults so ingeniously

32 taints of liberty: flaws resulting from his freedom

33 flash and outbreak of a fiery mind: sudden spontaneous outburst of a passionate mind

34 A savageness...assault: a wildness of untamed passion which can attack any young man

38 fetch of warrant: approved trick

39 sullies: blemishes

40 a little...working: as though Laertes has been just a little tarnished by his experiences

41 party in converse: the person you are talking to

42 prenominate: aforementioned

44 He closes...consequence: he agrees with you along these lines

48 does 'a this...marry: Polonius loses track of what he was saying and Reynaldo has to prompt him

POLONIUS	Ay, or drinking, fencing, swearing, quarrelling, 25
	Drabbing – you may go so far.
REYNALDO	My lord, that would dishonour him.
POLONIUS	<u>Faith no, as you may season it in the charge.</u>
	You must not put another scandal on him,
	That he is open to incontinency; 30
	That's not my meaning. But breathe his faults so quaintly,
	That they may seem the taints of liberty,
	The flash and outbreak of a fiery mind,
	A savageness in unreclaimed blood,
	Of general assault.
REYNALDO	But my good lord – 35
POLONIUS	Wherefore should you do this?
REYNALDO	Ay my lord,
	I would know that.
POLONIUS	Marry sir, here's my drift,
	And I believe it is a fetch of warrant.
	You laying these slight sullies on my son
	As 'twere a thing a little soiled i' th' working, 40
	Mark you, your party in converse, him you would sound,
	Having ever seen in the prenominate crimes
	The youth you breathe of guilty, be assured
	He closes with you in this consequence;
	'Good sir', or so, or 'friend', or 'gentleman', 45
	According to the phrase or the addition
	Of man and country.
REYNALDO	Very good my lord.
POLONIUS	And then, sir, does 'a this – he does – what was I
	about to say? By the mass I was about to say
	something. Where did I leave? 50
REYNALDO	At 'closes in the consequence', at 'friend or so',
	and, 'gentleman'.
POLONIUS	At 'closes in the consequence', ay marry.

[Handwritten marginalia: "loses conversation slightly lines 46-47"]

Polonius demonstrates to Reynaldo how lies will help to
discover the truth. He also tells him to observe Laertes on
his own account. Reynaldo leaves and Ophelia, very
agitated, comes to find her father. Hamlet has visited her
in a very dishevelled state and with a terrible expression.

57 o'ertook in 's rouse: found drunk
60 Videlicet: (Latin) that is to say
62 takes: catches
63 And thus...reach: and in this way, we who are both wise
and have a good grasp of affairs
64 With...bias: outflanking, and by indirect attempts
windlasses: crafty devices
assays: tests, trials
of bias: oblique
65 By indirections...out: find out the truth by indirect means
68 God buy ye: goodbye
70 in yourself: personally
72 And...music: and make sure he is carrying on with his
music
78 closet: private room
79 unbraced: unfastened
80 fouled: dirty
81 down-gyved: fallen down (so that they looked like 'gyves'
– chains round his ankles)
83 in purport: in its significance

> • *What is it in Hamlet's conduct that has frightened
> Ophelia?*

He closes thus: 'I know the gentleman;
I saw him yesterday, or th' other day,   55
Or then, or then; with such, or such; and as you
        say,
There was 'a gaming, there o'ertook in 's rouse,
There falling out at tennis', or perchance,
'I saw him enter such a house of sale',
Videlicet a brothel, or so forth.   60
See you now;
Your bait of falsehood takes this carp of truth.
And thus do we of wisdom, and of reach,
With windlasses, and with assays of bias,
By indirections find directions out;   65
So by my former lecture and advice
Shall you my son. You have me, have you not?

REYNALDO   My lord, I have.

POLONIUS   God buy ye, fare you well.

REYNALDO   Good my lord.

POLONIUS   Observe his inclination in yourself.   70

OBSERVE FOR HIMSELF NOT RELY ON WHAT OTHERS SAY.

REYNALDO   I shall my lord.

POLONIUS   And let him ply his music.

REYNALDO   Well, my lord.

POLONIUS' CHARACTER.

POLONIUS   Farewell.   [*Exit Reynaldo*

Enter OPHELIA

LIKES THE SOUND OF HIS OWN VIOCE

How now Ophelia, what's the matter?   75

INDICATION OF HER DISTR- AUGHT

OPHELIA   O my lord, my lord, I have been so affrighted.

POLONIUS   With what, i' th' name of God?

TERROR OF HAMLET'S BEHAVICE

OPHELIA   My lord, as I was sewing in my closet,
            Lord Hamlet with his doublet all unbraced,
            No hat upon his head, his stockings fouled,   80
            Ungartered, and down-gyved to his ankle,
            Pale as his shirt, his knees knocking each other,
            And with a look so piteous in purport
            As if he had been loosed out of hell
            To speak of horrors – he comes before me.   85

IMAGRY OF CLOTHING = DISGUISE. APPEARANCE OF MADNESS

DRAMATIC IRONY = WE KNOW HE'S ONLY TAKING THIS ON.

Ophelia reports how Hamlet acted in her presence, holding her by the wrist, gazing at her and sighing, and then keeping his eyes fixed on her as he left the room. When he hears this, Polonius concludes that Hamlet's love is genuine, after all, and that Ophelia's obedience in rejecting his advances has driven him mad. Polonius says they must go to the King.

91 **perusal**: study
92 **As 'a**: as if he
96 **bulk**: body, frame
101 **bended their light on me**: gazed at me
104 **Whose...itself**: the violent nature of which leads to self-destruction
113 **quoted**: observed
114 **wreck**: ruin
    beshrew my jealousy: curse my suspicious nature!
115 **it is as proper...discretion**: it is as common for old people to see too much in what goes on, as for the young ones to lack sound judgement in such matters

> • *Why do you think Hamlet (1) said nothing and (2) acted as he did in Ophelia's presence? From the evidence is it likely that Polonius has got it right?*

[handwritten: POLONIUS' ANSWER FOR HAMLET'S MADNESS.]

POLONIUS   Mad for thy love?

OPHELIA   My lord I do not know,
But truly I do fear it.

POLONIUS   What said he?

OPHELIA   He took me by the wrist, and held me hard;
Then goes he to the length of all his arm,
And with his other hand thus o'er his brow,   90
He falls to such perusal of my face
As 'a would draw it. Long stayed he so;   *[handwritten: SO INTENSE]*
At last, a little shaking of mine arm,
And thrice his head thus waving up and down,
He raised a sigh so piteous and profound   95
As it did seem to shatter all his bulk,   *[handwritten: HE CAN'T TELL HER.]*
And end his being; that done, he lets me go,
And with his head over his shoulder turned,   *[handwritten: HE'S LEAVING]*
He seemed to find his way without his eyes,   *[handwritten: HER FOR GOOD.]*
For out a-doors he went without their helps,   100
And to the last bended their light on me.

[handwritten left margin: AS WELL AS HIS STATE SHE GOES ON TO HIS BEHAVIOR. WHY? PART OF ACT "FRAILTY THY NAME IS WOMAN" AT OPHELIA AS SHE LIKE ALL WOMEN ARE WEAK]

POLONIUS   Come, go with me, I will go seek the King.
This is the very ecstasy of love,   *[handwritten: REINFORCES POLONIUS']*
Whose violent property fordoes itself,   *[handwritten: ANSWER]*
And leads the will to desperate undertakings   105
As oft as any passion under heaven
That does afflict our natures. I am sorry.
What, have you given him any hard words of late?

[handwritten left margin: HE WANTS TO CONFIDE IN HER]

OPHELIA   No my good lord, but as you did command,
I did repel his letters, and denied   110
His access to me.   *[handwritten: HASN'T REALLY HAD MUCH CONTACT.]*

POLONIUS   That hath made him mad.
I am sorry that with better heed and judgement
I had not quoted him. I feared he did but trifle,
And meant to wreck thee, but beshrew my jealousy.
By heaven it is as proper to our age   115
To cast beyond ourselves in our opinions,   *[handwritten: HAMLET'S]*
As it is common for the younger sort   *[handwritten: FEELINGS]*
To lack discretion. Come, go we to the King.   *[handwritten: FOR OPHELIA ARE MORE INTENSE THAN HE FIRST THOUGHT]*

[handwritten left margin: OPHELIA'S BEHAVIOR TO HAMLET HAS CAUSED THIS]

Polonius believes that it would be more dangerous to conceal what he sees now as Hamlet's true feelings than to reveal what he knows to the King and Queen.

119 **close**: secret
   which...love: this must be made known which, if it was concealed, might cause more grief

Claudius, with his Queen, is receiving Rosencrantz and Guildenstern, for whom he has sent. They have known Hamlet from his earliest years, Claudius says, and he hopes that if they keep company with Hamlet they may find out what is causing his present disturbed behaviour. The Queen supports him in this, and promises their gratitude.

2   **Moreover that**: in addition to the fact that
6   **Sith...that it was**: since neither his outward appearance nor his personality is as it was before
7   **that it was**: what it used to be
8   **put him...of himself**: so parted him from his right mind
12 **sith...haviour**: since that time you have been so close to his youthful interests
13 **vouchsafe your rest**: agree to stay
15 **to gather...remedy**: Claudius asks the two, as they keep Hamlet company, to take every opportunity to pick up any pointers to what is troubling Hamlet. Once this is discovered, Claudius says, perhaps he can help Hamlet.
21 **adheres**: feels himself close
22 **gentry**: courtesy
24 **supply and profit of our hope**: assistance and advancement of what we hope for
26 **remembrance**: recognition

> • *Look for truth and lies and diplomatic utterances cloaking villainy.*

This must be known, which, being kept close might
   move
More grief to hide than hate to utter love.   [*Exeunt* 120

Scene ❷

Flourish. Enter KING, QUEEN, ROSENCRANTZ,
GUILDENSTERN, *and Attendants*

LIKE POLONIUS -
THEY OBEY HE.
✓
WHO HAS
THE MOST
POWER

KING   Welcome dear Rosencrantz and Guildenstern.
Moreover that we much did long to see you,
The need we have <u>to use you</u> did provoke
Our hasty sending. Something have you heard
Of Hamlet's transformation; so call it,   5
<u>Sith nor th' exterior nor the inward man</u>
<u>Resembles that it was.</u> What it should be,
More than his father's death, that thus hath put
   him
So much from th' understanding of himself,
I cannot dream of. I entreat you both,   10
That being of so young days brought up with him,
And sith so neighboured to his youth and haviour,
That you vouchsafe your rest here in our court
Some little time, so by your companies
To draw him on to pleasures, and to gather,   15
So much as from occasion you may glean,
Whether aught to us unknown afflicts him thus
That opened lies within our remedy.

EVERYONE
IS BEING
"USED"
TO SPY

AN INTERNAL +
EXTERNAL
CHANGE

ASKING THEM
TO FIND OUT
WHAT IS
WRONG WITH
HAMLET.
SAYS HE CAN'T
THINK OF ⚹
ANOTHER
REASON →

⚹ THIS IS
AS WE
KNOW
UNTRUE.

QUEEN →   Good gentlemen, he hath much talked of you,
And sure I am, two men there are not living   20
To whom he more adheres. If it will please you
To show us so much gentry and good will,
As to expend your time with us awhile,
For the supply and profit of our hope,
Your visitation shall receive such thanks   25
As fits a King's remembrance.

THIS IS A PLAUSABLE EXCUSE
TO SPY ON HAMLET.

Rosencrantz and Guildenstern accept their mission, pointing out that they could have been ordered, not merely requested, to carry out this task. They are led away to Hamlet. Polonius comes to announce the return of ambassadors who had been sent to Norway. He also suggests that he has found the cause of Hamlet's madness, as he calls it.

27 by the sovereign power: ie because they are their king and queen

28 dread pleasures: *'dread'* was usually used in addressing royalty – as 'my dread lord'. A different phrase is created here, to sound excessive, and slightly silly.

30 bent: extent (as in a bow fully bent)

42 still: always

44 hold: maintain. My duty and my soul are God's and the King's to command.

47 Hunts...used to do: is not as hot on the trail of matters of state as it once was

52 fruit: fruit as dessert

53 grace: honour

TONE OF THE KING IS INFORMAL FRIENDLY MANNER

ROSENCRANTZ   Both your majesties *THEY COULD BE COMMA- NOTO*
     Might by the sovereign power you have of us,
     Put your dread pleasures more into command
     Than to entreaty.

NOT ASKED

GUILDENSTERN   But we both obey,
     And here give up ourselves, in the full bent,   30
PLAYFUL TONE   To lay our service freely at your feet   *BY DOING THIS IT*
     To be commanded.   *SEEMS THAT THE*

KING   Thanks Rosencrantz and gentle Guildenstern. *KING +*
                                             QUEEN
QUEEN   Thanks Guildenstern and gentle Rosencrantz. *ARE DOING*
NEED TO DISTINGUISH HAMLET   And I beseech you instantly to visit   *IT FOR*   35 *HAMLET*
(2)   My too much changed son. Go some of you,   *GOOD.*
     And bring these gentlemen where Hamlet is.

GUILDENSTERN Heavens make our presence and our practices
     Pleasant and helpful to him.

QUEEN   Ay, amen. *CLEVERLY MANIPULATE*

   [*Exeunt* ROSENCRANTZ, GUILDENSTERN, *and some* ATTENDANTS

     Enter POLONIUS

POLONIUS   Th' ambassadors from Norway, my good lord,   40
     Are joyfully returned.

KING   Thou still hast been the father of good news.

POLONIUS   Have I my lord? I assure my good liege,
     I hold my duty as I hold my soul,
     Both to my God, and to my gracious King.   45
     And I do think – or else this brain of mine
     Hunts not the trail of policy so sure
     As it hath used to do – that I have found
     The very cause of Hamlet's lunacy.

KING   O speak of that, that do I long to hear.   50

POLONIUS   Give first admittance to th' ambassadors;
     My news shall be the fruit to that great feast.

KING   Thyself do grace to them, and bring them in.

                                [*Exit* POLONIUS

Valtemand and Cornelius have been on a successful mission to Norway. The king, uncle of young Fortinbras, discovered that the army raised by his nephew was to march against Denmark. He put a stop to this, made the young man promise not to threaten Denmark again and asked for safe passage for the army through Denmark when it was sent against the Poles instead.

55 head: origin
> **distemper**: affliction, sickness
58 sift him: examine him closely
61 Upon our first: on the first expression of our views
66 impotence: helplessness
67 falsely borne in hand: taken advantage of
> **Was/sends**: note the change in style of the report here. So far, Valtemand has reported on the facts of the success of their mission in the past tense. From here on, the present tense and the omission of the subject of the sentence, when it is 'understood' makes for a more immediate and dramatic report – almost like a modern sports commentary. Claudius is meant to gain the impression that the ambassadors have been clever and efficient. Note, too, the diplomatic and face-saving elements in the gift of money to young Fortinbras, the discovery of a more satisfactory enemy, and the request for safe passage through Denmark.
69 in fine: in conclusion
71 assay: trial (of strength) – never again to take up arms
81 our more considered time: when we have more time for consideration

---

- *Note the second instalment of the Fortinbras story.*

He tells me, my dear Gertrude, he hath found
The head and source of all your son's distemper. 55

QUEEN   I doubt it is no other but the main,
His father's death, and our o'erhasty marriage.

She realises it too was hasty

KING   Well, we shall sift him.

Enter POLONIUS, *with* VALTEMAND *and* CORNELIUS

Welcome, my good friends.
Say Valtemand, what from our brother Norway?

VALTEMAND   Most fair return of greetings and desires. 60
Upon our first, he sent out to suppress
His nephew's levies, which to him appeared
To be a preparation 'gainst the Polack;
But better looked into, he truly found
It was against your highness; whereat grieved 65
That so his sickness, age, and impotence
Was falsely borne in hand, sends out arrests
On Fortinbras; which he in brief obeys,
Receives rebuke from Norway, and in fine,
Makes vow before his uncle never more 70
To give th' assay of arms against your majesty.
Whereon old Norway, overcome with joy,
Gives him three score thousand crowns in
    annual fee,
And his commission to employ those soldiers,
So levied, as before, against the Polack, 75
With an entreaty, herein further shown,

                    [*Giving a paper*

That it might please you to give quiet pass
Through your dominions for this enterprise,
On such regards of safety and allowance
As therein are set down.

KING   It likes us well; 80
And at our more considered time, we'll read,
Answer, and think upon this business.
Meantime, we thank you for your well-took labour.
Go to your rest, at night we'll feast together.

Handwritten margin notes:
- Result of the visit to Norway
- Thought they were going to attack Poland not Norway
- Will be no more trouble between the 2
- Round 'we' or involving Gertrude
- Important as we are unaware how much Gertrude knew of the situation

When Valtemand and Cornelius have left, Polonius indulges in a lengthy introduction to what he has discovered about Hamlet's sickness. He gets tied up in his own wordiness and then comes to the point and starts to read one of Hamlet's letters to Ophelia, which is in a very exaggerated style.

86 expostulate: set out one's views, discuss

90 wit: mental powers, intellect

91 tediousness: long-windedness
flourishes: ornaments, embellishments, decoration

93 Mad...let that go: Polonius has found himself trapped in a circular argument of his own making – '*to define true madness*' is to be '*mad*' – and hastily abandons it

95 More matter with less art: the Queen demands more substance with less ornamentation

98 figure: ie figure of speech

99 farewell it: say farewell to it

103 For this...by cause: this unfortunate madness we have observed does have a cause

105 Perpend: consider

108 gather and surmise: draw your conclusions

113 &c: (et cetera) the continuation of the greeting at the beginning of the letter, a recognized formula

115 faithful: true to you

- *Look at – or rather listen to – Polonius's way with words. Observe too, throughout the play, the fun Shakespeare has with language. In addition to Polonius, the list will include Rosencrantz and Guildenstern; the language of love letters; some 'dramatic' language; Osric; the grave-diggers. Notice how we are often led to understand the nonsense effect by people's reaction to what is said.*

Most welcome home.

[*Exeunt* VALTEMAND *and* CORNELIUS

POLONIUS   This business is well ended. 85

My liege, and madam, to expostulate

POLONIUS'

What majesty should be, what duty is,

POMPUS

Why day is day, night night, and time is time,

NATURE

Were nothing but to waste night, day, and time.

Therefore since brevity is the soul of wit,   90

And tediousness the limbs and outward flourishes,

I will be brief: your noble son is mad.

Mad call I it, for to define true madness,

What is 't but to be nothing else but mad?

But let that go.   *GET TO THE MEANING INSTEAD OF*

QUEEN   More matter with less art.   95

ELABORATE LANGUAGE

POLONIUS Madam, I swear I use no art at all.

That he's mad 'tis true, 'tis true 'tis pity,

And pity 'tis 'tis true – a foolish figure,

But farewell it, for I will use no art.

Mad let us grant him then, and now remains   100

That we find out the cause of this effect,

Or rather say, the cause of this defect,

For this effect defective comes by cause.

Thus it remains, and the remainder thus.

Perpend;   105

I have a daughter – have while she is mine –

Who in her duty and obedience, mark,

Hath given me this. Now gather and surmise.

[*Reads*

LETTER FROM HAMLET

'To the celestial and my soul's idol, the most

beautified Ophelia' – That's an ill phrase,   110

a vile phrase; 'beautified' is a vile phrase, but you

shall hear. Thus: 'In her excellent white bosom,

these, &c.'

QUEEN   Came this from Hamlet to her?

POLONIUS Good madam stay awhile; I will be faithful.   115

'Doubt thou the stars are fire;

HAVE TO ASSUME IT TO BE A GENUINE LETTER AS POLONIUS HAD STOPPED THEM SEEING EACH OTHER

³ELABORATE RHETORICAL LANGUAGE

MEANING OF THE SPEECH GET'S LOST

Polonius finishes reading Hamlet's love-letter and Claudius asks how Ophelia has received these declarations of love. Polonius protests that he is faithful to the King and Queen and that he told Ophelia not to see or speak to Hamlet. When Hamlet was rejected, Polonius continues, he became melancholy.

120 ill at these numbers: no good at writing verse

124 machine is to him: he still has this body

126 And more above...to mine ear: furthermore she has told me about all his approaches to her, as and when they happened, how they were communicated and where

131 fain: gladly

136 played the desk, or table-book: ie registered what was happening and let it continue

137 given...and dumb: flattered my feelings by turning a blind eye and saying nothing

138 Or...idle sight: gazed idly at this love without realizing what was going on

139 round: openly

141 out of thy star: above your position in life, out of your orbit

142 prescripts: instructions

143 resort: visit

144 tokens: little presents

145 took the fruits: reaped the benefit

146 he repelled: when he had been rejected, he...

148 Thence to a watch: from that to staying awake all night

149 lightness: lightheartedness
declension: downward slope

> • *We have further insights into Polonius's character and the way he regards his responsibilities.*

Doubt that the sun doth move;
Doubt truth to be a liar;
But never doubt I love.

IRONY
IT'S ALL AN ACT.

O dear Ophelia, I am ill at these numbers, I have   120
not art to reckon my groans; but that I love thee
best, O most best, believe it. Adieu.
　　Thine evermore most dear lady, whilst this
　　machine is to him, HAMLET.'
This in obedience hath my daughter shown me,   125
And more above, hath his solicitings,
As they fell out by time, by means, and place,
All given to mine ear.

KING
　　　　　　　　　　　　But how hath she
Received his love?

POLONIUS
　　　　　　　　　　What do you think of me?

KING
As of a man faithful and honourable.   130

POLONIUS
I would fain prove so. But what might you think,
When I had seen this hot love on the wing,
As I perceived it, I must tell you that,
Before my daughter told me, what might you,
Or my dear Majesty your Queen here think,   135
If I had played the desk, or table-book,
Or given my heart a winking, mute and dumb,
Or looked upon this love with idle sight;
What might you think? No, I went round to
　　work,
And my young mistress thus I did bespeak: 140
'Lord Hamlet is a prince out of thy star;
This must not be'. And then I prescripts gave her
That she should lock herself from his resort,
Admit no messengers, receive no tokens.
Which done, she took the fruits of my advice;   145
And he repelled, a short tale to make,
Fell into a sadness, then into a fast,
Thence to a watch, thence into a weakness,
Thence to a lightness, and, by this declension,

IT HE HAD
ALLOWED IT
TO
CONTINUE

BECAUSE POLONIUS FORBADE CONTACT HAMLET W LIKE HE W

Polonius finishes his explanation of Hamlet's decline into madness. He suggests that to check on his theory they secretly observe a meeting between Ophelia and Hamlet, which Polonius will contrive.

159 centre: centre of the earth, the most inaccessible place
    try: test
161 lobby: ante-room
162 loose: let loose. This suggests that Polonius looks on Ophelia as being in his keeping, more like a dog than a daughter. There is the added suggestion of 'loosing' an animal for breeding purposes.
163 arras: wall-hanging
165 be...thereon: has not lost his reason as a result
166 Let me...carters: if Polonius is wrong he will claim he is no longer fit to be a counsellor, but he'll run a farm and men who drive carts
170 board: speak to

ARt CRITICS WHO SAY HAMLETS
ATTRACTION TO HIS MOTHER IS
Sexual

Into the madness wherein now he raves,   150
And all we mourn for.

KING   Do you think 'tis this?

QUEEN   It may be, very like.

POLONIUS   Hath there been such a time – I would fain know
                that –
             That I have positively said ''Tis so',
             When it proved otherwise?

KING   Not that I know.   155

POLONIUS   [Points to his head and shoulder] Take this, from
                this, if this be otherwise.
             If circumstances lead me, I will find
             Where truth is hid, though it were hid indeed
             Within the centre.

KING   How may we try it further?

POLONIUS   You know sometimes he walks four hours   160
                together
             Here in the lobby.

QUEEN   So he does indeed.

POLONIUS   At such a time, I'll loose my daughter to him.
             Be you and I behind an arras then;
             Mark the encounter; if he love her not,
             And be not from his reason fall'n thereon,   165
             Let me be no assistant for a state,
             But keep a farm and carters.

KING   We will try it.

             Enter HAMLET

QUEEN   But look where sadly the poor wretch comes
                reading.

POLONIUS   Away, I do beseech you both, away.
             I'll board him presently.

                    [Exeunt KING, QUEEN, and ATTENDANTS

                              O give me leave   170

Handwritten annotations:
- WHEN HAS HE HAS EVER HAD REASON TO DOUBT HIM
- (RESPONSE TO CONVERSATION)
- NATURAL AFFECTION
- ONLY GERTRUDE WHO SHOWS SYMPATHY OR PITY FOR HAMLET = OBVIOUSLY WAS A STRONG BOND BETWEEN THEM.

Hamlet's replies when Polonius speaks to him seem to bear out the counsellor's opinion. The conversation sounds inconsequential and it soon turns on Ophelia. Hamlet's punning references and the quickness of his mind compared with his opponent's, make it easy for Polonius to draw the conclusions he wishes.

174 fishmonger: some see this merely as Hamlet's joke – to call the pompous, high-sounding counsellor a fishmonger. Others add the secondary meaning of 'pimp', since Polonius is about to send Ophelia to Hamlet.

181 For...carrion: it was thought that the action of the sun bred maggots in dead flesh – but maggots, of course, hatch from flies' eggs laid in the warm flesh. The carrion is sun-kissed and breeds maggots. If the son (the same punning reference was used in Act 1 scene 2) kisses the daughter, she may breed.

185 not...conceive: her child would be illegitimate

187 harping on: going on about

194 matter: the subject of the book (Hamlet is reading) *or* the quarrel. Hamlet chooses the meaning that Polonius does not intend.

197 satirical rogue: writer of the book. These contents enable Hamlet to be rude about Polonius indirectly, since it is 'in the book'.

199 purging thick amber: producing a yellowish discharge
plum-tree gum: a clear amber-coloured resin which is not only produced from the damaged tree bark, but also from the stone-end of the plum itself. It is very sticky.

200 wit: understanding

201 weak hams: weak muscles at the back of the thighs and in the buttocks

> • *Investigate the signs indicating real or assumed
> madness in Hamlet.*

1ST ILLUSTRATION OF HAMLET

HIS ANTIC DISPOSITION

IRONY OF SITUATION

How does my good Lord Hamlet?

HAMLET   Well, God-a-mercy.

POLONIUS   Do you know me my lord?

HAMLET   Excellent well, you are a fishmonger.

POLONIUS   Not I my lord. *ELIZABETHAN TIMES WAS A PIMP*   175

HAMLET   Then I would you were so honest a man.

POLONIUS   Honest, my lord?

HAMLET   Ay sir, to be honest as this world goes, is to be one
           man picked out of ten thousand.

POLONIUS   That's very true my lord.   180

WHILST OVERALL MEANING IS CLEAR

THERE IS IMPORTANT RELEVANCE IN WHAT IS SAID

HAMLET   For if the sun breed maggots in a dead dog,
           being a good kissing carrion – have you a daughter?

POLONIUS   I have my lord.

HAMLET   Let her not walk i' th' sun. Conception is a
           blessing, but not as your daughter may   185
           conceive – friend look to 't.

POLONIUS   [*Aside*] How say you by that? Still harping on my
           daughter. Yet he knew me not at first; 'a said I was a
           fishmonger: 'a is far gone, far gone, and truly
           in my youth I suffered much extremity for   190
           love, very near this. I'll speak to him again. What
           do you read my lord?

HAMLET   Words, words, words.

POLONIUS   What is the matter my lord?

HAMLET   Between who?   195

POLONIUS   I mean the matter that you read, my lord.

HAMLET   Slanders sir, for the satirical rogue says here that old
           men have grey beards, that their faces are wrinkled,
           their eyes purging thick amber and plum-tree
           gum, and that they have a plentiful lack of   200
           wit, together with most weak hams; all which sir,
           though I most powerfully and potently believe, yet

MORE CORRUPTION + SUBSTITUTE PROOF THAT ELSINORE IS UNHEALTHY.

HIS OBSESSION WITH THE RELATIONSHIP WITH CLAUDIUS + GERTRUDE SPILLED OVER TO HIS FEELINGS ON WOMEN GENERALLY

CRITICISM OF POLONIUS HIMSELF

ELEMENT FROM HAMLET OF DISLIKE + DISTRUST IN POLONIUS. TRIES TO MAKE P. LOOK FOOLISH AND CONFUSE HIM.

Hamlet continues to talk intelligent nonsense or nonsensical intelligence – Polonius in asides recognizes method in his madness. Polonius intends to proceed with the Ophelia plan and takes his leave. Rosencrantz and Guildenstern find Hamlet and the three exchange greetings, with Hamlet still in a rather provocative vein.

209 out of the air: this could be assumed to mean 'the open air' but they are in the ante-room. It could mean 'out of the draught' as he is considered to be sick, or similarly, out of an airy room into a darkened sickroom.

210 pregnant: quick-witted, full of meaning
     happiness: aptness, appropriateness

212 delivered of: this picks up the 'pregnant' metaphor

218 withal – except my life: with – and again the suggestion of suicide

229 As...earth: neither well nor badly, like most human beings

231 not the very button...shoe?: neither right at the top nor at the very bottom

---

- *Examine the double act of Rosencrantz and Guildenstern. Their names mean 'wreath (or garland) of roses' and 'golden star' – do you think these names might have any special significance?*

HAMLET IS AWARE HE IS BEING WATCHED
∴ IS DELIBERTLY CONFUSSING TO PUT
POLONIUS OFF.

	I hold it not honesty to have it thus set down; for yourself sir should be old as I am, if like a crab you could go backward.	205
POLONIUS	[*Aside*] Though this be madness, yet there is method in't. Will you walk out of the air my lord?	
HAMLET	Into my grave.	
POLONIUS	Indeed that's out of the air. [*Aside*] How pregnant sometimes his replies are; a happiness that often madness hits on, which reason and sanity could not so prosperously be delivered of. I will leave him, and suddenly contrive the means of meeting between him and my daughter – my honourable lord, I will most humbly take my leave of you.	210 215
HAMLET	You cannot sir take from me any thing that I will more willingly part withal – except my life, except my life, except my life.	
POLONIUS	Fare you well my lord.	220
HAMLET	These tedious old fools.	

Enter ROSENCRANTZ *and* GUILDENSTERN

POLONIUS	You go to seek the Lord Hamlet, there he is.	
ROSENCRANTZ	[*To Polonius*] God save you sir. [*Exit* POLONIUS	
GUILDENSTERN	My honoured lord	
ROSENCRANTZ	My most dear lord	225
HAMLET	My excellent good friends. How dost thou Guildenstern? Ah Rosencrantz. Good lads how do ye both?	
ROSENCRANTZ	As the indifferent children of the earth.	
GUILDENSTERN	Happy, in that we are not over-happy; On Fortune's cap we are not the very button.	230
HAMLET	Nor the soles of her shoe?	
ROSENCRANTZ	Neither my lord.	

Hamlet talks to Rosencrantz and Guildenstern in much the same style as he did with Polonius. He calls Denmark a prison and admits to bad dreams but he does not take these old acquaintances into his confidence.

234 the middle of her favours: Fortune's favours, with the suggestion of sexual favours

236 her privates we: we are her private parts *or* ordinary subjects *or*, rather against the sense so far, intimate

237 secret parts: private parts

238 strumpet: whore. The goddess Fortune is commonly accused of distributing her favours at random.

241 Then is doomsday near: the end of the world must be approaching because honesty and the world cannot exist together

248 confines, wards, and dungeons: places of imprisonment

252 nothing...thinking makes it so: it's all a question of mental attitude. A common theme in literature of the period.

260 Which dreams...dream: the dreams are themselves ambition, for the dream of the ambition comes first and the achievement copies, is the shadow of, the original dream.

266 Then are...shadows: Hamlet, in debating style, takes this clever argument to its conclusion. Beggars have no ambition, so they must be bodies and not shadows. Kings and heroes, presumably ambitious, must supply shadows for the beggars. The word *'outstretched'* is suitable for heroes who have reached out to grasp their ambition, or for long shadows.

> • *Can you distinguish any differences in the form Hamlet's madness takes, depending on the company he is in?*

BY THE END OF HIS CONVERSATION
WITH THESE TWO HE REALISES THEY
TOO ARE SPYING ON HIM

BEGINS WITH LIGHT MOMENTONESS

| HAMLET | Then you live about her waist, or in the middle or her favours? | 235 |

GUILDENSTERN Faith her privates we.

HAMLET In the secret parts of Fortune? O most true, she is a strumpet. What news?

ROSENCRANTZ None my lord, but that the world's grown honest. 240

HAMLET Then is doomsday near – but your news is not true. Let me question more in particular. What have you, my good friends, deserved at the hands of Fortune, that she sends you to prison hither?

GUILDENSTERN Prison my lord? 245

HAMLET Denmark's a prison.

ROSENCRANTZ Then is the world one.

HAMLET A goodly one, in which there are many confines, wards, and dungeons, Denmark being one o' th' worst. 250

ROSENCRANTZ We think not so my lord.

HAMLET Why then 'tis none to you; for there is nothing either good or bad but thinking makes it so. To me it is a prison.

ROSENCRANTZ Why then your ambition makes it one; 'tis too 255 narrow for your mind.

HAMLET O God, I could be bounded in a nutshell, and count myself a king of infinite space, were it not that I have bad dreams.

GUILDENSTERN Which dreams indeed are ambition, for the 260 very substance of the ambitious is merely the shadow of a dream.

HAMLET A dream itself is but a shadow.

ROSENCRANTZ Truly, and I hold ambition of so airy and light a quality, that it is but a shadow's shadow. 265

HAMLET Then are our beggars bodies, and our monarchs

Hamlet asks why they have come to Elsinore. He suggests they were sent for and gets them to admit it. He starts to tell them why, so that they need not break any promise of secrecy to the King and Queen.

268 fay: faith

270 sort you: class you, include you

272 I am...attended: I have useless servants, possibly also a reference to being *'attended'* by bad dreams

273 beaten way: beaten track

276 Beggar that I am: he refers to their earlier conversation, claiming he is without ambition

277 too dear a halfpenny: not worth much at all

278 Is it...visitation?: is it your own idea, have you come to visit of your own free will?

282 Why...purpose: Hamlet is reminding them ironically that they are not supposed to tell him the truth

284 modesties: sense of shame
craft: cunning

288 conjure you: make a solemn appeal to you

289 by the consonancy of our youth: by the way we got on together in our youth

291 by what...withal: by whatever is more dear, which a better proposer of oaths might think up, to charge you with

292 be even...with me: level with me

295 of: on

298 my anticipation prevent your discovery: my telling you first will prevent your having to tell me

---

- *Is it possible to make any useful distinctions between Rosencrantz and Guildenstern?*

HAMLET'S TONE BECOMES MORE DIRECT
+ DISCERNING WHEN HE REALISES
THEY ARE THERE AT THE KING'S REQUEST

and outstretched heroes the beggars' shadows.
Shall we to th' court, for by my fay I cannot reason?

ROSENCRANTZ ⎫
               ⎬ We'll wait upon you.
GUILDENSTERN ⎭

HAMLET   No such matter. I will not sort you with the   270
            rest of my servants; for to speak to you like an
            honest man, I am most dreadfully attended. But,
            in the beaten way of friendship, what make you at
            Elsinore?

ROSENCRANTZ To visit you my lord, no other occasion.   275

HAMLET   Beggar that I am, I am even poor in thanks, but I
            thank you; and sure, dear friends, my thanks are too
            dear a halfpenny. Were you not sent for? Is it your
            own inclining? Is it a free visitation? Come, come,
            deal justly with me. Come, come – nay, speak.   280

GUILDENSTERN What should we say my lord?

HAMLET   Why, any thing but to th' purpose. You were sent
            for, and there is a kind of confession in your looks,
            which your modesties have not craft enough to
            colour. I know the good King and Queen have   285
            sent for you.

ROSENCRANTZ To what end my lord?

HAMLET   That you must teach me. But let me conjure you,
            by the rights of our fellowship, by the consonancy
            of our youth, by the obligation of our ever-   290
            preserved love, and by what more dear a better
            proposer can charge you withal, be even and direct
            with me, whether you were sent for or no?

ROSENCRANTZ [*Aside to* GUILDENSTERN] What say you?

HAMLET   [*Aside*] Nay then I have an eye of you. If you   295
            love me, hold not off.

GUILDENSTERN My lord, we were sent for.

HAMLET   I will tell you why; so shall my anticipation prevent

Hamlet explains his present mood without giving much away. He builds up the conventional view of the earth and of man, only to destroy the illusion of beauty and excellence. A company of actors is on its way to the castle.

300 moult no feather: remain whole, keep its integrity

301 forgone...exercises: done without all my usual sporting activities

302 it goes...disposition: I am in such low spirits

303 that...promontory: that this splendid structure, the earth, seems to me a barren headland

305 brave o'erhanging firmament: fine sky hanging over us

306 fretted with golden fire: patterned with stars. These are references also to the theatre building.

308 pestilent...vapours: poisonous mass of foggy air

310 faculties: his abilities

form and moving: shape and movement

311 express: appropriate

312 apprehension: understanding

313 paragon: most perfect example

314 quintessence: the most essential element; in medieval philosophy the substance of which the stars and planets were made, and present in all things

321 lenten: entertainment in Lent, a time of fasting, would not be very lavish

322 coted: overtook

325 tribute on me: his dues from me – hospitality and payment

326 foil and target: sword and shield

327 gratis: (Latin) for nothing, in vain

the humorous man: a stock character; humour in the Elizabethan sense (see note Act 1 scene 4 line 27). This was an eccentric character who would quarrel and fall into rages.

329 tickle a th' sere: easily set off. The sere is the catch which keeps the hammer of a gun at full or half cock.

331 halt for 't: sound lame and stumbling as a result

333 tragedians: troupe of actors

334 Their residence...both ways: they were doubly better off when they stayed put

your discovery, and your secrecy to the King and
Queen moult no feather. I have of late, but   300
wherefore I know not, lost all my mirth, forgone all
custom of exercises; and indeed it goes so heavily
with my disposition, that this goodly frame the
earth, seems to me a sterile promontory, this most
excellent canopy the air, look you, this brave   305
o'erhanging firmament, this majestical roof fretted
with golden fire, why, it appears no other thing to
me but a foul and pestilent congregation of
vapours. What a piece of work is a man, how noble
in reason, how infinite in faculties, in form and   310
moving, how express and admirable in action, how
like an angel in apprehension, how like a god: the
beauty of the world, the paragon of animals. And
yet to me, what is this quintessence of dust? Man
delights not me; no, nor woman neither,   315
though by your smiling you seem to say so.

ROSENCRANTZ My lord, there was no such stuff in my thoughts.

HAMLET Why did ye laugh then, when I said 'man delights
not me'?

ROSENCRANTZ To think, my lord, if you delight not in man,   320
what lenten entertainment the players shall receive
from you. We coted them on the way, and hither
are they coming to offer you service.

HAMLET He that plays the king shall be welcome – his
majesty shall have tribute on me; the   325
adventurous knight shall use his foil and target, the
lover shall not sigh gratis, the humorous man shall
end his part in peace, the clown shall make those
laugh whose lungs are tickle a th' sere, and the lady
shall say her mind freely – or the blank verse   330
shall halt for 't. What players are they?

ROSENCRANTZ Even those you were wont to take such delight
in, the tragedians of the city.

HAMLET How chances it they travel? Their residence both in

Handwritten marginalia:

GIVES A DETAILED ACCOUNT OF IS BEHAVIOUR / IS MELANCHOLY.

OMITTING HE HAS LOST ALL HIS PLEASURE IN THE WORLD

IS HAMLET OFF ON THOUGHT

DEMONSTRATING A PLAN TO SET A TRAP FOR CLAUDIUS

MAN ULTIMATELY ENDS AS DUST

HIS DEPRESSION

GENUINELY ENTHUSIASTIC INSPIRE ABOUT

THE PLAYERS VISIT

The talk is of the current disputes in the London theatre. Newly-formed troupes of child actors are all the rage. Playwrights criticize and satirize established adult actors.

336 **I think...innovation**: I think they have been forbidden to play in the city because of the recent upheavals. This could mean the King's death, his widow's remarriage and the preparations for war. Some believe it also refers to the new children's acting companies, which had recently become popular, and the rebellion by the Earl of Essex in 1601.

338 **Do...followed?**: are they still as well thought of as when I was in the city? Do they still have such a following?

342 **endeavour**: efforts

343 **aery of children, little eyases**: brood of children, young hawks. The reference is to the young choristers of the Chapel Royal and St. Paul's, who acted plays.

344 **cry out on the top of question**: in their high voices they carry on the argument (the dispute about child actors)

345 **tyrannically**: unjustly

346 **berattle the common stages**: fill the public playhouses with the row they make

347 **that many...thither**: many young men wearing swords are afraid of (what may have been written by) goose quills and hardly dare show themselves at the theatre

349 **How...sing?**: How are they looked after financially? Will they only follow their profession until their voices break?

353 **common players**: professional actors
if their...better: if they find no better means of making a living

354 **their...succession**: their writers are damaging the children's future. They will be adult actors themselves one day.

357 **to do**: unruliness

358 **tarre them**: incite them, drive them on

359 **no money...question**: only plays where writers of children's plays and adult actors attacked each other made money

364 **carry it away?**: win

365 **Hercules and his load too**: Hercules' load is the world which he was often depicted as carrying on his back. This is also supposed to have been the symbol for the Globe Theatre.

368 **make mouths at him**: make faces at him (behind his back)

| | reputation and profit was better both ways. | 335 |

ROSENCRANTZ I think their inhibition comes by the means of
the late innovation.

HAMLET Do they hold the same estimation they did when I
was in the city? Are they so followed?

ROSENCRANTZ No indeed are they not.   340

HAMLET How comes it? Do they grow rusty?

ROSENCRANTZ Nay, their endeavour keeps in the wonted
pace; but there is sir, an aery of children, little
eyases, that cry out on the top of question, and are
most tyrannically clapped for 't; these are now   345
the fashion, and so berattle the common stages – so
they call them – that many wearing rapiers are
afraid of goose-quills, and dare scarce come thither.

HAMLET What, are they children? Who maintains 'em? How
are they escoted? Will they pursue the quality   350
no longer than they can sing? Will they not say
afterwards, if they should grow themselves to
common players – as it is most like, if their
means are no better – their writers do them wrong,
to make them exclaim against their own   355
succession?

ROSENCRANTZ Faith there has been much to do on both sides;
and the nation holds it no sin to tarre them to
controversy. There was for a while no money bid
for argument, unless the poet and the player   360
went to cuffs in the question.

HAMLET Is 't possible?

GUILDENSTERN O there has been much throwing about of brains.

HAMLET Do the boys carry it away?

ROSENCRANTZ Ay, that they do my lord, Hercules and his   365
load too.

HAMLET It is not very strange, for mine uncle is King of
Denmark, and those that would make mouths at

Hamlet talks about his madness, knowing that word will get
back to the King and Queen. He mocks Polonius, out of
earshot, and hears from him of the actors' arrival.

370 ducats: gold or silver coins
   in little: in miniature
371 'S blood: God's blood! – an exclamation
372 philosophy: science
374 Your hands: the formal welcome after the earlier
   exchange of greetings
375 appurtenance: accompaniment
376 fashion and ceremony: greeting proper to the time and
   the circumstances
   comply...garb: do what is right in this area
377 lest my extent...yours: in case the welcome I extend to
   the players, which I tell you must be made obvious,
   should seem to be better than the one I give you
383 I am but mad...southerly: a reference to the supposed
   influence of the weather on madness, and an insistence to
   Rosencrantz and Guildenstern that he is not mad all the
   time. Hamlet knows they will be reporting back and
   anything which might confuse them must be good for him.
384 a hawk from a handsaw: some commentators insist that
   Hamlet is saying he can tell one bird from another, or one
   tool from another. In this case 'handsaw' becomes
   'hernshaw' (heron) or 'hawk' becomes the small board
   which plasterers use. Others want to make his madness
   seem more extreme by his claiming to distinguish bird
   from tool. Another possibility is 'hawk' meaning 'hack' (a
   garden tool, like a hoe), but Hamlet may well have
   wanted to show Rosencrantz and Guildenstern that he
   regards them as birds of prey.
388 swaddling-clouts: clothes in which a baby was wrapped
   tightly
389 Happily: perhaps
390 twice a child: in his second childhood
392 you say right sir...indeed: Hamlet pretends there is a
   conversation going on which has not mentioned Polonius
395 When Roscius...Rome: a great and gifted Roman actor
398 Buz, buz!: a stock response to a rumour that is not
   believed

him while my father lived, give twenty, forty, fifty, a
hundred ducats apiece for his picture in little.   370
'S blood, there is something in this more than
natural, if philosophy could find it out.

[*Flourish of trumpets within*

GUILDENSTERN There are the players.

HAMLET   Gentlemen, you are welcome to Elsinore. Your
                       hands. Come then, th' appurtenance of   375
                       welcome is fashion and ceremony; let me comply
                       with you in this garb, lest my extent to the players,
                       which I tell you must show fairly outwards, should
                       more appear like entertainment than yours. You are
                       welcome; but my <u>uncle-father and aunt-mother</u> 380
                       are deceived. His UNNATURAL SITUATION .

GUILDENSTERN In what my dear lord? THEIR ROLE IS EMPHASISED .

HAMLET   I am but mad north-north-west; when the wind is
                       southerly I know a hawk from a handsaw. *

                       Enter POLONIUS ONLY AT CERTAIN TIMES HE
                                                       PUT'S ON AN ACT .

POLONIUS   Well be with you, gentlemen.   385

HAMLET   Hark you Guildenstern, and you too, at each ear
                       a hearer – that great baby you see there is not yet
                       out of his swaddling-clouts.

ROSENCRANTZ Happily he's the second time come to them,
                       for they say an old man is twice a child.   390

HAMLET   I will prophesy, he comes to tell me of the players,
                       mark it – you say right sir, a Monday morning,
                       'twas then indeed.

POLONIUS   My lord, I have news to tell you.

HAMLET   My lord, I have news to tell you. When Roscius 395
                       was an actor in Rome –

POLONIUS   The actors are come hither my lord.

HAMLET   Buz, buz!

POLONIUS   Upon mine honour –

Polonius continues to talk of the theatre, whereas Hamlet immediately returns to talk of daughters. The troupe of players arrives and Hamlet greets them like old friends.

400 on his ass: Hamlet may be using the repeat of upon/on to mock Polonius's honour, with a *punning* reference to 'arse'. (see GLOSSARY page 328)

401 tragedy...historical-pastoral: Polonius rattles through the categories of plays, but much drama could not even then sensibly be categorized like this, as Shakespeare is telling us.

404 scene individable...unlimited: in the first, the action takes place in one spot, whereas in *'poem unlimited'* there could be many scenes. Goethe, the eighteenth century German playwright, used Shakespeare's innovative work in this area as a pattern for the writing of short scenes which allowed dramatic changes of place and pace.

405 Seneca: Roman tragic dramatist

406 Plautus: Roman comic dramatist. Both would have been well known to Elizabethan audiences.
the law of writ and the liberty: Polonius claims they wrote plays that kept to the rules and sometimes remained free of them

408 Jephthah: Jephthah (*Judges 11 30–40*) vowed that if God gave him victory over the Ammonites, he would sacrifice the first living creature to come out of his house on his return. This was his only child, his daughter, and he had to sacrifice her. She begged for time to go into the hills to mourn the fact that she would die a virgin. Ophelia too will die a virgin.

421 As by lot...was: Hamlet quotes from a popular ballad called *Jephthah, Judge of Israel*

424 the first row...comes: the first line of the pious ballad will have to lead you in to the rest – for my recitation of it is cut short here (by the entrance of the actors)

428 valanced: fringed – he has grown a beard, hence the pun in *'beard me'* – confront me

431 nearer to heaven: taller

432 altitude of a chopine: height of a shoe with a thick cork sole

HAMLET	Then came each actor on his ass – *pun* 400
POLONIUS	The best actors in the world, either for tragedy,
Pompus /	comedy, history, pastoral, pastoral-comical,
Appear to	historical-pastoral, tragical-historical, tragical-
Be	comical-historical-pastoral, scene individable, or
Learned	poem unlimited. Seneca cannot be too heavy, 405
	nor Plautus too light for the law of writ and the
	liberty. These are the only men.
HAMLET	O Jephthah, judge of Israel, what a treasure hadst
	thou! *Reinforces Polonius*
POLONIUS	What a treasure had he my lord? *idea* 410
HAMLET	Why *That love for his*
Dramatic irony	'One fair daughter, and no more, *daughter is*
as Ophelia does	The which he loved passing well'. *making him*
die		*like her.*
POLONIUS	[*Aside*] Still on my daughter.
HAMLET	Am I not i' th' right old Jephthah? *religion* 415
POLONIUS	If you call me Jephthah my lord, I have a daughter
	that I love passing well. *being made*
HAMLET	Nay that follows not.
POLONIUS	What follows then my lord?
HAMLET	Why 420
Tone changes	'As by lot, God wot',
	and then you know
friendly	'It came to pass, as most like it was' –
outgoing	the first row of the pious chanson will show you
sincere,	more, for look where my abridgment comes. 425
happy	

Enter PLAYERS

You are welcome masters, welcome all, I am
glad to see thee well. Welcome good friends. O my
old friend, why thy face is valanced since I saw thee
last; com'st thou to beard me in Denmark? What,
my young lady and mistress; by 'r lady, your   430
ladyship is nearer to heaven than when I saw
you last by the altitude of a chopine. Pray God your

*Already formulated in his mind a
plan to force Claudius face his
guilt.*

Hamlet remembers a speech from a play the actors once performed and he quotes some of it. Its subject was the revenge killing for the death of a father.

433 piece of...the ring: if a crack spread from the edge of a coin to the ring containing the monarch's head it was no longer 'good'. 'Cracked' may also refer to loss of virginity or to the breaking of the boy's voice, spoiling his talent for female roles.

434 We'll e'en to 't...we see: falcons were trained to bring down one particular prey – but not in France. Hamlet intends to attack Claudius through the actors.

437 quality: professional skills

442 caviare to the general: an acquired taste, not for people in general

443 cried in the top of mine: were more valid than mine

444 well-digested in the scenes: the scenes well arranged

445 as much modesty as cunning: as much restraint as skill

447 sallets: salads – cold spicy dishes of a mix of vegetables sometimes with egg, meat or fish. Here 'no variety or spice'.

448 indict...affection: accuse the author of pretence

449 as wholesome...than fine: as sound as it was pleasing, owing more to a natural attractiveness than to a contrived magnificence

456 Pyrrhus: when Troy was under siege by the Greeks Pyrrhus went to avenge the death of Achilles, his father
Hyrcanian beast: tiger

458 rugged: rough

460 couched: hidden
ominous horse: the Greeks tricked the Trojans into accepting an enormous wooden horse into their city. It was full of fighting men. At night they killed the guards and let in the Greek army.

461 complexion: appearance

462 heraldry: used here for 'colour'. After the killing he is covered in blood; 'gules' is the heraldic word for red.

463 tricked: as in 'tricked out', decorated with

465 Baked...streets: baked on by the heat of the streets until it forms a crust

466 tyrannous: harsh

voice like a piece of uncurrent gold be not cracked
within the ring. Masters, you are all welcome. We'll
e'en to 't like French falconers, fly at any thing   435
we see. We'll have a speech straight; come give us a
taste of your quality; come, a passionate speech.

FIRST PLAYER   What speech my lord?

HAMLET   I heard thee speak me a speech once, but it was
never acted, or if it was, not above once, for   440
the play I remember pleased not the million, 'twas
caviare to the general; but it was, as I received it,
and others, whose judgments in such matters cried
in the top of mine, an excellent play, well digested in
the scenes, set down with as much modesty as   445
cunning. I remember one said there were no
sallets in the lines to make the matter savoury, nor
no matter in the phrase that might indict the author
of affection, but called it an honest method, as
wholesome as sweet, and by very much more   450
handsome than fine. One speech in it I chiefly
loved, 'twas Æneas' tale to Dido, and thereabout of
it especially where he speaks of Priam's slaughter. If
it live in your memory, begin at this line – let me
see, let me see –   455
'The rugged Pyrrhus, like th' Hyrcanian beast' –
'tis not so, it begins with Pyrrhus –
   'The rugged Pyrrhus, he whose sable arms,
   Black as his purpose, did the night resemble
   When he lay couched in th' ominous horse,   460
   Hath now this dread and black complexion
      smeared
   With heraldry more dismal; head to foot
   Now is he total gules, horridly tricked
   With blood of fathers, mothers, daughters, sons,
   Baked and impasted with the parching
      streets,   465
   That lend a tyrannous and a damned light
   To their lord's murder. Roasted in wrath

[handwritten margin note: HAMLET REMEMBERS A SPEECH WHICH CONNECTS WITH CLAUDIUS' HAMLET'S SITUATION]

The first player takes over the speech from Hamlet,
describing the death of Priam in lurid terms.

468 o'er-sized with coagulate gore: coated with sticky
clotted blood. 'Size' is a liquid glue.

469 carbuncles: precious stones, large and bulging and
supposed to dart rays of light

473 discretion: judgement
Anon he finds him: he soon finds Priam

474 antique: ancient

475 Rebellious to: refusing to obey

476 Repugnant to: resisting

478 with the whiff...sword: struck by the draught of this
dread sword. Shakespeare is here writing a *pastiche* (see
GLOSSARY page 328) of the heroic drama of his day.

479 unnerved: weakened, grown old and feeble
senseless Ilium: Troy, insensible

481 Stoops to his base: falls to the ground

482 Takes prisoner...to stick: Pyrrhus was distracted as he
heard the tremendous crash of the falling tower. His
sword, which was slicing down on old Priam's white head,
seemed to halt, held in mid-air.

485 painted tyrant: tyrant in a painting

486 like a neutral...matter: like someone who has not taken
sides, Pyrrhus stood unable to take action

488 against some storm: when a storm is near

489 the rack: the massed clouds

490 the orb below: the earth

492 Doth rend the region: tears the sky apart

494 Cyclops: giants with one eye in the middle of their
forehead. It was their job to forge iron for Vulcan, the
gods' blacksmith, on Mount Aetna.

495 Mars's armour: the god of war's armour
proof eterne: everlasting resistance

498 strumpet Fortune: Fortune, the whore – *personification*
of an abstract idea (see GLOSSARY page 328)

499 synod: assembly

500 fellies: wooden pieces forming the rim of a wheel

501 nave: hub of a wheel, navel, with a pun on 'knave'
meaning 'rogue'

and fire,
And thus o'er-sized with coagulate gore,
With eyes like carbuncles, the hellish Pyrrhus
Old grandsire Priam seeks'.   470
So proceed you.

POLONIUS   'Fore God my lord, well spoken, with good accent
and good discretion.

FIRST PLAYER   'Anon he finds him
Striking too short at Greeks; his antique sword,
Rebellious to his arm, lies where it falls,   475
Repugnant to command; unequal matched,
Pyrrhus at Priam drives, in rage strikes wide,
But with the whiff and wind of his fell sword
Th' unnerved father falls. Then senseless Ilium,
Seeming to feel this blow, with flaming top   480
Stoops to his base; and with a hideous crash
Takes prisoner Pyrrhus' ear; for lo, his sword
Which was declining on the milky head
Of reverend Priam, seemed i' th' air to stick;
So as a painted tyrant Pyrrhus stood,   485
And like a neutral to his will and matter,
Did nothing.
But as we often see against some storm
A silence in the heavens, the rack stand still,
The bold winds speechless, and the orb below 490
As hush as death, anon the dreadful thunder
Doth rend the region; so after Pyrrhus' pause,
Aroused vengeance sets him new a-work;
And never did the Cyclops' hammers fall
On Mars's armour forged for proof eterne   495
With less remorse than Pyrrhus' bleeding sword
Now falls on Priam.
Out, out, thou strumpet Fortune! All you gods,
In general synod take away her power,
Break all the spokes and fellies from her wheel, 500
And bowl the round nave down the hill of
heaven,

The first player continues his lines, as requested, with the speech about Hecuba, Priam's wife, and her reaction to his death. The actor is moved by his own acting, and Polonius calls a halt to it. Hamlet tells him to make sure the players are well looked after.

502 fiends: devils

505 jig or tale of bawdry: song and dance (with which a play often ended) or lewd tale

506 Hecuba: Priam's second wife, alleged to have borne him nineteen children

507 mobled: with her face muffled, covered up

511 bisson rheum: tears half-blinding her
a clout...diadem: a cloth wrapped around the head which recently wore a crown

513 About...loins: round about her shrunken loins, exhausted with child-bearing

515 Who this had seen...pronounced: anyone who had seen this would, with a poisonous tongue, have declared treason against the state ruled by Fortune

517 did see: had seen

520 instant burst of clamour: sudden scream

522 Would have made milch...gods': would have made the burning stars weep tears of milk and created passion in the gods' eyes

524 Look, whe'r: (whether) see if

528 bestowed: lodged

529 abstract...of the time: summing-up and a brief contemporary history

As low as to the fiends.'

POLONIUS   This is too long.

HAMLET   It shall to the barber's with your beard. Prithee, say
             on – he's for a jig or a tale of bawdry, or he   505
             sleeps – say on, come to Hecuba. (wife) F

FIRST PLAYER 'But who, ah woe, had seen the mobled queen –'

HAMLET   'The mobled queen'?   LINK WITH
                                                          GERTRUDE.
POLONIUS   That's good, 'mobled queen' is good.

FIRST PLAYER 'Run barefoot up and down, threat'ning the
                   flames   510
             With bisson rheum, a clout upon that head
             Where late the diadem stood, and for a robe,
             About her lank and all o'er-teemed loins,
             A blanket in the alarm of fear caught up –
             Who this had seen, with tongue in venom
                   steeped,   515
             'Gainst Fortune's state would treason have
                   pronounced;
             But if the gods themselves did see her then,
             When she saw Pyrrhus make malicious sport
             In mincing with his sword her husband's limbs,
             The instant burst of clamour that she made,   520
             Unless things mortal move them not at all,
             Would have made milch the burning eyes of
                   heaven,
             And passion in the gods'.

POLONIUS   Look, whe'r he has not turned his colour, and has
             tears in 's eyes – prithee no more.   525

HAMLET   'Tis well, I'll have thee speak out the rest of
             this soon. Good my lord, will you see the players
             well bestowed? Do you hear, let them be well used,
             for they are the abstract and brief chronicles of the
             time; after your death you were better have a   530
             bad epitaph than their ill report while you live.

POLONIUS   My lord, I will use them according to their desert.

Handwritten margin notes: GRIEF OF HER HUSBANDS DEATH / IRONIC WE / DON'T SEE THIS / FROM GERTRUDE

As Polonius leads the players away, Hamlet detains the first player and asks for a particular play – *The Murder of Gonzago* – the following evening. He also asks if the player could learn an extra speech and insert it in the play. The actor agrees. Hamlet, when he is alone, comments on the way the actor seemed moved by his lines, whereas he, with a very real cause for grief, can say nothing.

533 God's bodkin: an oath, replacing 'God's bodykins' – God's little body
534 'scape whipping: escape being whipped – the legal punishment for unlicensed actors, who were considered to be vagabonds
536 bounty: generosity
548 look you mock him not: Hamlet may be concerned that the players have noticed his attitude to Polonius and be tempted to imitate it
554 peasant slave: low rascal
557 conceit: imagination
558 his visage wanned: his face grew pale
559 distraction in his aspect: madness in his looks
560 whole function...conceit: his every action, every gesture, suiting his imagined mood

> • *What is Hamlet's mood in his second soliloquy and what has contributed to it?*

HAMLET IMAGINES HIMSELF TO BE A SURGEON WHO WILL "TENT (CLAUDIUS) TO THE QUICK"

THAT HE SHOWS REGRET, FOR LACK OF EMOTION, DOUBT + REMORSE. HE IS LEARNING HIS WEAKNESSES, HE ASKS A SERIES OF RHETORICAL QUESTIONS THEN EXPRESSES WEAKNESS AGAIN, HE USES SELF-CONDEMNATION ALSO) ALTHOUGH HE RECOGNISES THAT HE IS NOT ACTING HE CONTINUES TO DO SO.

IT DOES SHOW DEVELOPMENT IN HAMLET. HE STEPS FORWARD + BEGINS TO FORMULATE A PLAN. DECIDES THE PLAY WILL GIVE HIM PROOF. IS THIS ANOTHER DELAY TACTIC BY HAMLET. AS HE IS FRIGHTENED OR IS HE BEING CAUTIOUS WITH THIS ELABORATE PLAN.

HAMLET God's bodkin man, much better. Use every man
after his desert, and who shall 'scape whipping?
Use them after your own honour and dignity: 535
the less they deserve, the more merit is in your
bounty. Take them in.

POLONIUS Come sirs.

HAMLET Follow him friends, we'll hear a play tomorrow.
[*Exit* POLONIUS *with all the* PLAYERS *but the* FIRST.]

Dost thou hear me old friend, can you play the   540
Murder of Gonzago?   *PLAYER WILL PERFORM WITH*

EXTRA LINES ADDED

FIRST PLAYER Ay my lord.   *SHOW CLAUDIUS*

HAMLET We'll ha 't tomorrow night. You could for a need   *GUILT*
study a speech of some dozen or sixteen lines,
which I would set down and insert in 't,   545
could you not? HK

FIRST PLAYER Ay my lord.

HAMLET Very well. Follow that lord, and look you mock
him not. [*Exit* FIRST PLAYER] My good friends, I'll
leave you till night. You are welcome to   550
Elsinore.

ROSENCRANTZ Good my lord.

* HAMLET Ay, so God buy to you   [*Exeunt* ROSENCRANTZ *and*
GUILDENSTERN]
Now I am alone.
O what a rogue and peasant slave am I!   *sadness.*
Is it not monstrous that this player here,   555
But in a fiction, in a dream of passion,
Could force his soul so to his own conceit,
That from her working all his visage wanned;   *ALL FOR*
Tears in his eyes, distraction in his aspect,   *AN*
A broken voice, and his whole function suiting   560   *ACT*
With forms to his conceit – and all for nothing?
For Hecuba!
What's Hecuba to him, or he to Hecuba,
That he should weep for her? What would he do,

How he regrets his inactivity at this stage. An actor can be more moved by stage tragedy than Hamlet is with real life

Hamlet blames himself for not yet having taken revenge for
his father's murder. He calls himself a coward for making use
of words, not deeds. He has had the idea that, when
presented with a play telling the story of what they have
done, murderers have confessed their crimes. He will arrange
for the players to act such a play before his uncle, and he will
watch him carefully.

567 **cleave the general ear**: split the audience's ears
    horrid: causing horror, dreadful
568 **the free**: those free of guilt
569 **Confound**: confuse, perplex
    amaze: bewilder
572 **muddy-mettled**: dull of spirit (mettle) and mud-
    coloured, tarnished metal
    peak: droop around the place (cf modern English 'peaky')
573 **John-a-dreams**: the name for a stupid, dreamy fellow
    unpregnant of: unmoved by
575 **property**: the man he was, his whole personality
576 **defeat**: destruction
577 **pate**: head
579 **gives me the lie i' the throat...lungs**: accuses me of lying
    (cf modern English 'he's lying in his teeth'). Lying *'As
    deep as to the lungs'* must mean a very serious lie indeed.
582 **'Swounds**: God's wounds, an oath
583 **pigeon-livered and lack gall**: the pigeon, seen as a mild
    bird was thought to have no gall, the alleged source of
    bitterness
585 **the region kites**: the kites of the air (birds of prey and
    also scavengers)
587 **kindless**: unnatural
592 **unpack my heart**: unburden, relieve my heart
593 **drab**: whore, slatternly woman
594 **stallion**: male whore *or* 'scullion', kitchen maid, used as
    term of abuse – a loud, low woman
595 **About**: set about your task

Had he the motive and the cue for passion   565
That I have? He would <u>drown</u> the stage with
    tears,
And <u>cleave the general ear</u> with horrid speech,
Make mad the guilty, and appal the free,
Confound the ignorant, and amaze indeed
The very faculties of eyes and ears.   570
Yet I,
<u>A dull and muddy-mettled rascal</u>, peak,
Like John-a-dreams, unpregnant of my cause,
And can say nothing; no, <u>not for a King</u>,
<u>Upon whose property and most dear life</u>   575
<u>A damned defeat was made.</u> Am I a coward?
Who calls me villain, breaks my pate across,
Plucks off my beard, and blows it in my face,
Tweaks me by the nose, gives me the lie i' the
    throat,
As deep as to the lungs – who does me this?   580
Ha!
'Swounds, I should take it; for it cannot be
But I am pigeon-livered and lack gall
To make oppression bitter, or ere this
I should ha' fatted all the region kites   585
With this slave's offal. Bloody, bawdy villain,
Remorseless, treacherous, lecherous, kindless
    villain!
O vengeance!
Why, <u>what an ass am I</u>. This is most brave,
That I, the son of a dear father murdered,   590
Prompted to my revenge by heaven and hell,
Must, like a whore, unpack my heart with words,
And fall a-cursing like a very drab,
A stallion!
Fie upon 't, foh! About, my brains; hum, I have
    heard   595
That guilty creatures sitting at a play
Have by the very cunning of the scene

Hamlet is not prepared to act against Claudius until he can be sure that the ghost is telling him the truth. He is conscious that in his melancholy state he is particularly liable to be deceived in this way. He will use the play to get some form of proof.

598 presently: instantly, straightaway
599 malefactions: misdeeds, crimes
601 organ: although murder hasn't the power of speech, it will find some way of expressing itself
604 tent: probe
   blench: flinch
609 potent: skilful in his use of, powerfully effective with
610 Abuses me: deceives, deludes me
   grounds More relative than this: more substantial reasons

- *Why does Hamlet need to be satisfied on the question of Claudius's guilt?*

*FIRST MOVE FORWARD BY HAMLET —
FORMULATEING A
PLAN.*

Been struck so to the soul, that presently
They have proclaimed their malefactions.
For murder, though it have no tongue, will
 speak   600
With most miraculous organ. I'll have these
 players
Play something like the murder of my father
Before mine uncle; I'll observe his looks,
I'll tent him to the quick; if 'a do blench,
I know my course. The spirit that I have seen   605
May be a devil, and the devil hath power
T' assume a pleasing shape; yea, and perhaps,
Out of my weakness and my melancholy,

HE WANTS As he is very potent with such spirits,
MORE   Abuses me to damn me. I'll have grounds   610
PROOF - AS More relative than this – the play's the thing
        Wherein I'll catch the conscience of the King. [*Exit*

*THE GHOST   STARTS TO ELABORATE ON THE PLAN.
MAY BE THE   GOING TO PUT ON THE PLAY — CF
DEVIL   CLAUDIUS + OLD HAMLET.
IN
DISGUISE.*

WHOLE ACT

SPYING

WATCHING

ACTIVITIES

Keeping track

Scene 1

1 The scene begins with Polonius sending one of his servants to Paris to spy on Laertes. How exactly is Reynaldo to discover what Laertes is doing?

2 How does this short section confirm or extend your first impressions of Polonius?

3 When Ophelia enters the scene she describes an encounter with Hamlet which has taken place off-stage. What exactly did Hamlet do in this meeting with Ophelia?

4 How does Polonius explain Hamlet's behaviour, and what evidence does he have to support this theory?

5 Why do you think he decides to tell the king?

6 There has obviously been some lapse of time between Act 1 and the opening of Act 2. Does this report of Hamlet's appearance and behaviour surprise you?

Scene 2

1 Why have Rosencrantz and Guildenstern appeared in Elsinore, and how do Claudius and Gertrude persuade them to co-operate with their plans?

2 Why do you think Rosencrantz and Guildenstern co-operate so willingly?

3 The return of the ambassadors brings news of a diplomatic success for Claudius. What are the terms of the treaty which has been negotiated?

4 What is Polonius's explanation of Hamlet's behaviour?

5 How does Polonius propose to test his theory?

6 How does Hamlet behave towards Polonius when he enters the scene?

7 Is there 'method' in Hamlet's madness?

8 As Polonius leaves the stage, Rosencrantz and Guildenstern enter. What possible explanation does Rosencrantz suggest for Hamlet's 'loss of mirth'?

9 How does Hamlet react to their probing?

10 The arrival of the Players prompts Hamlet to ask for a performance of a particular speech, describing the killing of Priam by Pyrrhus (lines 456–502). What impression do you get of Pyrrhus, and how

does the language of the speech create this impression?

11 The focus of the speech changes to Hecuba's reaction to the cold –
blooded slaughter of her husband (lines 507–523). How does
Hecuba react to the killing of Priam, and how does the Player react
to the speech he is performing?

12 Why do you think Hamlet asked for this particular speech: in what
ways is Pyrrhus of interest to him? Are there any parallels between
Hecuba and Gertrude?

Drama

1 Ophelia
   • The actress playing Ophelia feels that she does not want to portray
     her as a weakling. How can she achieve this? Look at her lines in
     Scene 1. In small groups, help one actress find ways of making the
     lines strong.
   • Hotseat Ophelia before and after she sees the mad Hamlet.
   • Young women in Elizabethan times had less power than teenage
     girls today. How do you think you would take the idea of your
     father reading your love letters to his boss's son out loud in public?
     Imagine the scene immediately after this, when Ophelia comes face
     to face with her father.

2 Look at the exchange between Hamlet and Polonius (Act 2 scene 2
   lines 169–219).
   Work in threes and practise these lines.
   • Perform them very fast.
   • Imagine Reynaldo is there to receive Polonius's asides.
   • Repeat them to find out Polonius's non-verbal responses to
     Hamlet's baffling twists and turns.
   • How mad is Hamlet at this point?
   • How can the actor show the variations in madness or antic
     disposition?

3 Rosencrantz and Guildenstern
   • Look at the exchanges between Hamlet, Rosencrantz and
     Guildenstern in Scene 2. There are some clever word plays. In
     threes, work on any sequence of ten or so lines. Sort out the
     wordplays and deliver them in a snappy manner. Work out the
     subtext, working out the interplay of Hamlet's suspicion and their
     subterfuge. When Guildenstern is speaking to Hamlet, what is
     Rosencrantz doing?
     Following these exchanges, Rosencrantz and Guildenstern report
     back to Claudius, but they don't tell the whole story. In pairs,
     imagine the two men planning what they will say to Claudius and
     what suspicions they will leave unsaid. Remember they are in a
     difficult position and must be careful what they say.

Key elements

In Act 2 these are:
- the major characters (mainly Hamlet, Ophelia and Polonius)
- Ophelia's description of the '*antic disposition*'
- Hamlet's exchange with Rosencrantz and Guildenstern
- the Player's speech
- Hamlet's second soliloquy.

The key scene

Hamlet's second soliloquy: scene 2 lines 553–612

Keying it in

1 This speech comes after the Player's demonstration of visible emotion
   as he describes the death of Priam and Hecuba's grief.
   - What has Hamlet actually been doing since he vowed to avenge
     his father?
   - What state of mind is he in during this part of the play?
   - Does he seem to have a clear focus on revenge?
   - Does he have any clear plan at this stage of the action?

The speech itself

2 Look at lines 553–562.
      It is conceivable that the Player's speech could have affected
   Hamlet in several ways. For example, it is possible that he could have
   been inspired into bloody action by the description of Pyrrhus.
   - How does he react to the Player's speech?
   - How do the language and structure of these lines convey the
     strength of Hamlet's feelings?
   - Why does the Player provoke such an intense response from
     Hamlet?
3 Look at lines 563–589.
      In these lines Hamlet compares his own behaviour with the
   emotion shown by the Player. He concludes that his failure to act has
   two possible explanations.
   - What are they?
   - How does Hamlet feel about himself?
   - Do you agree with him?
      Towards the end of this section of the speech his mood changes as
   his passion turns outside himself and he launches into a violent tirade
   against Claudius.

- How does the language convey his feelings here?
- What is revealed by the stress on both 'bloody' and 'bawdy' in his abuse of his uncle?

4 Look at lines 590–594.

   The tone of the speech changes again in these lines.

   - How would you describe the tone of these lines?
   - How does Hamlet feel about the way he has just spoken about Claudius?
   - How does language convey his feelings?

5 Look at lines 595–612.

   Hamlet now begins to construct a plan of action.

   - What exactly is he proposing to do?
   - What reasons does he give for this course of action?
   - How would you describe his mood by the end of the speech?

Overview

If the keynote of the first soliloquy is the mood of profound disillusion then, here, it is the overwhelming sense of self-disgust which leads to his plan to stage the inner play, in an attempt to prove whether or not Claudius is guilty of murder.

- Why is Hamlet so disgusted with himself?
- Choose two quotations which illustrate his self-disgust.

The speech contains several twists and turns and also some dramatic changes of mood.

- Look closely at the argumentative structure of the speech. How does Hamlet get from '*O what a rogue and peasant slave am I!*' to '*the play's the thing*'?
- What emotions does he experience during this speech?

Close study

Act 2 scene 2 lines 298–316

1 What view of the world does Hamlet express here?
2 What view of human beings does he express here?
3 How does the language of the speech convey Hamlet's feelings?
4 For what purposes does the speech use sharp contrasts?
5 Is Hamlet telling the 'truth' to Rosencrantz and Guildenstern in this speech?
6 How far do you think this is a genuine statement of Hamlet's feelings?
7 Do you think it is simply an evasive tactic?
8 Where else in the play so far has Hamlet expressed similar views?

Hamlet and revenge

1 After the initial surge of 'blood' when the Ghost reveals the 'truth' about Claudius, Hamlet could have pursued his target in one of two ways. He could have confronted Claudius in a mood of passionate fury or he could have engaged in devious, calculated scheming designed to achieve his revenge. He does neither. He does not act against Claudius either immediately or decisively. It is in this space between the end of Act 1 and the end of Act 2 that Hamlet hesitates.

   Look at what he says and does during this time.
   • Does he have a single focus on revenge?
   • What are his other preoccupations?
   • Do they distract him from his purpose?
   • Do you share his sense of disgust at his failure to act?

2 The Player's speech is chosen by Hamlet and you may see in it a dramatization of the active, implacable revenger in the figure of Pyrrhus. This is perhaps what Hamlet wants to be, or may have to become.
   • Do you think he is capable of acting like Pyrrhus?
   • Do you want him to be like Pyrrhus?

3 The speech also stresses Hecuba's grief and in a way it is an indictment of Gertrude's failure to mourn, and her lack of loyalty to her husband.
   • Can you find any other examples of Hamlet being distracted from revenge by his feelings about women and sex?

4 The second soliloquy explores the possibilities that his failure to take action is evidence either of a lack of real feeling for his father or straightforward cowardice. Hamlet admits that he has done nothing, is disgusted with himself and frustrated by his own aimlessness.

   He then argues that he needs firm proof before he can safely proceed against Claudius.
   • Are his doubts genuine?
   • How do you make sense of '*It is an honest ghost*' and '*the spirit that I have seen may be a devil*'?
   • Are his doubts simply a rationalization of his failure to take action?

5 By the end of Act 2, Hamlet has improvised a plan which may unmask Claudius. However, he has plunged into confusion and uncertainty and he is experiencing violent swings of mood.

Assignments

1 Hamlet's '*antic disposition*' is a matter of concern for several characters. Make a list of the various explanations given in this Act for Hamlet's apparent madness.

Essay

2 How does the arrival of the Players in Elsinore influence Hamlet and his actions?

Claudius asks Rosencrantz and Guildenstern what they have
learnt about Hamlet's madness. They tell him that they were
well received and that Hamlet spoke to them quite freely. He
seemed pleased, they say, to hear about the arrival of the
troupe of actors.

1 **drift of conference**: leading of the conversation
2 **puts on this confusion**: pretends to be mentally disturbed
3 **Grating**: jarring on
7 **forward**: inclined
8 **crafty madness**: a pretended madness
12 **forcing of his disposition**: a self–imposed politeness which
   he did not really feel
13 **Niggard of question**: asking few questions
14 **assay him To**: suggest to him
17 **o'er-raught**: overtook

> • *How effective have Rosencrantz and Guildenstern been
> at carrying out the first part of their task?*

SOLILOQUY

HE REFERS TO SUICIDE AGAIN AITHOUGH HE DOESN'T
SEEM AS BITTER + DEPRESSED; HE IS AGAINST
SUICIDE. HE SEE'S LIFE AS A BURDEN + TAKES ON A
NEGATIVE ROLE. EITHER HIM OR CLAUDIUS NEED TO DIE.
AGAIN SHOWING FEAR THROUGH RHETORICAL QUESTIONS
ABOUT WHAT COMES AFTER DEATH. HAMLET DOESN'T
ACT AS HE IS AFRAID OF THE CONSEQUENCES. IT
SHOWS HIS NEED FOR REVENGE BUT ALSO HIS
INADEQUACY IN DOING SO. WE SEE HIS WEAKNESS
IS THE FEAR OF DEATH.
SHAKESPEARE HAS ILLUSTRATED HERE; HOW HAMLET
THINKS + SPEAKS RATHER THAN ACT.
SHOWS HE IS CHARACTERISTICALLY DEMENTED, REFLECTIV
ANALYTIC + MORAL, TEMPERAMENTALLY UNLIKE THE
ACTIVE SIMPLE-MINDED FIGURES OF OLD HAMLET, FORTINBRE
+ HIS SON, + THE RASH LAERTES. (Pg 136)

Act three

Scene 1

Enter KING, QUEEN, POLONIUS, OPHELIA,
ROSENCRANTZ *and* GUILDENSTERN

HE SUSPECTS THAT HAMLET IS ACTING.

KING	And can you, by no drift of conference,
	Get from him why he puts on this confusion,
	Grating so harshly all his days of quiet
	With turbulent and dangerous lunacy?

ROSENCRANTZ He does confess he feels himself distracted   5
But from what cause 'a will by no means speak.

THEY CONFESS NO FINDING ANYTHING

GUILDENSTERN Nor do we find him forward to be sounded,
THEY TOO SEE HE PUTS ON MADNESS. But with a crafty madness keeps aloof,
When we would bring him on to some confession
Of his true state.

QUEEN   Did he receive you well?   10

ROSENCRANTZ Most like a gentleman.

GUILDENSTERN But with much forcing of his disposition. *NOT A TRUE ACCOUNT*

ROSENCRANTZ Niggard of question, but of our demands
Most free in his reply. *HAMLET GUESSED WHY THEY WERE THERE. DIDN'T WANT TO NAME HAMLET THIS.*

QUEEN   Did you assay him
To any pastime?   15

ROSENCRANTZ Madam, it so fell out that certain players
We o'er-raught on the way; of these we told him,
And there did seem in him a kind of joy
To hear of it. They are about the court,
And as I think, they have already order   20
This night to play before him.

POLONIUS   'Tis most true.
And he beseeched me to entreat your majesties
To hear and see the matter.

Claudius asks Rosencrantz and Guildenstern to encourage Hamlet's interest in the players. He asks Gertrude to leave as he and Polonius intend to arrange a 'chance' meeting between Hamlet and Ophelia in order to spy on them. Polonius hopes to prove that Hamlet is in love with her.

26 give him...edge: stimulate his interest even more
27 drive his purpose: encourage him
29 closely: secretly
31 Affront Ophelia: come face to face with Ophelia
32 lawful espials: legitimate spies
33 bestow: position
35 as he is behaved: according to his behaviour
41 wonted: usual, accustomed
43 Gracious: (your) gracious (majesty) – to the king
45 colour Your loneliness: explain away the fact that you are alone
47 devotion's visage...himself: we often put on a holy face and appear to be doing pious deeds to hide the devil's work
50 How...conscience: how that whiplash stings my conscience
51 The harlot's...it: the cheek of a loose woman, made beautiful with make-up thickly applied, is not more ugly compared to the cosmetics, than is my deed to the falsely painted words I'm covering it up with. Claudius in this *aside* (see GLOSSARY page 326) is acknowledging his guilt to us before the test Hamlet is planning for him.

> • *The parents are solemnly arranging to spy on what may be an intimate conversation between their adult son and daughter. Is there really any serious justification for this, or is it just another symptom of the moral sickness that has invaded the castle? Which is the phrase in which Claudius feels he has to justify himself and Polonius?*

APPEARANT / REALITY (handwritten)

KING	With all my heart, and it doth much content me
	To hear him so inclined. 25
	Good gentlemen, give him a further edge,
	And drive his purpose into these delights.
ROSENCRANTZ	We shall my lord.

[*Exeunt* ROSENCRANTZ *and* GUILDENSTERN

KING   Sweet Gertrude leave us too,
For we have closely sent for Hamlet hither,
That he, as 'twere by accident, may here 30
Affront Ophelia.
Her father and myself, lawful espials,
Will so bestow ourselves that, seeing unseen,
We may of their encounter frankly judge,
And gather by him, as he is behaved, 35
If 't be th' affliction of his love or no
That thus he suffers for.

QUEEN   I shall obey you.
And for your part Ophelia, I do wish
That your good beauties be the happy cause
Of Hamlet's wildness; so shall I hope your virtues 40
Will bring him to his wonted way again,
To both your honours.

OPHELIA   Madam, I wish it may.

[*Exit* QUEEN

POLONIUS   Ophelia, walk you here. Gracious, so please you,
We will bestow ourselves. – Read on this book,
That show of such an exercise may colour 45
Your loneliness. – We are oft to blame in this;
'Tis too much proved, that with devotion's visage
And pious action we do sugar o'er
The devil himself.

KING   [*Aside*]   O 'tis too true.
How smart a lash that speech doth give my
conscience. 50
The harlot's cheek, beautied with plast'ring art,
Is not more ugly to the thing that helps it

(Handwritten annotations:)
KEEP ON WATCHING CONTINUES.
DON'T WANT TO THINK IT'S WRONG.
TWO MEN WILL WATCH HAMLET + OPHELIA
ACTING RELIGIOUSLY COVERS UP EVIL
APPEARANCE U'S REALITY.
PROSTITUTE COVERS UP WITH MAKE-UP
ATTRACTIVE EXTERIOR COVERS UP EVILNESS WITHIN.

Hamlet comes in debating whether death is simply the end of life, the absence of everything and so of all problems; or possibly, and frighteningly, the beginning of something that we cannot know or even guess at.

56 To be, or not to be: to go on existing, or to cease to exist. Hamlet is mentally testing the continuation of his life, against its absence.

58 slings: some suspect a misprint for 'stings', but slings were used from earliest times to hurl missiles at the enemy

60 To die...no more: in literature as in life, sleep is often welcome. But sleep can be disturbed by nightmares and in line 65 Hamlet realizes this.

61 by a sleep...heir to: just by being human we are subject to *'shocks'*. 'Shock' is the term for the blow of sword on sword in battle. Hamlet here is still occupied with the hope that death equals sleep equals an end.

63 consummation: satisfactory conclusion, perfect fulfilment

65 rub: difficulty, hindrance. A metaphor from the game of bowls – any impediment to the course of the bowl.

67 shuffled off...coil: got rid of this business of being alive – *'shuffle off'* contains a sense of shiftiness, of being evasive

68 there's...long life: that's the consideration that makes calamity so long-lived (with the echo 'long life itself is a calamity')

70 of time: that merely living through time brings

71 contumely: scorn

73 the spurns...takes: the disdain which someone who deserves better has to put up with from unworthy people

75 quietus: death – a legal term for full payment of a debt, but also carrying the suggestion of rest and quiet

76 a bare bodkin: just a dagger
fardels: burdens

79 bourn: boundary

83 conscience: (1) inward knowledge or consciousness. Here, the ability to work things out, to understand that things may not be as we first thought or as we might like them to be. (2) conscience in the sense of the knowledge of right and wrong.

84 native hue of resolution...thought: resolution, being a bold and positive product of the sanguine humour would be red. Converted into indecisiveness it turns pale.

Than is my deed to my most painted word.
O heavy burthen!

POLONIUS   I hear him coming, let's withdraw my lord.   55

[*Exeunt* KING *and* POLONIUS

Enter HAMLET

HAMLET   To be, or not to be, that is the question:
Whether 'tis nobler in the mind to suffer
The slings and arrows of outrageous fortune,
Or to take arms against a sea of troubles,
And by opposing end them? To die, to sleep –   60
No more; and by a sleep to say we end
The heart-ache, and the thousand natural shocks
That flesh is heir to; 'tis a consummation
Devoutly to be wished. To die, to sleep –
To sleep, perchance to dream, ay there's the rub,   65
For in that sleep of death what dreams may come
When we have shuffled off this mortal coil,
Must give us pause; there's the respect
That makes calamity of so long life.
For who would bear the whips and scorns of
       time,   70
Th' oppressor's wrong, the proud man's
       contumely,
The pangs of despised love, the law's delay,
The insolence of office, and the spurns
That patient merit of th' unworthy takes
When he himself might his quietus make   75
With a bare bodkin? Who would fardels bear,
To grunt and sweat under a weary life,
But that the dread of something after death,
The undiscovered country from whose bourn
No traveller returns, puzzles the will,   80
And makes us rather bear those ills we have,
Than fly to others that we know not of?
Thus conscience does make cowards of us all,
And thus the native hue of resolution

This fear of the unknown, Hamlet suggests, numbs us into inaction. He becomes aware that Ophelia is there. She offers to return his gifts, which Hamlet denies sending her. He speaks abruptly to her, making similar connections between chastity, beauty and immorality as her father and brother have already done.

86 pitch and moment: scope and importance
87 With this regard: on this account
their currents turn awry: change their intended direction
88 Soft you now: hush, be silent
89 Nymph: beautiful girl, maiden
orisons: prayers
93 remembrances: gifts
96 aught: anything
98 with them...composed: accompanied by such charming words
99 their perfume lost: since the affection with which they were given no longer exists
101 wax: grow, become
103 honest: chaste
108 admit no discourse: not hold any conversation, ie chastity and beauty are a dangerous combination
109 commerce: dealings
111 the power...a bawd: it is easier for the power of beauty to turn chastity to prostitution
113 his: its
114 paradox: something which cannot be accounted for by using reason

> • *How can we account for Hamlet's behaviour towards Ophelia? Do you find any comparisons with her father's and brother's lectures to her?*

SOLILOQUY IS BLANK VERSE

CONVERSATION IS PROSE

THE TONE IS MORE TENSE; THE EMOTION PATTERNING SHOWS THE CHANGE.

MAJORITY OF PLAY IS BLANK VERSE.

[handwritten top margin: STRIKING SIMILARITIES BETWEEN THIS + THE CONVERSATION HE HAD WITH GERTRUDE IN ACT 3 SCH. THE EMOTIONAL STRUCTURE DIFFERS DUE TO THE PRESENCE OF CLAUDIUS + POLONIUS HERE]

[handwritten left margin: WE ARE AFRAID OF THE CONSEQUENCES OF OUR ACTIONS]

Is sicklied o'er with the pale cast of thought,   85
And enterprises of great pitch and moment
With this regard their currents turn awry,
And lose the name of action. Soft you now,
The fair Ophelia. – Nymph, in thy orisons
Be all my sins remembered.

[handwritten: TENDERNESS NO AGGRESSIVE REACTION.]

OPHELIA   *[handwritten: IN THE SONNETS, TRUE, KIND + TRUE DESCRIBE QUALITIES WHICH WE ADMIRE IN THOSE WE LOVE]* Good my lord,   90
[handwritten left: CONCERNED] How does your honour for this many a day?

[handwritten: TO HIMSELF TELLING HIMSELF TO CALM]

HAMLET   I humbly thank you, well, well, well.

OPHELIA   My lord, I have remembrances of yours
That I have longed long to re-deliver.
I pray you now receive them.

[handwritten: HE IS HAMLET HIMSELF.]

HAMLET   *[handwritten: NOT THE SAME HAMLET WHO GAVE HER THIS TOKEN OF LOVE]* No, not I,   95
I never gave you aught.   *[handwritten: OR HE NEVER LOVED HER ANYWAY.]*

OPHELIA   My honoured lord, you know right well you did,
And with them words of so sweet breath composed
As made these things more rich. Their perfume
        lost,
Take these again, for to the noble mind   100
Rich gifts wax poor when givers prove unkind.
There my lord.

[handwritten left: BUILDS UP TO A FURIOUS ATTACK]

HAMLET   Ha, ha, are you honest?   *[handwritten: * PROSE. THROUGH HER FORMAL, FORCED, SELF CONCIOUS LANGUAGE]*

OPHELIA   My lord?   *[handwritten: KNOWS HE'S BEING WATCHED]*

HAMLET   Are you fair?   105

OPHELIA   What means your lordship?   *[handwritten: ANTIC DISPOSITION IS]*

HAMLET   That if you be honest and fair, your honesty should   *[handwritten: AGGRESSIVE]*
admit no discourse to your beauty.

OPHELIA   Could beauty, my lord, have better commerce than
with honesty?   110

HAMLET   Ay truly, for the power of beauty will sooner   *[handwritten: APPEARANCE vs REALITY]*
transform honesty from what it is to a bawd, than
the force of honesty can translate beauty into his
likeness. This was sometime a paradox, but now the
time gives it proof. I did love you once.   115

[handwritten bottom: BEAUTIFUL WOMEN ARE DECIEVERS. WE BELIEVE HAMLET IN ACTS "LOVED OPHELIA" THEN WE CAN UNDERSTAND HIS SHOCK OF HER BETRAYAL.]

Hamlet continues to reject Ophelia, to her considerable
distress. His insistence that she should go to a nunnery, with
his ranting speech and violent sentiments, convince her he is
mentally unbalanced.

117 for virtue...relish of it: *'inoculate'* and *'stock'* are
technical terms borrowed from horticulture. A graft
(containing a bud or 'eye' – Latin 'oculus') is taken from
a rose bush or fruit tree and inserted into the stem of a
stock of the same species. The graft is usually attractive
while the stock is vigorous. The resulting plant should
share the best qualities of both. Hamlet is saying that the
characteristics of the old stock will persist.

118 relish: trace, taste, tinge

121 Get thee to a nunnery: a place where Ophelia can
remain chaste and not continue the procreation of wicked
sinful creatures. Even the most ordinary men are full of
sins: Hamlet enumerates his.

122 indifferent honest: fairly virtuous

126 at my beck: waiting to be called on

129 arrant knaves: notorious rogues, out and out villains

130 Go...nunnery: perhaps speaking as a father might to an
errant daughter reminds Hamlet of Polonius. There is no
indication in the text that he knows he is being spied on –
he might have had more verbal fun with it if he had known.

137 be thou: even if you are

138 calumny: slander

141 monsters: a husband, deceived by his wife, was said to be
a 'cuckold' and to grow horns, thus to look like a monster

144 paintings: using cosmetics

146 you jig, you amble: dance steps. The word *'jig'* suggests
a rapid, jerky action, *'amble'* an easy more gliding
motion. The word *'jig'* can also refer to singing or playing
a tune in this style.
you lisp, you nickname: you speak affectedly and
childishly, you give made-up names. Hamlet is
commenting unfavourably on the flirtatious tricks women
get up to, to attract men.

149 on't: of it

this DISGUST WITH HER BECOMES LIKE HIS MOTHERS
TURNING TO SEXUAL DEPRAVITY,

Although Gertrude is on stage she has no part in the... preparing us for her later change of heart. (handwritten top margin)

OPHELIA	Indeed my lord you made me believe so.
HAMLET	You should not have believed me, for virtue cannot so inoculate our old stock, but we shall relish of it. I loved you not.
OPHELIA	I was the more deceived. 120
HAMLET	Get thee to a nunnery, why wouldst thou be a breeder of sinners? I am myself indifferent honest, but yet I could accuse me of such things, that it were better my mother had not borne me. I am very proud, revengeful, ambitious, with more 125 offences at my beck, than I have thoughts to put them in, imagination to give them shape, or time to act them in. What should such fellows as I do crawling between earth and heaven? We are arrant knaves all, believe none of us. Go thy ways to a 130 nunnery. Where's your father?
OPHELIA	At home my lord.
HAMLET	Let the doors be shut upon him, that he may play the fool no where but in 's own house. Farewell.
OPHELIA	O help him, you sweet heavens! 135
HAMLET	If thou dost marry, I'll give thee this plague for thy dowry – be thou as chaste as ice, as pure as snow, thou shalt not escape calumny. Get thee to a nunnery, go farewell. Or if thou wilt needs marry, marry a fool for wise men know well enough 140 what monsters you make of them. To a nunnery go, and quickly too. Farewell.
OPHELIA	O heavenly powers, restore him!
HAMLET	I have heard of your paintings too, well enough; God has given you one face, and you make 145 yourselves another; you jig, you amble, and you lisp, you nickname God's creatures, and make your wantonness your ignorance. Go to, I'll no more on 't; it hath made me mad. I say we will have no more marriage. Those that are married already, 150

(handwritten annotations:)
NO CONTACT (PROTECTION) WITH WORLD.
DISTORTED VIEW OF WOMEN.
HAMLET HAS A SENSE OF FOREBODING. NEGATIVE QUALITIES OF HIMSELF, TO HELP OPHELIA DESTROY HER AFFECTION
APPLY MORE TO OMINOUS THING HAMLET
LIES — PROVES WOMEN ARE DECEIVERS. HAMLET KNOWS HERE
IT MUST BE CLEAR WHICH OF HAMLET'S WORDS ARE AIMED AT OPHELIA + THOSE LISTENING.
TREACHERY OF WOMEN
RESPONDS TO OPHELIA LIE.
HE SEES HER AS A WHORE.

When Hamlet leaves Ophelia, she expresses her grief at his state of mind and we glimpse what hopes she – and others – had of him. Claudius cannot see love in what he has observed and has plans to send Hamlet away for a change of scene. Polonius still puts Hamlet's derangement down to neglected love.

151 shall live: shall remain (married)
    keep as they are: remain single
155 Th' expectancy and rose: the great hope, the incomparable prince
156 The glass of fashion and the mould of form: a pattern for others to follow, a model of behaviour
157 observed: honoured by, looked up to by
159 musicked vows: his vows sounded like music to her
162 blown youth: youth in full bloom (like a rose)
163 ecstasy: madness
168 sits on brood: like a bird on a clutch of eggs
169 doubt: fear
    disclose: bringing out
172 set it down: decided, determined
173 neglected tribute: money, called Danegeld, paid annually by Anglo-Saxons in the eleventh century to buy off attacks by the Danes
176 This...heart: to settle (here) is to sink to the bottom like dregs or sediment in wine. What it is that has '*something -settled*' in Hamlet's heart should be unclear to the observers, but Claudius has taken fright.
178 fashion of himself: behaviour normal to him

> • *In Ophelia's sad reaction, we have the chance to see Hamlet as he was observed by her before the dramatic changes brought about by his father's murder. Be aware of similar suggestions elsewhere in the play.*
> • *What impressions does Claudius have now of Hamlet's madness?*

(CLAUDIUS)

all but one, shall live, the rest shall keep as they are.
To a nunnery go.   [Exit

OPHELIA

O what a noble mind is here o'erthrown!
The courtier's, soldier's, scholar's, eye, tongue, sword,
Th' expectancy and rose of the fair state,   155
The glass of fashion, and the mould of form,
Th' observed of all observers, quite, quite down,
And I of ladies most deject and wretched,
That sucked the honey of his musicked vows,
Now see that noble and most sovereign reason,   160
Like sweet bells jangled, out of time and harsh;
That unmatched form and feature of blown youth
Blasted with ecstasy. O woe is me,
T' have seen what I have seen, see what I see.

Enter KING *and* POLONIUS

KING

Love? His affections do not that way tend;   165
Nor what he spake, though it lacked form a little,
Was not like madness. There's something in his soul
O'er which his melancholy sits on brood,
And I do doubt the hatch and the disclose
Will be some danger; which for to prevent,   170
I have in quick determination
Thus set it down: he shall with speed to England,
For the demand of our neglected tribute.
Haply the seas and countries different,
With variable objects, shall expel   175
This something-settled matter in his heart,
Whereon his brains still beating puts him thus
From fashion of himself. What think you on 't?

POLONIUS

It shall do well. But yet do I believe
The origin and commencement of his grief   180
Sprung from neglected love. How now Ophelia?
You need not tell us what Lord Hamlet said;
We heard it all. My lord, do as you please,
But if you hold it fit, after the play

Polonius sets up a tête-à-tête between Hamlet and Gertrude, his mother, in the hope that she can find out the truth.

186 round: direct, plain-spoken
187 in the ear...conference: where I can hear everything that is being said
188 If she finds him not: if she cannot discover what is at the bottom of this

Hamlet instructs the actors in the performance of the speech he has given them to introduce into the play. At the same time he criticizes acting which is overdone and also ignorant elements in the audience.

3 I had as lief: I would just as soon
7 acquire...a temperance: get for yourselves and then produce in your acting a moderation
9 robustious: boisterous
10 periwig-pated: wearing a wig
11 groundlings: the section of the audience which stood in front of and around the stage in the cheapest part of the theatre
12 are capable of nothing but: respond only to
13 inexplicable dumb shows: mime, where the meaning is not always clear
14 o'erdoing Termagant: overdoing Termagant – an imaginary god supposed by Christians to be worshipped by Muslims and represented in mystery plays as a violent character
15 Herod: also portrayed as a violent man in the mystery plays and, of course, traditionally the murderer of innocent children killed on his orders
20 modesty: self-control, restraint
21 from: a long way from
22 end: intention

- *Do you detect any indirect comment on Hamlet's own predicament in his instructions to the players?*

HAMLET SPEAK TO HIS MOTHER.
+ BE WATCHED.

Let his queen mother all alone entreat him   185
To show his grief; let her be round with him,
And I'll be placed, so please you, in the ear
Of all their conference. If she finds him not,
To England send him; or confine him where
Your wisdom best shall think.

KING   It shall be so.   190
Madness in great ones must not unwatched go.
[*Exeunt*

SENDING
HAMLET TO HIS
DEATH.

Scene 2

PROSE

BEFORE RUNNING
THROUGH THE
SPEECH.

Enter HAMLET *and three of the Players* ↑

HAMLET   Speak the speech I pray you as I pronounced it to
you, trippingly on the tongue; but if you mouth it
as many of our players do, I had as lief the town-
crier spoke my lines. Nor do not saw the air too
much with your hand thus, but use all gently; for   5
in the very torrent, tempest, and as I may say, the
whirlwind of your passion, you must acquire and
beget a temperance that may give it smoothness.
O it offends me to the soul, to hear a robustious
periwig-pated fellow tear a passion to tatters, to   10
very rags, to split the ears of the groundlings, who
for the most part are capable of nothing but
inexplicable dumb shows and noise. I would have
such a fellow whipped for o'erdoing Termagant; it
outherods Herod, pray you avoid it.   15

WE KNOW
THERE'S AN
EXTRA
SPEECH.
THIS ADVICE
COULD BE BASED
ON THAT.

FIRST PLAYER I warrant your honour.

HAMLET   Be not too tame neither, but let your own
discretion be your tutor. Suit the action to the
word, the word to the action, with this special
observance, that you o'erstep not the modesty   20
of nature. For any thing so o'erdone is from the
purpose of playing, whose end both at the first, and

Hamlet continues to set down what he considers the true purpose of theatre and to castigate bad actors and clowns who extemporize too freely. Polonius assures him that both the King and Queen will see the play.

25 the very age...and pressure: a true reflection of the period – pinpointing the shape it takes and the influences on it

26 Now this...theatre of others: when something is overacted or done badly, although it may make foolish spectators laugh, it must make sensible people feel sad; the judgement of one of these sensible people must, you will agree, be of more significance than that of a theatre full of the foolish ones

overdone...tardy off: overacted or done badly

27 unskilful: ignorant

28 the censure of the which one: the judgment of one of whom

32 profanely: irreverently

35 nature's journeymen: apprentices of Nature, still learning the craft of making people

38 indifferently: reasonably well

41 no more...for them: clowns in plays traditionally improvized, rather like some stand-up comics today.

43 barren spectators: members of the audience who are not responding

44 in the mean time...considered: by doing this some important element of the plot may need to be put across

49 piece of work: artistic composition

51 presently: immediately

*

IT CAPTURES H. FEELINGS OF BEING UNEQUAL TO THE TASK THAT HAS BEEN ASSIGNED TO HIM. THE REST OF HIS SPEECH IS FLUENT. THE IDEAS IT EXPLORES ARE EXPRESSED AS GENERAL TRUTHS (LINE 83) MOST FAMOUS SOLILOQUY NO MENTION OF MUM + DAD, UNCLE OR PLANS FOR REVENGE. WHEN WE HAVE DEATH DESCRIBED AS (LINE 79) IT SEEMS HAMLET HAS FORGOTTEN THE GHOST LIKE HIS - 80 FATHER TELLING HIM THE HORRORS OF PURGATORY. SOLILOQUY IS UNLIKE THE OTHERS SHAKESPEARE GIVES HAMLET THERE IS A DEJECTED UNIFORMITY OF TONE. NONE OF THE ASSION PREVIOUSLY SEEN FROM CONFUSED HAMLET: IT SERVES AS A POIGNANT DRAMATIC CONTRAST TO WHAT COMES NEXT.

PURPOSE OF ACTING IS TO IMMITATE NATURE (HR)

BALANCED PERFORMANCE HAVE CLOSE RELATIONSHIP BETWEEN + DRAMA.

now, was and is, to hold as 'twere the mirror up to
nature; to show virtue her own feature, scorn her
own image, and the very age and body of the   25
time his form and pressure. Now this overdone, or
come tardy off, though it makes the unskilful laugh,
cannot but make the judicious grieve; the censure
of the which one must in your allowance o'erweigh
a whole theatre of others. O there be players that   30
I have seen play, and heard others praise, and that
highly – not to speak it profanely – that neither
having th' accent of Christians, nor the gait of
Christian, pagan, nor man, have so strutted and
bellowed, that I have thought some of nature's   35
journeymen had made men, and not made them
well, they imitated humanity so abominably.

FIRST PLAYER   I hope we have reformed that indifferently with us
sir.

HAMLET   O reform it altogether; and let those that play   40
your clowns speak no more than is set down for
them, for there be of them that will themselves
laugh, to set on some quantity of barren spectators
to laugh too, though in the mean time some
necessary question of the play be then to be   45
considered; that's villainous, and shows a most
pitiful ambition in the fool that uses it. Go make
you ready.   [*Exeunt* PLAYERS

DOESN'T WANT THEM TO IMPROVISE MEANING WOULD BE LOST.

Enter POLONIUS, ROSENCRANTZ, *and* GUILDENSTERN

How now my lord, will the King hear this piece of
work?   50

POLONIUS   And the Queen too, and that presently.

HAMLET   Bid the players make haste. [*Exit* POLONIUS] Will
you two help to hasten them?

ROSENCRANTZ   }
GUILDENSTERN }   Ay my lord.

[*Exeunt* ROSENCRANTZ *and* GUILDENSTERN

Hamlet calls on Horatio to observe the King, during the progress of the play, so that they may compare notes afterwards on his reactions and make a judgement about whether he is guilty of the murder of Hamlet's father. But first he tells Horatio how much he values him.

57 just: honourable

58 my conversation coped withal: as I have ever met with in all my dealings

60 advancement: promotion, favours

63 candied tongue: sugared tongue

64 crook the pregnant hinges: bend the eager joints – kneel

65 thrift: gain, rewards

67 of men distinguish: discriminate between people
election: choice

72 blood and judgment...co-meddled: passion and reason are so well balanced

73 a pipe for Fortune's finger: an instrument on which Fortune can play her tunes. Hamlet is praising people like Horatio who are more likely to make things happen than to be victims of chance.

79 circumstance: details

81 afoot: being played out

82 Even with...mine uncle: watch my uncle as closely as though your soul itself were expected to comment on the result.

83 occulted: hidden, secret

84 unkennel: used in fox-hunting of driving a fox from its lair. Here 'disclose' or 'bring to light'.

> • *Hamlet gives Horatio an assessment of what true friendship is. Is it possible for a man in his position to have a friend with whom he can be completely open? Is he completely open with Horatio?*

BLANK VERSE.

| HAMLET | What ho, Horatio! | 55 |

Enter HORATIO

HORATIO	Here sweet lord, at your service.
HAMLET	Horatio, thou art e'en as just a man
	As e'er my conversation coped withal.

TRUSTWORTHY
CLOSENESS OF
THEIR RELATIONSHIP
IS REINFORCED

| HORATIO | O my dear lord – |
| HAMLET | Nay, do not think I flatter, |

For what advancement may I hope from thee   60
That no revenue hast but thy good spirits
To feed and clothe thee? Why should the poor be
    flattered?
No, let the candied tongue lick absurd pomp,
And crook the pregnant hinges of the knee
Where thrift may follow fawning. Dost thou
    hear?   65
Since my dear soul was mistress of her choice,
And could of men distinguish, her election
Hath sealed thee for herself, for thou hast been
As one in suffering all that suffers nothing,
A man that Fortune's buffets and rewards   70
Hast ta'en with equal thanks; and blest are those
Whose blood and judgment are so well
    co-meddled,
That they are not a pipe for Fortune's finger
To sound what stop she please. Give me that man
That is not passion's slave, and I will wear him   75
In my heart's core, ay in my heart of heart,
As I do thee – something too much of this –
There is a play tonight before the King;
One scene of it comes near the circumstance
Which I have told thee of my father's death.   80
I prithee when thou seest that act afoot,
Even with the very comment of thy soul
Observe mine uncle. If his occulted guilt
Do not itself unkennel in one speech,

IMPLICIT CRITICISM OF CHARACTERS LIKE POLONIUS

REASON + PASSION

DUAL NATURE OF MAN — BRINGS THE QUESTION TO MIND; WHICH CNUC WILL FINALLY PORTRAY → CP IS A TRUE PERSON MADE OF THE RECONCILIATION OF BOTH

HORATIO + HAMLET ADMIRES MOST HIS WELL BALANCED NATURE — NOT CARRIED AWAY BY PASSION.

Horatio agrees to Hamlet's plan for observing the King. At the entry of the King and Queen, Polonius, Ophelia and other members of the court, Hamlet's apparently inconsequential, punning and challenging style of speech returns.

85 a damned ghost: a ghost from Hell, telling lies and trying to damn Hamlet's soul

87 Vulcan's stithy: Vulcan's forge. Vulcan was the gods' blacksmith, the forge was on the volcanic Mount Aetna. One of his jobs was to make thunderbolts for Jove.

90 In censure of his seeming: and form our opinion from the way he looks and acts

93 I must be idle: Hamlet is concerned that he must not be seen to be busily and intelligently occupied in conversation with Horatio, which might arouse his uncle's suspicions. The word *'idle'* also means 'crazy'. He must put on his madness again.

95 How fares...Hamlet?: how is ...getting on? The word *'cousin'* is any close relation. Hamlet chooses to answer another meaning of *'fare'* – 'to live on', 'to eat'.

96 the chameleon's dish: the chameleon, a tropical lizard-like creature which can adapt its colouring to its surroundings, was commonly supposed to live on air

97 capons: cockerels, castrated to keep them plump and tender, fattened up for roasting

107 calf: a stupid or meek and harmless person

111 metal more attractive: a more magnetic metal, with a play on the word 'mettle' meaning 'spirit', 'temperament' or 'disposition' (see *pun*, GLOSSARY page 328)

TRUST
TELLS OF HIS
PLAN .

> It is a damned ghost that we have seen,   85
> And my imaginations are as foul
> As Vulcan's stithy. Give him heedful note,
> For I mine eyes will rivet to his face,   *DOESN'T*
> And after we will both our judgments join   *TRUST HIS*
> In censure of his seeming.   *OWN*
>   *JUDGMENT*

HORATIO   Well my lord;   90
> If 'a steal aught the whilst this play is playing,
> And 'scape detecting, I will pay the theft.

HAMLET   They are coming to the play; I must be idle.
> Get you a place.   *ANTIC DISPOSIT-*
>   *ION.*

> *Danish march. A flourish. Enter* KING, QUEEN,
> POLONIUS, OPHELIA, ROSENCRANTZ, GUILDENSTERN,
> *and others*

KING   How fares our cousin Hamlet?   95

HAMLET   Excellent i' faith, of the chameleon's dish; I eat the
> air, promise-crammed, you cannot feed capons so.

KING   I have nothing with this answer, Hamlet; these
> words are not mine.

HAMLET   No, nor mine now. [*To* POLONIUS] My lord,   100
> you played once i' th' university, you say?

POLONIUS That did I my lord, and was accounted a good
> actor.

HAMLET   What did you enact?

POLONIUS I did enact Julius Caesar, I was killed i' th'   105
> Capitol; Brutus killed me.

HAMLET   It was a brute part of him to kill so capital a calf
> there. Be the players ready?

ROSENCRANTZ Ay my lord, they stay upon your patience.

QUEEN   Come hither my dear Hamlet, sit by me.   110

HAMLET   No, good mother, here's metal more attractive.

POLONIUS [*To the* KING] O ho, do you mark that?

HAMLET   Lady, shall I lie in your lap?

Hamlet disconcerts Ophelia with thinly-veiled sexual backchat. He refers again to his father's recent death and his mother's cheerfulness. The mime element of the actors' play begins with an affectionate king and queen. The queen leaves the king asleep in the garden whereupon a man comes in, removes the crown, kisses it and pours poison in the king's ears.

117 **country matters**: the rather more basic and direct approach to sex, supposed to be common among unsophisticated rural people, but also the sexual pun intended in the first syllable of 'country'

121 **Nothing**: 'thing' is also used for the male or female sexual organ

125 **your only jig-maker**: your one and only entertainer

131 **sables**: rich, lustrous dark furs, and the heraldic word for black, which is used in mourning

135 **not thinking on**: being forgotten
the hobby-horse: one of the characters in the traditional Morris dance. The hobby-horse too represents a lustful person.

136 **For O, for...forgot**: a line of a ballad popular at the time

> • *Hamlet's conversation with Ophelia consists of very broad sexual innuendo. What do you think is the point of this?*

OPHELIA	No my lord.
HAMLET	I mean, my head upon your lap. 115
OPHELIA	Ay my lord.
HAMLET	Do you think I meant country matters?
OPHELIA	I think nothing, my lord.
HAMLET	That's a fair thought to lie between maid's legs.
OPHELIA	What is, my lord? 120
HAMLET	Nothing.
OPHELIA	You are merry my lord.
HAMLET	Who, I?
OPHELIA	Ay my lord.
HAMLET	O God, your only jig-maker. What should a 125 man do but be merry, for look you how cheerfully my mother looks, and my father died within these two hours.
OPHELIA	Nay, 'tis twice two months, my lord.
HAMLET	So long? Nay then let the devil wear black, for 130 I'll have a suit of sables. O heavens, die two months ago, and not forgotten yet? Then there's hope a great man's memory may outlive his life half a year, but by 'r lady he must build churches then, or else shall 'a suffer not thinking on, with the hobby- 135 horse, whose epitaph is 'For O, for O, the hobby-horse is forgot'.

Trumpets sound. The Dumb Show enters (*PLAY SET OUT IN MIME*)

Enter a KING *and a* QUEEN *very lovingly; the* QUEEN *embracing him, and he her. She kneels, and makes show of protestation unto him. He takes her up, and declines his head upon her neck: lays him down upon a bank of flowers: she, seeing him asleep, leaves him. Anon comes in a fellow, takes off his crown, kisses it, and pours poison in the* KING'S *ears, and exits. The* QUEEN *returns; finds the* KING *dead, and makes*

[Handwritten annotation:] HAMLET IS BRINGING HIS FATHERS DEATH TO THE FRONT.

[Handwritten annotation:] INSIGHT INTO THEATRE (IN DANISH THEATRE)

The mime continues with the poisoner appearing to mourn the dead king. He then courts the queen who, after hesitation, accepts him. Ophelia has difficulty understanding the Dumb Show. There is a very brief spoken prologue and the play proper begins with the Player King and Queen commenting on thirty years of marriage.

139 miching mallecho: form, origin and meaning are uncertain, but the best sense is taken to be 'skulking mischief'

140 Belike...play: perhaps this dumb show is to tell us what the play is about

142 The players...tell all: the actors cannot keep a secret, they'll let it all spill out

145 Ay or any show...show him: Hamlet continues the sexual innuendo with a play on words meaning 'exposure'

148 naught: Ophelia takes the point and calls him 'bad', 'offensive'

150 clemency: indulgence

152 posy of a ring: a necessarily short message or verse inscribed in a ring given as a present or token of love (cf *The Merchant of Venice* where the message in a ring is *'love me and leave me not'*)

155 Phoebus' cart: the chariot of the sun. The idea was that the sun god's progress through the skies lit the world from dawn to dusk.

156 Neptune's salt-wash...orbed ground: the sea and the earth

159 Since love...bands: since we were married. A six-line speech conveys the information that they have been married for thirty years.

Hymen: god of marriage, a sort of overgrown Cupid. He is symbolized by the bridal-torch and veil he carries.

Play

GIVES INSIGHT INTO ELIZABETHAN DRAMA.

Hamlet + Horatio → close, warm relationship reinforced, role of Horatio creates relationship with audience. Eg political background

+ Act 4 concern for Ophelia's welfare.

Loyal to Hamlet. Hamlet sees qualities in him that he hasn't got.

passionate action. The POISONER, *with some two or*
three MUTES, *comes in again, seeming to lament with*
her. The dead body is carried away. The POISONER
woos the QUEEN *with gifts: she seems harsh awhile, but*
in the end accepts his love.   [*Exeunt*

OPHELIA   What means this, my lord?

HAMLET   Marry, this is miching mallecho; it means mischief.

OPHELIA   Belike this show imports the argument of the   140
           play.

           Enter PROLOGUE

HAMLET   We shall know by this fellow. The players cannot
           keep counsel, they'll tell all.

OPHELIA   Will a' tell us what the show meant?

HAMLET   Ay or any show that you will show him. Be not   145
           ashamed to show, he'll not shame to tell you
           what it means.

OPHELIA   You are naught, you are naught. I'll mark the play.

PROLOGUE   For us, and for our tragedy,
           Here stooping to your clemency,   150
           We beg your hearing patiently.   [*Exit*

HAMLET   Is this a prologue, or the posy of a ring?

OPHELIA   'Tis brief, my lord.   THE PLAY

HAMLET   As woman's love.

           Enter two PLAYERS, KING *and* QUEEN

PLAYER KING   Full thirty times hath Phœbus' cart gone round   155
              Neptune's salt-wash, and Tellus' orbed ground,   RHETORICAL
              And thirty dozen moons with borrowed sheen   LANGUAGE
              About the world have times twelve thirties been,
              Since love our hearts, and Hymen did our hands
              Unite commutual in most sacred bands.   160

PLAYER QUEEN So many journeys may the sun and moon
              Make us again count o'er ere love be done.

The stage king and queen now speak of the king's poor health and the queen vehemently denies that she would ever marry again if he were to die. She says that to marry another husband when the first has died would be like causing his death for a second time. He says that circumstances change what were our firm intentions.

165 distrust you: am concerned (about your health)
167 women's fear and love...in extremity: fear and love in a woman go together – either all or nothing
169 proof: testing, experience of it
174 operant...to do: my active powers stop working
180 None wed...the first: Hamlet has not been told by the ghost that Gertrude connived at her husband's murder, but in marrying Claudius she appears guilty by association
181 wormwood: the plant *Artemisia Absintium*, known for its bitter taste and used as a *metaphor* (see GLOSSARY page 328) for bitterness, unpleasantness
182 instances...move: causes that motivate a second marriage
183 respects of thrift: concern for advantage
186 think: believe
188 slave to memory: entirely subservient to memory
189 of violent birth: powerful when it first comes to life
poor validity: not very robust
192 Most necessary 'tis: inevitable
196 The violence...destroy: the strength of grief or joy prevents either being translated into action

> • *Look for comparisons and contrasts between the Player Queen and Gertrude.*

WORDS + MEANING IS
LOST THROUGH
TRYING TO MAKE
IT RHYMN.

HAMLET + PLAYER
PROSE.
HAMLET + HORATIO →
BLANK VERSE.

shows skull of the Shakespeare (handwritten annotation)

But woe is me, you are so sick of late,
So far from cheer, and from your former state,
That I distrust you. Yet though I distrust, 165
Discomfort you my lord it nothing must.
For women's fear and love hold quantity;
In neither aught, or in extremity.
Now, what my love is, proof hath made you know,
And as my love is sized, my fear is so. 170
Where love is great, the littlest doubts are fear;
Where little fears grow great, great love grows
there.

PLAYER KING Faith I must leave thee love, and shortly too,
My operant powers their functions leave to do,
And thou shalt live in this fair world behind, 175
Honoured, beloved, and haply one as kind
For husband shalt thou –

PLAYER QUEEN   O confound the rest,
Such love must needs be treason in my breast.
In second husband let me be accurst;
None wed the second but who killed the first. 180

irony beginning (handwritten annotation)

HAMLET [*Aside*] That's wormwood, wormwood.

bitter. His anticipation building up. (handwritten annotation)

PLAYER QUEEN The instances that second marriage move
Are base respects of thrift, but none of love.
A second time I kill my husband dead,
When second husband kisses me in bed. 185

PLAYER KING I do believe you think what now you speak,
But what we do determine, oft we break.
Purpose is but the slave to memory,
Of violent birth, but poor validity,
Which now like fruit unripe sticks on the tree, 190
But fall unshaken when they mellow be,
Most necessary 'tis that we forget
To pay ourselves what to ourselves is debt.
What to ourselves in passion we propose,
The passion ending, doth the purpose lose. 195
The violence of either grief or joy

The stage king declares that human life is full of uncertainty. Although we may make plans, circumstances are bound to change. His queen protests she would not remarry after his death. She leaves him to rest. Hamlet asks Gertrude's opinion of the play.

198 Where joy...accident: people who experience strong emotions will feel grief or joy with equal intensity and one emotion can easily swing to the opposite extreme

200 for aye: for ever

202 prove: put to the test

204 The great man...flies: if a great man is brought down, you will see the man who was his favourite run for cover

205 The poor advanced: poor man given promotion

206 hitherto: up to this point

208 who...doth try: someone who in need turns to a friend who does not help him

209 seasons him: turns him into

212 devices: plans
still: continually

219 An anchor's cheer: such food and drink as a hermit (an anchorite) might have
scope: limit, extent

220 Each opposite...and it destroy: let each contrary force that is able to make joy turn pale, oppose what I hope will turn out well and destroy it

222 here and hence: in the present life and in the next world

224 If she...now!: supposing she were to break her word now!

226 fain I would beguile: I'd like to while away

228 mischance: bad luck, ill fortune

230 doth protest too much: makes too many vows

- *In lines 216–223 the Player Queen has sworn an oath depriving herself of practically everything that makes day-to-day human life pleasant, or at least tolerable, if she were to marry again after becoming a widow. What effect would you expect this speech to have on Gertrude?*

Handwritten margin note (top): REPETITIVE STYLE OF WRITING.

Handwritten margin note (left): RHETORIC + COMPLEX LANGUAGE CONTINUES UNTILL HAMLET BREAKS IT + BY EXCITMENT ANTICIPATION.

Their own enactures with themselves destroy.
Where joy most revels, grief doth most lament;
Grief joys, joy grieves, on slender accident.
This world is not for aye, nor 'tis not strange   200
That even our loves should with our fortunes
          change;
For 'tis a question left us yet to prove,
Whether love lead fortune, or else fortune love.
The great man down, you mark his favourite flies,
The poor advanced makes friends of enemies.   205
And hitherto doth love on fortune tend;
For who not needs shall never lack a friend,
And who in want a hollow friend doth try,
Directly seasons him his enemy.
But orderly to end where I begun,   210
Our wills and fates do so contrary run
That our devices still are overthrown;
Our thoughts are ours, their ends none of our own.
So think thou wilt no second husband wed,
But die thy thoughts when thy first lord is dead. 215

PLAYER QUEEN Nor earth to me give food, nor heaven light,
Sport and repose lock from me day and night,
To desperation turn my trust and hope,
An anchor's cheer in prison be my scope,
Each opposite that blanks the face of joy   220
Meet what I would have well, and it destroy.
Both here and hence pursue me lasting strife,
If once a widow, ever I be wife.

HAMLET If she should break it now!

PLAYER KING 'Tis deeply sworn. Sweet, leave me here awhile; 225
My spirits grow dull, and fain I would beguile
The tedious day with sleep.   [*Sleeps*

PLAYER QUEEN   Sleep rock thy brain,
And never come mischance between us twain. [*Exit*

HAMLET Madam, how like you this play?

Handwritten margin note: HAMLET FOCUSES ON GERTRUDE

QUEEN The lady doth protest too much, methinks.   230

Handwritten margin note: LIKELY SHE IS ALREADY UNCOMFORTABLE.

Claudius asks anxiously about any offensive material there might be in the play. Hamlet reassures him ambiguously, continues his conversation, still full of sexual innuendo, with Ophelia, but is eager for the play to proceed.

232 argument: plot (of the play)
offence: anything to cause offence

237 Tropically: figuratively and possibly also a play on the word 'trap', which is the use Hamlet is making of the play. 'Trope' is a figure of speech where a word or phrase is used in a sense different from the one proper to it.

242 galled jade: a worn-out horse with saddle sores

243 withers: the highest part of a horse's back, between the shoulder blades
unwrung: not chafed

245 chorus: in classical Greek plays the chorus would explain the action of the play or tell what happened off stage

247 puppets dallying: the flirtation of the characters in a puppet play. In line with Hamlet's recent remarks to Ophelia some sexual reference is suspected, but is unclear.

248 keen: sharp

249 It would...mine edge: you would be forced to groan if you, a virgin, were to relieve my need for sex (take the keen edge off my sexual appetite)

250 Still better and worse: ever more clever and more offensive

251 mis-take: take wrongly or falsely

252 pox...faces: curse it, stop pulling your damned faces – ie leave off the dumb show

253 'the croaking raven...revenge': a quotation from two lines of an anonymous play about Richard III

254 apt: ready

255 Confederate season: time conspires with him
else no creature: no other creature

256 midnight weeds: plants for the witches' brew gathered at midnight would be more effective

257 Hecate's ban: the curse of the goddess who presides over witchcraft

258 dire property: evil quality

259 usurps: intrudes on, infests

260 estate: position in life

Handwritten annotations (top): HAMLET MAKES CRUDE JOKES ABOUT OPHELIA WHICH R, INAPPROPRIATE

HAMLET	O but she'll keep her word. *[UNLIKE GERTRUDE. 'DIG AT HER']*
KING	Have you heard the argument? Is there no offence in't?
HAMLET	No, no, they do but jest, poison in jest, no offence i' th' world. *[IMAGERY WHICH]* 235
KING	What do you call the play? *[RE-ACCURS IN THE PLAY]*
HAMLET	The Mouse-trap. Marry how? Tropically. This play *[ALSO TIES IN LITERALLY HERE]* is the image of a murder done in Vienna. Gonzago is the duke's name, his wife, Baptista; you shall see anon; 'tis a knavish piece of work, but what o' 240 that? Your majesty and we that have free souls, it touches us not. Let the galled jade wince, our withers are unwrung.

[DIDN'T PAY MUCH ATTENTION]

[SIGNIFICANT IMAGE OF A TRAP TO CATCH THE KING]

Enter LUCIANUS

	This is one Lucianus, nephew to the king.
OPHELIA	You are as good as a chorus my lord. 245
HAMLET	I could interpret between you and your love, if I could see the puppets dallying.
OPHELIA	You are keen my lord, you are keen.
HAMLET	It would cost you a groaning to take off mine edge.
OPHELIA	Still better, and worse. 250
HAMLET	So you mis-take your husbands. Begin, murderer; pox, leave thy damnable faces, and begin. Come, 'the croaking raven doth bellow for revenge'.
LUCIANUS	Thoughts black, hands apt, drugs fit, and time agreeing;
	Confederate season, else no creature seeing; 255
	Thou mixture rank, of midnight weeds collected, *[CORRUPTION]*
	With Hecate's ban thrice blasted, thrice infected, *[EVIL]*
	Thy natural magic and dire property,
	On wholesome life usurps immediately.
	[Pours the poison in his ears
HAMLET	'A poisons him i' th' garden for his estate. His 260

As Hamlet tells Claudius the story of the play, the King rises, calls for lights and leaves – soon only Hamlet and Horatio remain. Hamlet is elated at the King's unease and they agree that the King has demonstrated his guilt.

261 is extant: still exists
265 false fire: guns firing blanks
270 Why, let...world away: a song or ballad
   stricken: wounded in the hunt
271 ungalled: uninjured
272 watch: stay awake
274 forest of feathers: the plumes of feathers worn in men's hats, particularly as part of theatre costume
275 turn Turk with me: round on me, desert me
276 Provincial roses...razed shoes: roses of Provence – 'rosettes on my cut shoes'. Shoes were sometimes 'slashed' to leave a slit or show a coloured facing.
277 cry of players: Hamlet's collective noun for a troupe of actors, taken from the word for a pack of hounds. In lines 270–277 Hamlet, fired by his success at getting a reaction from Claudius, claims that he could make his living in the theatre.
280 O Damon dear: Damon and Pythias were inseparable friends in ancient Syracuse. Condemned to death by the ruler, Damon needed to sort out his affairs and Pythias stayed as hostage for him. When Damon returned, the tyrant, impressed, spared them both.
281 This realm...himself: the kingdom was stripped of Jove – the chief of the gods – Hamlet's father
283 peacock: Horatio says Hamlet could have rhymed, presumably with 'ass'. He seems to have chosen something worse. The 'peacock' was associated with vicious qualities. It is also read as 'pajock', or 'patchock' a brute, or 'paddock' a toad, thought then to be poisonous.

> • *At which point does Claudius rise and stop the performance? Why did he not do so at a similar point in the Dumb Show? How does Hamlet react?*

name's Gonzago, the story is extant, and written in very choice Italian. You shall see anon how the murderer gets the love of Gonzago's wife.

OPHELIA	The King rises. *WHAT HAMLET WANTED!*
HAMLET	What, frighted with false fire! 265
QUEEN	How fares my lord?
POLONIUS	Give o'er the play. *METAPHORICALLY*
KING	Give me some light – away! *SYMBOLIC OF EVIL + GUILT.*
ALL	Lights, lights, lights.

[*Exeunt all but* HAMLET *and* HORATIO

HAMLET	Why, let the stricken deer go weep, 270
	The hart ungalled play, *HUNTING – HAMLET*
	For some must watch while some must sleep, *HAS*
	HUNTED
	So runs the world away. *THIS*
	Would not this, sir, and a forest of feathers, if the *PLAY*
	rest of my fortunes turn Turk with me, with 275
	two Provincial roses on my razed shoes, get me a
	fellowship in a cry of players, sir?
HORATIO	Half a share.
HAMLET	A whole one, I.
	For thou dost know, O Damon dear, 280
	This realm dismantled was
	Of Jove himself, and now reigns here
	A very, very – peacock.
HORATIO	You might have rhymed.
HAMLET	O good Horatio, I'll take the ghost's word for 285
	a thousand pound. Didst perceive? *HE HAS*
	DEFINATE PROOF.
HORATIO	Very well, my lord. *HE SHOULD NOW*
HAMLET	Upon the talk of the poisoning? *TAKE ACTION.*
HORATIO	I did very well note him.
HAMLET	Ah ha! Come, some music! Come, the
	recorders! 290
	For if the King like not the comedy,

THIS IS WHAT HAMLET HAS WANTED

Guildenstern comes in to say the King is out of sorts, angry at what has happened. Hamlet pretends at first to think Claudius is drunk, then talks of doctors. Guildenstern has been sent by Gertrude. Hamlet explains that he is not in his right mind.

292 perdy: Pardieu (by God), a mild oath

294 vouchsafe: grant

298 distempered: out of sorts, or drunk, which is the meaning Hamlet chooses to take up

300 choler: anger, Hamlet chooses the meaning 'bile'

303 purgation: both clearing of waste matter from the body by means of a laxative, and cleansing the soul of guilt by confession

305 put...frame: structure your conversation more logically

306 start not...from my affair: do not jump away so suddenly from my subject

307 tame: well–behaved, docile

313 wholesome: healthy – (here) sane, sensible

314 pardon: permission to go

320 command: have at your service

WRITTEN IN PROSE
SHOWS THEIR LOWER SOCIAL RANK.
+ LESS IMPORTANT CHARACTERS IN PLAY.

Why then belike, he likes it not, perdy.
Come, some music!

Enter ROSENCRANTZ *and* GUILDENSTERN

GUILDENSTERN Good my lord, vouchsafe me a word with you.

HAMLET Sir, a whole history. *EVIDENTLY ON* 295
KING'S SIDE.

GUILDENSTERN The King, sir –

HAMLET Ay sir, what of him? *ANGRY OR UPSET IN MIND + BODY.*

GUILDENSTERN Is in his retirement marvellous distempered.

HAMLET With drink sir?

GUILDENSTERN No my lord, rather with choler. 300

HAMLET Your wisdom should show itself more richer to
signify this to his doctor; for, for me to put him to
his purgation would perhaps plunge him into far
more choler.

CONTINUES HIS ANTIC DISPOSITION

GUILDENSTERN Good my lord, put your discourse into some 305
frame, and start not so wildly from my affair.

HAMLET I am tame sir, pronounce.

GUILDENSTERN The Queen your mother in most great
affliction of spirit, hath sent me to you.

HAMLET You are welcome. 310

GUILDENSTERN Nay good my lord, this courtesy is not of the
right breed. If it shall please you to make me a
wholesome answer, I will do your mother's
commandment; if not, your pardon and my return
shall be the end of my business. 315

HAMLET Sir, I cannot.

GUILDENSTERN What, my lord? *HIS BEHAVIOR / ANTIC DISPOSITION.*

HAMLET Make you a wholesome answer; my wit's diseased.
But sir, such answer as I can make, you shall
command, or rather as you say, my mother: 320
therefore no more, but to the matter. My mother,
you say –

Rosencrantz tells Hamlet his mother wants to speak to him
before he goes to bed. He accuses Hamlet of not being open
with his friends, not sharing his troubles. Hamlet suggests
they are trying to trap him. Picking up a recorder, Hamlet
asks Guildenstern to play.

324 amazement and admiration: bewilderment and wonder
331 trade: dealings
333 pickers and stealers: hands. The reference is to the
   catechism in *The Book of Common Prayer*.
335 bar the door...liberty: if Hamlet keeps his problems
   bottled up, instead of confiding in his friend, he cannot
   free his mind
337 I lack advancement: Hamlet gives the reason that
   Rosencrantz originally suggested for his mood
340 'While the grass grows': completed by 'the horse starves'
342 To withdraw with you: Hamlet takes Rosencrantz aside
343 recover the wind...toil: get to windward of me again as if
   you wanted to drive me into a net. The fox, if he got the
   scent of a huntsman, would run away and this knowledge
   could be used to make him run into a net.
345 if my duty...unmannerly: if Hamlet finds the duty
   Guildenstern owes him too assertive, then love itself, from
   which duty stems, must be ill–mannered
347 I...that: it is Guildenstern's profession of love that
   Hamlet claims not to understand, not his whole remark
348 pipe: recorder

> • *Rosencrantz and Guildenstern are still observing*
>   *Hamlet. What could they have learnt about his*
>   *attitude to them if they had really listened?*

SHOWS HIS BITTERNESS TOWARDS THE TWO .

ROSENCRANTZ Then thus she says, your behaviour hath
struck her into amazement and admiration.

HAMLET O wonderful son that can so stonish a mother! 325
But is there no sequel at the heels of this mother's
admiration? Impart.

ROSENCRANTZ She desires to speak with you in her closet ere
you go to bed.

HAMLET We shall obey, were she ten times our mother. 330
Have you any further trade with us?

ROSENCRANTZ My lord, you once did love me.

HAMLET So I do still, by these pickers and stealers.

ROSENCRANTZ Good my lord, what is your cause of distemper? You do surely bar the door upon your 335
own liberty, if you deny your griefs to your friend.

HAMLET Sir, I lack advancement.

ROSENCRANTZ How can that be, when you have the voice of
the King himself for your succession in Denmark?

HAMLET Ay sir, but 'While the grass grows' – the proverb 340
is something musty.

Enter PLAYERS *with recorders*

O the recorders – let me see one. To withdraw with
you – why do you go about to recover the wind of
me, as if you would drive me into a toil?

GUILDENSTERN O my lord, if my duty be too bold, my love 345
is too unmannerly.

HAMLET I do not well understand that. Will you play upon
this pipe?

GUILDENSTERN My lord, I cannot.

HAMLET I pray you. 350

GUILDENSTERN Believe me, I cannot.

HAMLET I do beseech you.

GUILDENSTERN I know no touch of it my lord.

When Guildenstern absolutely refuses to play, saying he does not know how to, Hamlet rebukes him for thinking he can manipulate him like a musical instrument. When Polonius comes by to give Hamlet the message that Gertrude wishes to speak to him, Hamlet again has fun at the old diplomat's expense.

354 ventages: holes
364 compass: range
366 little organ: the recorder
369 fret me: the frets are the raised bars under the strings of some instruments (lute, guitar) to regulate the fingering. The word *'fret'* (here) is the verb – to supply with frets, with a play on the meaning 'irritate'.
380 by and by: shortly
381 the top of my bent: my absolute limit

SOLILOQUY

SHOWS HAMLET READY FOR REVENGE, UNLIKE
PREVIOUS SOLILOQUY, HE SHOWS HERE HIS "WANT"
FOR REVENGE, HE SHOWS CRUELTY TOWARDS HIS
MOTHER, BY SAYING SHE WILL SUFFER THROUGH
HER GUILT, EMOTIONALLY NOT PHYSICALLY,
"I WILL SPEAK IN DAGGERS ..."
HE SEEMS TO BE GAINING STRENGTH AS THE
PLAY PROGRESSES.
THE MORE HE THINKS OF IT THE THE MORE APPEALING
IT SOUNDS.   (REVENGE)

HAMLET	It is as easy as lying; govern these ventages with your fingers and thumb, give it breath with 355 your mouth, and it will discourse most eloquent music. Look you, these are the stops.
GUILDENSTERN	But these cannot I command to any utterance of harmony; I have not the skill.
HAMLET	Why look you now how unworthy a thing 360 you make of me. You would play upon me, you would seem to know my stops, you would pluck out the heart of my mystery, you would sound me from my lowest note to the top of my compass; and there is much music, excellent voice in this 365 little organ, yet cannot you make it speak. 'Sblood do you think I am easier to be played on than a pipe? Call me what instrument you will, though you can fret me, yet you cannot play upon me.

Enter POLONIUS

	God bless you sir. 370
POLONIUS	My lord, the Queen would speak with you, and presently.
HAMLET	Do you see yonder cloud that's almost in shape of a camel?
POLONIUS	By th' mass and 'tis, like a camel indeed. 375
HAMLET	Methinks it is like a weasel.
POLONIUS	It is backed like a weasel.
HAMLET	Or like a whale?
POLONIUS	Very like a whale.
HAMLET	Then I will come to my mother by and by. 380 They fool me to the top of my bent – I will come by and by.
POLONIUS	I will say so.
HAMLET	By and by is easily said. [*Exit* POLONIUS] Leave me friends. 385

Hamlet, now as sure as he can be of Claudius's guilt, tries to convince himself that he can take revenge. He prepares for the interview with his mother.

386 witching time: the time of night appropriate for witchcraft and other supernatural occurrences

388 Contagion: plague, pestilence

Now...hot blood: this sounds unlikely on Hamlet's lips, but by using the language of horror he hopes to nerve himself to murder

390 Soft: enough of this

391 nature: feelings of a son for his mother

392 Nero: a Roman emperor who arranged the death of his mother Agrippina. She had poisoned her husband.

396 How...shent: however she may be punished with words

397 To give...consent: may my soul never agree to these words becoming deeds

> • *Does Hamlet intend following the Ghost's*
> *instructions, as far as his mother is concerned?*

Claudius tells Rosencrantz and Guildenstern that because Hamlet is now clearly a danger they must take him to England at once. They tell the King that while the safety of any individual is important, it is vital that he, on whom so many depend, should not come to harm.

1 I like him not: I do not like the way he is behaving

with us: with me (the royal plural)

3 I your...dispatch: I will have your warrant quickly prepared

5 The terms of our estate: the circumstances of my position (royal plural again)

6 Hazard: danger

grow Out of his brows: is apparent from the way he looks

7 provide: equip

11 peculiar: individual

13 noyance: harm, injury

14 weal: well-being

(handwritten margin notes:) Soliloquy. Insight into how he is ready for revenge. He wants to speak to his mother cruelly but no intention to hurt her physically. Shows the only time he can be himself is when he is alone. When we are not murdering + scheming he is unsure (unaware)

Soliloquy
He wants to act.
He seems at this point ready for revenge.

> [*Exeunt all but* HAMLET

'Tis now the very witching time of night,
When churchyards yawn, and hell itself breathes out
Contagion to this world. Now could I drink hot blood,
And do such bitter business as the day
Would quake to look on. Soft, now to my mother.   390

Imagery of supernatural

O heart, lose not thy nature, let not ever
The soul of Nero enter this firm bosom.
Let me be cruel, not unnatural,   *Not hurt his mother*
I will speak daggers to her, but use none;
My tongue and soul in this be hypocrites,   395   *Musical*
How in my words somever she be shent,
To give them seals never my soul consent.   [*Exit*

Scene 3

This is what the ghost asked - her guilt will punish her.

Enter KING, ROSENCRANTZ, *and* GUILDENSTERN

KING

I like him not, nor stands it safe with us   *Hamlet is a danger to the country.*
To let his madness range, therefore prepare you;
I your commission will forthwith dispatch,
And he to England shall along with you.
The terms of our estate may not endure   5
Hazard so near us as doth hourly grow
Out of his brows.

Realistically he is a danger to civilians

GUILDENSTERN   We will ourselves provide.
Most holy and religious fear it is
To keep those many many bodies safe   10
That live and feed upon your majesty.

Role of king is to keep everyone safe. 'Kings' said to be appointed by God.

ROSENCRANTZ The single and peculiar life is bound,
With all the strength and armour of the mind,
To keep itself from noyance, but much more
That spirit, upon whose weal depend and rest

Getting involved in what they don't understand.

Rosencrantz continues to praise the importance of kingship.
The King wants to speed their journey. When they have left
the King, Polonius arrives to say that Hamlet is on the way
to his mother's room and that he will go and conceal himself
so that a true version of their conversation can be told.
Alone, Claudius is struck by the horror of his deed. His guilt
makes him incapable of praying.

15 cess: cessation, death

16 gulf: whirlpool

17 massy: massive

20 mortised: fastened

21 Each small annexment: every small thing which is joined on
    consequence: attachment

22 bois'trous: violent and noisy

24 Arm you: get ready

27 closet: private room

28 arras: wall-hanging

29 the process: what goes on
    tax him home: take him to task, tell him the score

31 meet: appropriate, sensible

33 of vantage: from a convenient position

36 rank: foul, evil-smelling

37 primal eldest curse: God laid a curse on Cain for the
    murder of his brother Abel. The word '*primal*' is used
    because they were the sons of Adam and Eve (the book of
    Genesis in the *Bible*) and this is the first recorded curse of
    God on man.

39 Though inclination...intent: though my desire to pray is
    as strong as my determination to do so, my guilt , which is
    stronger still, defeats my intention

41 And...begin: like someone with two courses of action open
    to him, I pause, not knowing where to start. The word
    '*bound*' is taken to be in the sense of 'bound for a
    destination'. Here the two courses of action are 'to pray or
    not to pray' and echo Hamlet's own indecisions.

> • *Taking Claudius's speech which opens the scene, and
> this soliloquy together, what do you make of the man?*

The lives of many. The cess of majesty   15
Dies not alone; but like a gulf doth draw
What's near it with it. It is a massy wheel
Fixed on the summit of the highest mount,
To whose huge spokes ten thousand lesser things
Are mortised and adjoined; which when it falls   20
Each small annexment, petty consequence,
Attends the boist'rous ruin. Never alone
Did the king sigh, but with a general groan.

KING   Arm you I pray you to this speedy voyage,
For we will fetters put upon this fear (CHAINS)   25
Which now goes too free-footed.

ROSENCRANTZ }
GUILDENSTERN }   We will haste us.

Exeunt ROSENCRANTZ *and* GUILDENSTERN

Enter POLONIUS

POLONIUS   My lord, he's going to his mother's closet.
Behind the arras I'll convey myself
To hear the process. I'll warrant she'll tax him
    home,
And as you said, and wisely was it said,   30
'Tis meet that some more audience than a mother,
Since nature makes them partial, should o'erhear
The speech of vantage. Fare you well, my liege,
I'll call upon you ere you go to bed,
And tell you what I know.

KING   Thanks dear my lord. 35
                              [*Exit* POLONIUS
O my offence is rank, it smells to heaven;
It hath the primal eldest curse upon't,
A brother's murder. Pray can I not,
Though inclination be as sharp as will.
My stronger guilt defeats my strong intent,   40
And like a man to double business bound,
I stand in pause when I shall first begin,

Claudius cannot be pardoned as he still enjoys all he gained from fratricide, and he cannot repent. He begs the angels for help. It would be easy to kill him, but he seems to be praying.

46 Whereto...of offence: what is God's mercy for, if not to come face to face with sin?

49 To be forestalled...being down?: to be prevented from falling – or having fallen, to be forgiven?

54 effects: those things and that position

56 retain th' offence: keep the gains. If you asked for pardon you should make what restitution you could, and not continue to benefit from your offence

58 gilded: supplied with money or gold
shove by: push aside

60 Buys out the law: in this world corruption can override justice

61 There: above, in Heaven
shuffling: evasiveness, deception
the action lies: the case is before the court

62 his: its

63 Even to the teeth...in evidence: to give evidence about the worst aspects of our sins

64 rests: remains

65 Try...can: see what repentance can do

68 limed: birds were caught in a sticky substance (called birdlime) smeared on the branches.

69 make assay: make the attempt. An appeal to the angels, presumably including his own guardian angel, to intercede on his behalf.

73 Now...pat: now would be an opportune moment to do it.

75 That...scanned: either 'that needs further consideration' or, imagining the deed already done in these particular circumstances, 'people would interpret this "revenge" as...'

> • *What chiefly stands in the way of forgiveness and then repentance for Claudius?*

And both neglect. What if this cursed hand
Were thicker than itself with brother's blood,
Is there not rain enough in the sweet heavens   45
To wash it white as snow? Whereto serves mercy
But to confront the visage of offence?
And what's in prayer but this two-fold force,
To be forestalled ere we come to fall,
Or pardoned being down? Then I'll look up;   50
My fault is past. But o what form of prayer
Can serve my turn? 'Forgive me my foul murder'?
That cannot be since I am still possessed
Of those effects for which I did the murder,
My crown, mine own ambition, and my Queen.   55
May one be pardoned and retain th' offence?
In the corrupted currents of this world
Offence's gilded hand may shove by justice,
And oft 'tis seen the wicked prize itself
Buys out the law. But 'tis not so above;   60
There is no shuffling, there the action lies
In his true nature, and we ourselves compelled,
Even to the teeth and forehead of our faults
To give in evidence. What then? What rests?
Try what repentance can – what can it not?   65
Yet what can it, when one can not repent?
O wretched state, o bosom black as death,
O limed soul, that struggling to be free,
Art more engaged! Help, angels, make assay.
Bow stubborn knees, and heart with strings of
    steel,   70
Be soft as sinews of the new-born babe.
All may be well.   [Kneels

Enter HAMLET

HAMLET   Now might I do it pat, now he is praying;
And now I'll do 't – and so he goes to heaven;
And so am I revenged. That would be scanned: 75
A villain kills my father, and for that,

THeme

FAOOURITE SHAKESPEAREAN IS DISCREPANCY BETWEEN APPEARANCE + REALITY

Hamlet compares what he knows of his father's murder with his proposed killing of Claudius. His father died without confession or absolution. It would be preferable, as vengeance, to kill a drunken or raging Claudius, not after confession and at prayer. Claudius rises, unable to pray.

79 this is...not revenge : this is reward, not revenge
80 grossly: in a state of gross sinfulness
81 broad blown: in full blossom
  flush: vigorous
82 audit: reckoning
83 in our...thought: as our thoughts go – in an indirect way. Shakespeare is using two nouns in place of a noun and an adjective
84 'Tis heavy with him: he is in a bad way
85 purging of his soul: confessing his sins
86 seasoned: prepared
88 Up: back in your scabbard
  hent: both 'grasp' and 'occasion' – the sword must wait to be used on an occasion which might be more likely to send Claudius straight to hell
91 At game: gambling
92 relish: trace
93 may kick at heaven: as he is forced to dive headfirst into hell
96 physic: medicine – ie being saved from death

> • *On a false premise, Hamlet lets his thoughts persuade him not to act. Are you disappointed?*

Polonius instructs Gertrude to be severe with Hamlet. He gets ready to hide as Hamlet calls out to his mother.

1 lay home to him: take him to task
2 pranks: outrageous tricks
4 silence me: hide myself and listen silently. Either ironic, since Polonius does not keep silent and thus invites his death, or a misreading.
5 round: direct

DISCREPANCY BETWEEN WHAT HAMLET SAYS HE WILL DO + THIS SUBSEQUENT BEHAVIOUR.

his sole son do this same villain send
To heaven.
Why, this is hire and salary, not revenge.
'A took my father grossly full of bread,   80
With all his crimes broad blown, as flush as May,
And how his audit stands who knows save heaven?
But in our circumstance and course of thought,
'Tis heavy with him; and am I then revenged,
To take him in the purging of his soul,   85
When he is fit and seasoned for his passage?
No.
Up sword, and know thou a more horrid hent,
When he is drunk asleep, or in his rage,
Or in th' incestuous pleasure of his bed,   90
At game, a-swearing, or about some act
That has no relish of salvation in 't –
Then trip him that his heels may kick at heaven,
And that his soul may be as damned and black
As hell whereto it goes. My mother stays.   95
This physic but prolongs thy sickly days.   [*Exit*

KING   [*Rising*] My words fly up, my thoughts remain below.
Words without thoughts never to heaven go.   [*Exit*

Scene 4

Enter QUEEN *and* POLONIUS

POLONIUS   'A will come straight. Look you lay home to him,
Tell him his pranks have been too broad to bear with,
And that your grace hath screened and stood between
Much heat and him. I'll silence me even here.
Pray you be round with him.   5

HAMLET   [*Within*] Mother, mother, mother!

Polonius hides as Hamlet enters. The Queen starts to rebuke him, but Hamlet will not accept what she says and in turn points out that she has made an illicit marriage. She is about to send for someone he will listen to, when Hamlet sits her down, promising to show her to herself. Alarmed she calls for help and Polonius, forgetting the need for silence, does so too. Hamlet pulls out his rapier and kills him, unseen, through the arras, thinking it might be Claudius.

11 idle: useless, silly
14 rood: the cross of Christ
17 I'll set...speak: I'll fetch people to whom you'll have to listen
24 Dead for a ducat: possibly a bet with himself that the thrust will kill the man, or an indication that someone who spies is not worth much anyway

> • *Hamlet does not hesitate to kill the man behind the arras. What are the differences between the situations where he fails to kill Claudius, yet whips out his sword and kills whoever is hiding?*

PASSION JUXTAPOSED WITH REASON.

SOLILOQUY ON (165)
THIS AGAIN SHOWS DELAY IN HAMLET. HE SAYS
HE CAN'T KILL CLAUDIUS WHEN PRAYING AS HE
WILL GO TO HEAVEN.
"I HIS SOLE SON ...
AGAIN ONLY THINKING HE DOESN'T FOLLOW
THROUGH WITH ACTIONS.
THIS SOLILOQUY CONTRASTS STRONGLY WITH
FOLLOWING SCENE WITH THE DEATH OF POLONIUS.
HAMLET DOES NOT STOP + THINK WHEN HE
SHOULD + DOES WHEN HE SHOULDN'T.
THIS DELAY IS INEVITABLE IN REVENGE TRAGEDY

DOES NOT PROGRESS IN ACTION BUT DOES IN
MIND.

Handwritten note at top: TONE :- CYNICAL / MOCKING

QUEEN	I'll warrant you,
	Fear me not. Withdraw, I hear him coming.

[POLONIUS *hides behind the arras*

Enter HAMLET

HAMLET	Now mother, what's the matter?
QUEEN	Hamlet, thou hast thy father much offended.
HAMLET	Mother, you have my father much offended.
QUEEN	Come, come, you answer with an idle tongue.
HAMLET	Go, go, you question with a wicked tongue.
QUEEN	Why, how now Hamlet!
HAMLET	What's the matter now?
QUEEN	Have you forgot me?
HAMLET	No by the rood, not so.
	You are the Queen, your husband's brother's wife,
	And would it were not so, you are my mother.
QUEEN	Nay, then I'll set those to you that can speak.
HAMLET	Come, come, and sit you down, you shall not budge.
	You go not till I set you up a glass
	Where you may see the inmost part of you.
QUEEN	What wilt thou do, thou wilt not murder me?
	Help, help, ho!
POLONIUS	[*Behind*] What ho, help, help, help!
HAMLET	[*Drawing*] How now! A rat? Dead for a ducat, dead.

[*Makes a pass through the arras*

POLONIUS	[*Behind*] O I am slain!

[*Falls and dies*

QUEEN	O me, what hast thou done?
HAMLET	Nay I know not,
	Is it the King?

Line numbers in margin: 10, 15, 20, 25

Handwritten notes in right margin: GERTRUDE CALLS FOR HELP. POLONIUS COMES IN H/E KILLS HIM THINKS IT'S CLAUDIUS

Handwritten note under "Dead for a ducat": FOR NOTHING

Handwritten note at bottom: HIS PASSION MOTIVATES HIM.

Hamlet, having killed, likens the deed to his mother's actions. When he discovers he has killed Polonius he delivers a heartfelt epitaph, then turns to his mother. He sets out in blunt language to make her fully aware of what she has done, as he sees it. When she seems not to understand, he shows her the portraits of the two brothers.

30 As kill...brother: not necessarily an accusation of complicity in murder. This would be going far beyond the Ghost's brief. But in accepting the marriage with Claudius so soon after her husband's death she is almost an accessory after the fact.

38 brazed it: made it brazen, hammered it hard, like brass

39 proof and bulwark: tried and proved, a defence

43 the rose: the fresh bloom

45 blister: an indication of disease or a reference to the practice of branding prostitutes on the forehead

47 As from ...The very soul: as makes an empty farce of contracts (particularly the marriage vows)

49 rhapsody: a meaningless string of words
Heaven's face...solidity: the heavens flush red above the solid mass of the earth, and the earth itself, with glowing face, as though foretelling doomsday, is immensely distressed at the act. Alternative readings are 'Yea' for 'O'er' and 'tristful' (sad) for 'heated'.

53 index: table of contents, preface

55 counterfeit presentment: portrait

- *We see here for the first time Hamlet's pent-up anger and frustration being vented directly at one of the guilty parties – not at his own inadequacy. Are you convinced that this is the first time that Gertrude has confronted her own dubious behaviour?*

THE VIOLENT JUXTAPOSITION OF IMAGES; THE
BEAUTIFUL, FRAGRANT, FRAGILE ROSE, SYMBOLIC OF
YOUTH & INNOCENT, SET ALONGSIDE THE BLISTERED
FOREHEAD OF A BRANDED PROSTITUTE IS SHOCKING.
INTERESTINGLY CLAUDIUS COMPARES HIMSELF TO A
WHORE BEING WHIPPED THROUGH THE STREETS
ACT 3 SC 1 LINE 50-3)

QUEEN	O what a rash and bloody deed is this!
HAMLET	A bloody deed, almost as bad, good mother,
	As kill a king, and marry with his brother. 30
QUEEN	As kill a king? *didn't know*
HAMLET	Ay, lady, it was my word.

[Lifts up the arras and discovers POLONIUS

Polonius' character role

Thou wretched rash, intruding fool, farewell.
I took thee for thy better, take thy fortune; *paid the price for spying*
Thou find'st to be too busy is some danger.
Leave wringing of your hands; peace, sit you down, 35
And let me wring your heart, for so I shall,
If it be made of penetrable stuff;
If damned custom have not brazed it so
That it be proof and bulwark against sense.

QUEEN	What have I done, that thou dar'st wag thy tongue 40
	In noise so rude against me?
HAMLET	Such an act *focus on marriage*

imagery of prostitution — Hamlet likens the woman to Hamlet's view of the ideal descent in "mousetrap" reticularly turbing picture

That blurs the grace and blush of modesty,
Calls virtue hypocrite, takes off the rose
From the fair forehead of an innocent love,
And sets a blister there, makes marriage vows 45
As false as dicers' oaths, o such a deed
As from the body of contraction plucks
The very soul, and sweet religion makes
A rhapsody of words. Heaven's face does glow
O'er this solidity and compound mass 50
With heated visage, as against the doom,
Is thought-sick at the act.

QUEEN	Ay me, what act,
	That roars so loud, and thunders in the index?
HAMLET	Look here upon this picture, and on this;
	The counterfeit presentment of two brothers. 55
	See what a grace was seated on this brow,

Hamlet sees Gertrude's sexual misconduct as a source of moral pollution that has tarnished his relationship with Ophelia

Hamlet makes a hard-hitting comparison between
Gertrude's two husbands. He asks what could possibly have
made her desert his father for his uncle. He seeks to shame
her and succeeds.

57 **front**: forehead
   Jove: the chief god in Roman mythology
59 **station**: stance, bearing
   Mercury: the messenger of the gods, usually depicted with
   wings on his heels
60 **New-lighted**: just alighted, having just landed
65 **mildewed ear**: diseased ear of corn
66 **Blasting**: infecting and destroying
67 **leave to feed**: stop grazing
68 **batten**: fatten yourself up
70 **hey-day in the blood**: excitement in passion, sexual drive
72 **Sense**: your senses
74 **apoplexed**: made numb
   madness...err: madness would not go so far astray
75 **Nor...thralled**: nor would the senses ever be made so
   captive by a state of hallucination
76 **But...difference**: but that they kept in reserve some
   capacity to choose between such different alternatives
78 **cozened you at hoodman-blind?**: deceived you into a
   game of blindman's buff?
80 **sans**: (French) without
82 **Could not so mope**: could not be so bewildered, so dazed
83 **Rebellious...own fire**: if the urge for sex, inspired by the
   devil, can still be so strong in a mature woman, there is no
   hope for virtue in passionate youth – it will just melt away
   like wax
84 **mutine**: mutiny
   matron: a married woman with the sense 'an older woman'
87 **compulsive...the charge**: irresistible passion signals the
   attack
88 **frost itself**: the older woman's passions, which should by
   rights be cold
89 **reason panders will**: reason procures what passion desires
91 **grained**: ingrained, dyed in

CLASSICAL IMAGE.

Hyperion's curls, the front of Jove himself,

OLD HAMLET

An eye like Mars, to threaten and command,
A station like the herald Mercury,
New-lighted on a heaven-kissing hill,   60
A combination and a form indeed,
Where every god did seem to set his seal
To give the world assurance of a man.   CONTRAST
This was your husband. Look you now what
        follows:
Here is your husband like a mildewed ear,   CLAUDIUS · 65
Blasting his wholesome brother. Have you eyes?
Could you on this fair mountain leave to feed, NATURAL
And batten on this moor? Ha, have you eyes?
You cannot call it love, for at your age
The hey-day in the blood is tame, it's humble,   70
And waits upon the judgment; and what judgment
Would step from this to this? Sense sure you have,
Else could you not have motion; but sure that sense
Is apoplexed, for madness would not err,
Nor sense to ecstasy was ne'er so thralled   75
But it reserved some quantity of choice
To serve in such a difference. What devil was 't   BITTER
That thus hath cozened you at hoodman-blind?   TONE,
Eyes without feeling, feeling without sight,   SHAME HERE.
Ears without hands or eyes, smelling sans all,   80
Or but a sickly part of one true sense
Could not so mope.
O shame, where is thy blush? Rebellious hell,
If thou canst mutine in a matron's bones,
To flaming youth let virtue be as wax,   85
And melt in her own fire. Proclaim no shame
When the compulsive ardour gives the charge,
Since frost itself as actively doth burn
And reason panders will.

PASSION v REASON
(HOT + COLD)

QUEEN   O Hamlet speak no more,
Thou turn'st mine eyes into my very soul,   90
And there I see such black and grained spots

His mother now begs him to stop, but Hamlet is well launched on his theme – until the Ghost of his father reappears. Hamlet assumes the Ghost intends to chide him for not taking vengeance. Gertrude cannot see the Ghost, who tells Hamlet to speak to her. He does so.

92 leave their tinct: give up their colour, allow their colour to fade

93 enseamed: greasy

94 Stewed: bathed in sweat, with the secondary meaning of 'brothel'. These were commonly called 'stews'.
corruption: moral corruption and also putrefaction
honeying: using sweet words, talking fondly
making love: talking fondly – not the present meaning of indulging in the sexual act itself

98 tithe: a tenth part, also the annual payment due to the church or other authority

99 precedent: former
vice: another word for the clown, or jester, in dramas of the time, but also suggesting the idea of 'mischief' and 'villainy'

100 cutpurse: thief – when purses were bags on strings and could be cut off
rule: good government

104 of shreds and patches: literally made up of rags and scraps, and so unlike her first husband. But the phrase also recalls the multi-coloured or patchwork costume traditional for the vice or clown, who was also called 'the patch'.

106 heavenly guards: angels

108 tardy: slow to act, late

109 lapsed in time and passion: who has let slip time and moments of passionate hatred

112 whet: sharpen

113 amazement: bewilderment

115 Conceit: imagination

- *Why can Gertrude not see the Ghost? What effect does Hamlet's conversation with him have on her?*

EXPRESSING HER OWN GUILT.

As will not leave their tinct.

HAMLET   Nay but to live
** In the rank sweat of an enseamed bed
Stewed in corruption, honeying, and making love
Over the nasty sty.

QUEEN   O, speak to me no more;   95
These words, like daggers, enter in mine ears;
No more, sweet Hamlet!

HAMLET   A murderer and a villain,
A slave that is not twentieth part the tithe
Of your precedent lord, a vice of kings,
A cutpurse of the empire and the rule,   100
That from a shelf the precious diadem stole
And put it in his pocket. *NO BETTER THAN A COMMON THIEF.*

QUEEN   No more.

HAMLET   A king of shreds and patches –
NOT WHOLE.

Enter GHOST

Save me and hover o'er me with your wings,   105
You heavenly guards – what would your gracious
    figure?

QUEEN   Alas he's mad.   *SLOW.*   *INTERVENTION OF THE GHOST STOPS HIM*

HAMLET   Do you not come your tardy son to chide,
GUILT FOR NOT ACTING That lapsed in time and passion lets go by
Th' important acting of your dread command?   110
O say.

GHOST   Do not forget, this visitation
SYMPATHY LIES WITH GERTRUDE Is but to whet thy almost blunted purpose.
But look, amazement on thy mother sits;   *HE SEE'S THE BATTLE WITH GUILT*
O step between her and her fighting soul –
Conceit in weakest bodies strongest works –   115
Speak to her Hamlet.

HAMLET   How is it with you lady?

QUEEN   Alas how is 't with you,
That you do bend your eye on vacancy,

Gertrude, alarmed to see Hamlet talking to the air, is convinced of his madness. He fears that pity for the Ghost will drive out vengeance. Gertrude must not make Hamlet's madness her excuse to continue in her sin.

119 incorporal: (incorporeal) without material existence, empty air

120 Forth...peep: the vital spirits were supposed to be subtle, highly refined substances which suffused the blood and, as here, in moments of great agitation might show themselves

121 sleeping...alarm: like soldiers raised suddenly from sleep when the trumpet calls to arms

122 excrements: in addition to the modern meaning of the word – what the body gets rid of – also what grows out of the body, like hair and nails. The *simile* (see GLOSSARY page 329) suggests that as though it were like the soldiers, Hamlet's hair suddenly stands on end.

126 glares: not necessarily an angry stare, but a fixed gaze.

127 His form...capable: at the sight of him, and knowing what has happened, even stones would be moved to action

128 Do not...blood: Hamlet begs to be spared another gaze from his father, fearing pity will take over from revenge

136 habit: clothes

137 portal: door

138 very coinage: mere creation

139 This bodiless...cunning in: madness is good at creating 'ghosts' or 'visions'
    ecstasy: madness, hallucination
    cunning: skilful;

145 gambol from: start away, shy away from

146 unction: ointment

148 skin and film: if skin grows over an abscess, the infection continuing underneath becomes more serious

---

- *Where is the irony in Gertrude's perception of Hamlet's madness in this scene?*
- *What is Hamlet's warning to his mother (lines 140–156)?*

	And with th' incorporal air do hold discourse?
	Forth at your eyes your spirits wildly peep, 120
	And as the sleeping soldiers in th' alarm,
	Your bedded hair like life in excrements
	Start up and stand an end. O gentle son,
	Upon the heat and flame of thy distemper
	Sprinkle cool patience. Whereon do you look? 125

HAMLET   On him, on him. Look you how pale he glares.
His form and cause conjoined, preaching to stones,
Would make them capable. Do not look upon me,
Lest with this piteous action you convert
My stern effects; then what I have to do   130
Will want true colour, tears perchance for blood.

QUEEN   To whom do you speak this?

HAMLET   Do you see nothing there?

QUEEN   Nothing at all, yet all that is I see.

HAMLET   Nor did you nothing hear?

QUEEN   No, nothing but ourselves.

HAMLET   Why look you there, look how it steals away –   135
My father in his habit as he lived – *NOT IN HIS ARMOUR – more AS FATHER THAN KING*
Look where he goes, even now out at the portal.

                              [*Exit* GHOST

QUEEN   This is the very coinage of your brain;   *PROOF*
This bodiless creation ecstasy   *FOR MADNESS.*
Is very cunning in.

HAMLET   Ecstasy?   140
My pulse as yours doth temperately keep time,
And makes as healthful music. It is not madness
That I have uttered; bring me to the test,   *FACE UP TO YOUR SINS*
And I the matter will re-word, which madness
Would gambol from. Mother, for love of grace,   145
Lay not that flattering unction to your soul,
That not your trespass, but my madness speaks.
It will but skin and film the ulcerous place,
Whiles rank corruption mining all within

Hamlet begs his mother to change her ways, saying that habit can replicate evil actions, but equally, if she stays apart from Claudius for one night, it will be easier the second time and so on until this abstinence becomes habit. Hamlet says he repents of the killing of Polonius but in a rather offhand way. Before he goes he answers his mother's request for advice.

152 do not...them ranker: do not encourage the weeds to grow even more vigorously by spreading fertile soil on them. Hamlet is concerned that she is discounting her own misdeeds by comforting herself that what Hamlet has been saying to her are the words of a madman.

154 fatness: grossness
pursy: fat, corpulent through self-indulgence

156 curb: (here) bow

157 cleft: split

162 That monster custom...is put on: habit is a monster because people get so used to their bad habits that they don't consider them any more – on the other hand the same can become true of good habits.

169 use: habitual practice

170 either....the devil: a verb is missing. The sense would seem to demand either a (one syllable) verb meaning 'entertain', such as 'house' *or* 'get the better of' – 'quell' has been suggested.

176 their scourge and minister: 'heaven' has become 'the heavens' to produce the possessive 'their': administer their punishment

177 bestow: dispose of
answer well: give a good account of

183 bloat: bloated, presumably with food and drink

184 wanton: lecherously

• *Hamlet approves of habit. What is his argument?*

INFECTION/CORRUPTION of DENMARK + THE RELATIONSHIP.

Infects unseen. Confess yourself to heaven,   150
Repent what's past, avoid what is to come,
And do not spread the compost on the weeds   *EVIL everywhere*
To make them ranker. Forgive me this my virtue,
For in the fatness of these pursy times
Virtue itself of vice must pardon beg,   155
Yea curb and woo for leave to do him good.

QUEEN   O Hamlet thou hast cleft my heart in twain.

HAMLET   O throw away the worser part of it,   *DISGARD CINUOUS*
And live the purer with the other half.
Good night: but go not to my uncle's bed,   160
Assume a virtue if you have it not.   *FIRST MOVE TO*
That monster custom, who all sense doth eat   *DESTROY*
Of habits evil, is angel yet in this,   *EVIL*
That to the use of actions fair and good
He likewise gives a frock or livery   165
That aptly is put on. Refrain tonight,
And that shall lend a kind of easiness
To the next abstinence, the next more easy;
For use almost can change the stamp of nature,
And either....the devil, or throw him out   170
With wondrous potency. Once more good night,
And when you are desirous to be blessed,
I'll blessing beg of you. For this same lord,
I do repent; but heaven hath pleased it so,
To punish me with this, and this with me,   175
That I must be their scourge and minister.   *USED BY HEAVEN*
I will bestow him, and will answer well   *TO REVENGE.*
The death I gave him. So again good night.
I must be cruel only to be kind.
Thus bad begins, and worse remains behind.   180
One word more good lady.

QUEEN   What shall I do?

HAMLET   Not this by no means that I bid you do:
Let the bloat king tempt you again to bed,
Pinch wanton on your cheek, call you his mouse,

Hamlet forbids Gertrude to tell Claudius the truth about his madness. Rosencrantz and Guildenstern are to escort him to England. He shows her he knows they are his enemies. He drags Polonius's body away with a fitting obituary.

185 reechy: filthy, squalid
186 paddling in: fondling
187 ravel...out: disentangle
189 in craft: by design
190 For who...hide: what good, beautiful, clever queen, such as you, would keep matters of such relevant concern from a toad, a bat, a tomcat? These three creatures are familiars of witches and sorcerers.
194 Unpeg the basket...neck down: there was a fable where an ape let birds fly from a wicker cage or basket on the roof and then himself got into the cage and tried to repeat the performance, assuming that he too could fly out. This whole set of instructions to Gertrude is, of course, governed by line 182 'Not...that I bid you do'.
205 bear the mandate: have their instructions from the king
sweep my way: clear my path
206 marshal me to knavery: lead me on to their trickery
enginer: engineer, designer of military machines to use in war, particularly to end sieges
208 Hoist with his own petard: blown up by his own bomb. A petard was a metal or wooden container of explosive, fired by a fuse, used for blowing in doors or gates, or making large holes in castle walls
and 't: and it
211 in one line...directly meet: plot and counter-plot meet
212 This man...packing: the fact that he has killed Polonius will speed his departure
217 to draw...with you: bring our association to an end

- *Why does Gertrude put up with Hamlet's treatment of her? Is she relieved he is going to England?*
- *Note that Hamlet can confide in her about his enemies.*

OBSESSION —

DISGUST IN THEIR RELATIONSHIP

GERTRUDE IS WITH CLAUDIUS. C IS NOT MAD

And let him for a pair of reechy kisses,   185
Or paddling in your neck with his damned fingers,
Make you to ravel all this matter out
That I essentially am not in madness,
But mad in craft. 'Twere good you let him know,
For who that's but a queen, fair, sober, wise,   190
Would from a paddock, from a bat, a gib,
Such dear concernings hide, who would do so?
No, in despite of sense and secrecy,
Unpeg the basket on the house's top,
Let the birds fly, and like the famous ape,   195
To try conclusions in the basket creep,
And break your own neck down.

QUEEN   Be thou assured, if words be made of breath,
          And breath of life, I have no life to breathe
          What thou hast said to me.   200

HAMLET   I must to England, you know that?

QUEEN   Alack,
          I had forgot. 'Tis so concluded on.

HAMLET   There's letters sealed, and my two schoolfellows,
          Whom I will trust as I will adders fanged,
          They bear the mandate; they must sweep my
              way,   205
          And marshal me to knavery. Let it work,
          For 'tis the sport to have the enginer
          Hoist with his own petard; and 't shall go hard
          But I will delve one yard below their mines,
          And blow them at the moon. O 'tis most sweet 210
          When in one line two crafts directly meet.
          This man shall set me packing.
          I'll lug the guts into the neighbour room.
          Mother, good night. Indeed this counsellor
          Is now most still, most secret, and most grave, 215
          Who was in life a foolish prating knave.
          Come sir, to draw towards an end with you.
          Good night, mother.

                    [*Exit* HAMLET *dragging in* POLONIUS

ACTIVITIES

Keeping track

Scene 1

1 This scene opens with Rosencrantz and Guildenstern reporting back to Claudius and Gertrude after their attempt to discover the reasons for Hamlet's madness. What do they have to tell Claudius and Gertrude? Is there anything new in this?

2 What is Polonius suggesting when he says that *'with devotion's visage'* we *'sugar o'er the devil himself'* (lines 47–49)?

3 How does Claudius react to this comment and what is revealed about him here?

4 Hamlet's third soliloquy shows him once more in a mood of brooding introspection. What is troubling Hamlet at this point in the play? What conclusions does he reach?

5 Lines 88–191 are often referred to as 'the nunnery scene'. This encounter has been deliberately contrived by Polonius. What is the plan, and what exactly is Polonius trying to prove?

6 It is not clear whether Hamlet knows he is being overheard. Do you think it makes any difference to the dramatic effect? Can you find any evidence to suggest that Hamlet knows that Claudius and Polonius are listening?

7 How does Hamlet behave towards Ophelia? Does his behaviour affect your thoughts and feelings about him? How does Ophelia react to Hamlet in this part of the scene?

8 What conclusion does Claudius reach and what action does he decide to take?

9 What is Polonius's reaction to what they have overheard?

Scene 2

1 The first part of this scene shows Hamlet offering advice to the Players on the subject of acting. Can you see any ways in which his words are relevant to his own situation?

2 In his conversation with Horatio (lines 55–94), Hamlet reveals his plan to trap Claudius. Why do you think he does this?

3 He also defines the 'ideal man': how does he define this ideal? How close is Hamlet to his own ideal?

4 Just before the beginning of the 'inner play', Hamlet continues his attack on Ophelia. What is his mood here? How and why does he attack Ophelia? What do you think of his behaviour?

5 The Dumb Show enacts the events surrounding the murder of Hamlet's father. Claudius does not appear to react. Why do you think this is?

6 The inner play also enacts the events leading to the murder of Hamlet's father. Much of the emphasis is on the words of the Player Queen. How does Gertrude react? What does Claudius learn from the inner play? What does Hamlet learn?

7 How does Hamlet react to the success of the inner play?

8 What does he plan to do when he speaks to his mother?

Scene 3

1 At the beginning of this scene Claudius confirms his decision to remove Hamlet to England. What insight do we gain into his private thoughts and feelings in his soliloquy? Does this change your view of Claudius in any way? Why does his attempt to pray for forgiveness fail?

2 When the king is kneeling in prayer, Hamlet appears to have the perfect opportunity to exact his revenge. However, he does not take his chance. What reasons does he give for not killing Claudius? In what way is this ironic? Do you accept his reasons?

Scene 4

1 This encounter is the result of a plan constructed by Polonius. What is the plan? Why has it been set up and what part is Polonius going to play in it?

2 Hamlet has obeyed the summons come to his mother's closet and, in doing so, missed an opportunity to kill Claudius. Does this tell us anything about Hamlet's real priorities? Is Claudius the only target of his bloody thoughts? Is he the main target?

3 How does Gertrude try to begin the scene and how does Hamlet attempt to seize the initiative? Does he succeed?

4 Why does Gertrude think that Hamlet is going to murder her?

5 Who does Hamlet think he is stabbing?

6 How does he justify his action? What are his feelings about what he has done?

7 When Gertrude asks, 'What have I done', Hamlet launches into a denunciation of her conduct. How would you describe his tone? What has made him speak to her in this way?

8 How does Gertrude respond to Hamlet's attack on her?

9 What advice does Hamlet give to his mother and how does she react to this advice?

10 Has Gertrude been changed by this encounter?

Drama

1   Imagine you are psychologists dealing with the young Hamlet. You have acquired a diary entry which contains the famous soliloquy *'To be, or not to be'*.

Work through the speech analysing the patient's mental health and report back to a case conference on your findings. Some of you could be working in an unprejudiced manner, but others could have been employed by Claudius.

Having discussed the patient, you could then interview him to try to help your diagnosis. You could have Hamlet played by a varying number of people to represent the different voices in his head: the revengeful son, the doubting fearer of damnation, the woman/mother-hater, the playful word-player, etc.

2   Imagine one of the servants is present at the play. The press are desperate to know what went on, but official channels are playing it down. Improvise the telephone conversation between one of you as the servant, and a partner as a newspaper reporter looking for some royal scandal. Write up the ensuing article using exaggeration and sensationalist language.

3   Work in two groups: some of you rehearse and perform the Dumb Show, while others rehearse the reactions of the royal audience. Bring the two together.

4   Work in threes on the exchanges between Hamlet, Rosencrantz and Guildenstern (Act 3 scene 2 lines 294–369). Choose a section and work on getting the level of vicious wordplay – compare this with their earlier exchanges.

5   In pairs, learn the exchange between Hamlet and Gertrude (Act 3 scene 4 lines 8–21).

Rehearse this scene to explore the complex relationship between mother and son. As an audience, we have a very good idea of what is going on in Hamlet's mind, but what is Gertrude thinking? We only have her public utterances to help us. Did she recognize herself in the *Murder of Gonzago*?

What was the relationship like between mother and son before the death of the father? Hotseat the two characters to help you.

6   Using Act 3 scene 4 lines 54–89 work in groups of about six. One person should represent Gertrude, while the other five represent five Hamlets all attacking her using the words as weapons.

7   Use FORUM THEATRE (see page 299) to explore these key moments:
   • the moment when Hamlet says *'No, not I, I never gave you aught.'* (Act 3 scene 1 line 95)
   • the moment when *'The King rises.'* (Act 3 scene 2 line 264)
   • the arrival of the Ghost (Act 3 scene 4 line 104).

Key elements

In Act 3 these are:
• the third soliloquy
• the 'nunnery scene'
• the inner play
• Claudius at prayer
• the closet scene.

The key scene

Hamlet's third soliloquy: Act 3 scene 1

Keying it in

1 This speech is Hamlet's first appearance after his decision to unmask Claudius by using the inner play. Look back across the opening two acts of the play.
• What moods has Hamlet experienced so far?
• Is there any pattern to his feelings?

The speech itself

1 Critics have debated what *'the question'* actually is and it is probably fair to say that this famous soliloquy is by no means transparent in meaning.
• What do you think he means by *'To be, or not to be'*?
  Look at lines 56–65.
• How does Hamlet describe life in these lines?
• How do the language and imagery convey his feelings about life?
• How does Hamlet describe death in these lines?
• How do the language and imagery convey his feelings about death?
• In which direction is the argument leading?
2 Look at lines 66–82.
  In this part of the speech, the argument changes direction: life is still presented as an inescapable torment.
• What exactly are the torments of life?
• How does the language convey Hamlet's feelings?
  However, Hamlet recognizes the fact that we endure the agony of existence, even though death offers an escape from 'the heart-ache' of life.
• Why do we choose to go on living, according to Hamlet?
• Choose two quotations which illustrate this point.

3 Look at lines 83–88.

    In these lines Hamlet reaches two conclusions:
'conscience does make cowards of us all, '
and
    'the native hue of resolution
Is sicklied o'er with the pale cast of thought'.

- What do you understand by the word *'conscience'* here?
- Is there any significant difference between these two conclusions?
- Is it possible that *'thought'* and *'conscience'* mean much the same thing to Hamlet?
- What is the effect of *'thought'* on *'resolution'*?
- How does Hamlet's choice of language indicate his attitude to the result of *'thought'*?

Overview

In this soliloquy the keynote is the mood of despair and frustration as Hamlet grapples with apparently insoluble contradictions. Inaction – the product of conscience and thought – makes us cowards, but action – the product of blood and instinct – makes us less than human. Hamlet feels trapped in that paradox.

- Compare this soliloquy with *'O that this too too solid flesh'* and *'O what a rogue and peasant slave am I!'*
- What connections can you find between these three speeches?
- Taken together what do they reveal about Hamlet?
- How far do they explain his 'delay' in killing Claudius?

Close study

Act 3 scene 3 lines 73–96
1 How difficult does the task of killing Claudius appear at first?
2 What does Hamlet mean when he says *'That would be scanned'*?
3 Compare what is happening here with Hamlet's conclusions in the *'To be, or not to be'* soliloquy.
4 In what way would killing Claudius at prayer be *'hire and salary'*?
5 In what circumstances does Hamlet say he wants to kill Claudius?
6 How does the language indicate Hamlet's inner feelings?
7 Dr Johnson commented that this speech was 'too terrible to be read or uttered'.
- In what ways is it 'terrible'?
- Why do you think Dr Johnson felt like that?
  Do you agree with him?
8 How do you react to Hamlet at this point in the play?

Hamlet and revenge

1 At the end of Act 2 Hamlet had expressed a need for proof of Claudius's guilt, but he did seem to have discovered a sense of purpose and a momentum of a kind. However, the third soliloquy returns to a mood of brooding introspection as Hamlet struggles to make sense of his feelings and his situation.

   The attack on Ophelia in the 'nunnery scene' reveals that his problems go beyond just killing Claudius. He has not succeeded in achieving the sustained, single-minded fury of the conventional revenger and his anger does not have a single focus.
   • Why does he attack Ophelia so cruelly?
   • What makes this scene so painful?

2 The success of the inner play rouses Hamlet to a mood where he could *'drink hot blood'* and perform *'bitter business'*.
   • Is he pleased or alarmed by this?
   • Do you want him to be like the figure of Pyrrhus?

3 At this point Hamlet is presented with an opportunity to kill Claudius. However, he does not kill him.
   • Why does he not kill him?
   • Is it significant that he is on his way to his mother's closet?
   • Does this reveal something about Hamlet's real priorities?

4 Interestingly the confrontation with Gertrude seems to give a release to much of Hamlet's frustration. He agrees to go to England without protest.
   • Why do you think he agrees to this so readily?
   • Where does this leave his revenge on Claudius?

5 By the end of Act 3, Hamlet has fulfilled the Ghost's demands as far as Gertrude is concerned and he has proved beyond any doubt that Claudius is a murderer. However, he is still entangled in the intellectual and moral complexities of revenge and the King is still alive and dangerous. It is worth noting that Hamlet's killing of Polonius has also made him an object of revenge and that Claudius, as a result of the inner play, now knows that Hamlet is aware of his guilt.

Assignments

Essays

1 Look at the inner play. What dramatic opportunities does this scene offer?
2 Look at the closet scene. Where do your sympathies lie in this scene?
3 Why has Hamlet not killed Claudius by the end of Act 3?

When Rosencrantz and Guildenstern have left the King and
Queen together, Gertrude explains her distress. Claudius
immediately sees that he was the potential target when
Polonius was killed and blames himself for not having
restricted Hamlet's movements. He wants to know where
Hamlet is.

   1 **There's...must translate**: you must explain the cause of
     these heavy sighs
   4 **Bestow this place on us**: leave us
  11 **brainish apprehension**: deluded conviction
  13 **It...there**: I would have been his victim if I'd been hiding
     there. (The royal plural again, as throughout this speech.)
  17 **laid to us**: blamed on me
     providence: foresight
  18 **kept short**: kept on a short rein
     out of haunt: away from places where people gather
  22 **divulging**: becoming generally known
  23 **pith**: essential tissue
  25 **ore**: precious metal, often gold

> * *Is Gertrude keeping faith with Hamlet, or telling
>   Claudius what she really believes?*
> * *We can learn a lot from the order of priorities in
>   Claudius's speech on this page...*

Act four

3 fairly short scenes to push on plot.

Scene ❶

Enter KING, ROSENCRANTZ, *and* GUILDENSTERN

KING

jealous it was meant for him

There's matter in these sighs, these profound
     heaves.
You must translate, 'tis fit we understand them.
Where is your son?

QUEEN

Bestow this place on us a little while.
          [*Exeunt* ROSENCRANTZ *and* GUILDENSTERN
Ah mine own lord, what have I seen tonight!   5

KING

What, Gertrude? How does Hamlet?

QUEEN

Mad as the sea and wind when both contend
Which is the mightier. In his lawless fit,
Behind this arras hearing something stir,
Whips out his rapier, cries, 'A rat, a rat!'   10
And in this brainish apprehension kills
The unseen good old man.

KING

                              O heavy deed!

Hamlet is more secure posing as he's a murderer

It had been so with us, had we been there.
His liberty is full of threats to all;
To you yourself, to us, to every one.   15
Alas, how shall this bloody deed be answered?
It will be laid to us, whose providence
Should have kept short, restrained and out of haunt
This mad young man; but so much was our love,
We would not understand what was most fit,   20
But like the owner of a foul disease,   *evoking sympathy for himself*
To keep it from divulging, let it feed
Even on the pith of life. Where is he gone?

QUEEN

To draw apart the body he hath killed,
O'er whom his very madness, like some ore   25

While Gertrude speaks of Hamlet's remorse, Claudius is planning to get him out of the country. He tells Rosencrantz and Guildenstern to find Hamlet and the body of Polonius, which must be taken to the chapel. His next thought is to talk things over with trusted friends, to find a way of ensuring that no blame may attach to him.

26 mineral: mine
    metals base: not precious metals
32 countenance: face up to, acknowledge
41 the world's diameter: from one end of the world to the other
42 blank: either the white mark in the centre of a target (cf French 'blanc' – white) or 'point-blank' – on a level line of fire

Hamlet, having temporarily disposed of the corpse, hears Rosencrantz and Guildenstern calling him.

H. POSITIONS IN COURT WEAKENS HIS STRENGTH OF CHARACTER GROWS.

Among a mineral of metals base,
Shows itself pure; 'a weeps for what is done.

KING   O Gertrude, come away.
The sun no sooner shall the mountains touch,
But we will ship him hence, and this vile deed   30
We must with all our majesty and skill,
Both countenance and excuse. Ho Guildenstern!

Enter ROSENCRANTZ *and* GUILDENSTERN

Friends both, go join you with some further aid.
Hamlet in madness hath Polonius slain,
And from his mother's closet hath he dragged
    him.   35

THINKS QUICKLY:

Go seek him out, speak fair, and bring the body
Into the chapel; I pray you haste in this.
            [*Exeunt* ROSENCRANTZ *and* GUILDENSTERN
Come Gertrude, we'll call up our wisest friends;
And let them know both what we mean to do
And what's untimely done; so haply slander –   40
Whose whisper o'er the world's diameter,
As level as the cannon to his blank,
Transports his poisoned shot, may miss our name,
And hit the woundless air. O come away,
My soul is full of discord and dismay.   45 [*Exeunt*

WON'T TARNISH THEIR REPUTATION

Scene 2

REFUSES TO SAY WHERE P. BODY IS HIDDEN

Enter HAMLET

HAMLET   Safely stowed.

ROSENCRANTZ ⎫   [*Within*] Hamlet, Lord Hamlet!
GUILDENSTERN ⎭

HAMLET   But soft, what noise? Who calls on Hamlet? O here
they come.

Enter ROSENCRANTZ *and* GUILDENSTERN

When Rosencrantz and Guildenstern ask Hamlet where the corpse is, he answers ambiguously, making it clear at the same time that he knows the King is using them as informers. The three of them go to the King.

6 **Compounded**: mixed
11 **keep your...mine own**: keep your secret and not my own. Hamlet is sure that Rosencrantz and Guildenstern have 'plans' for him. He will not reveal what his counter-measures might be.
12 **demanded**: questioned
13 **replication**: reply
15 **countenance**: expressions of favour
18 **in the corner of his jaw**: some apes have cheek pouches where they store food for eating later
20 **it is...dry again**: presumably, once an agent has served a king in this way, he may be of no further use...or even dangerous
23 **a knavish speech...ear**: Hamlet makes this sound like a proverb, but he means: you are probably too stupid to understand my carefully crafted insult
27 <u>**The body...body**: Polonius's body is in the same building as the King, but the King is not dead, he is not in the same state as the body</u>
28 **The King is a thing**: since he lacks any proper authority to be the King, Claudius is – nothing
30 **Hide fox, and all after**: omitted in Q2. Probably a reference to a children's game like hide-and-seek.

• *Why do both Rosencrantz and Guildenstern apparently refuse to understand Hamlet's potentially dangerous dislike of them?*

ROSENCRANTZ	What have you done my lord with the dead body? 5
HAMLET	Compounded it with dust whereto 'tis kin.
ROSENCRANTZ	Tell us where 'tis that we may take it thence, And bear it to the chapel.
HAMLET	Do not believe it.
ROSENCRANTZ	Believe what? 10
HAMLET	That I can keep your counsel, and not mine own. Besides, to be demanded of a sponge, what replication should be made by the son of a king?
ROSENCRANTZ	Take you me for a sponge my lord?
HAMLET	Ay sir, that soaks up the King's countenance, his 15 rewards, his authorities. But such officers do the King best service in the end; he keeps them like an ape in the corner of his jaw, first mouthed to be last swallowed. When he needs what you have gleaned, it is but squeezing you, and, sponge, you shall 20 be dry again.
ROSENCRANTZ	I understand you not my lord.
HAMLET	I am glad of it; a knavish speech sleeps in a foolish ear.
ROSENCRANTZ	My lord, you must tell us where the body is, and 25 go with us to the King.
HAMLET	The body is with the King, but the King is not with the body. The King is a thing –
GUILDENSTERN	A thing my lord!
HAMLET	Of nothing. Bring me to him. Hide fox, and all 30 after.

[*Exeunt*

The King, attended possibly by those he has been consulting, is musing on the fact that Hamlet is popular with the people. Claudius has decided that sending Hamlet away is best on all counts. Hamlet is now guarded. When he is brought in, he jokes about the supper-dish Polonius is providing for the worms.

4 **distracted**: bewildered

6 **scourge**: punishment. The severity of the punishment is considered, but not the gravity of the offence.

7 **To bear...and even**: to manage matters so that everything runs smoothly

9 **Deliberate pause**: well-weighed reflection, consideration
Diseases...relieved: a proverb – desperate ills need desperate remedies

21 **convocation**: assembly
politic: shrewd, with the additional sense of diplomatic, or meddling in politics
e'en: at this very moment

22 **Your worm...for diet**: possibly a reminder of the Diet of Worms – every pupil's joke, but they have been beaten to it by Hamlet. Emperor Charles V called a meeting (diet) in the German city of Worms, in 1521. At this convocation Martin Luther was excommunicated for refusing to deny his Reformist beliefs.

22 **we fat...fat us**: generally we fatten up animals so that they can feed us

Scene 3

soliloquy. [handwritten annotation]

Enter KING, *attended*

KING   I have sent to seek him, and to find the body.
How dangerous is it that this man goes loose.
Yet must not we put the strong law on him.
He's loved of the distracted multitude,
Who like not in their judgment, but their eyes, 5
And where 'tis so, th' offender's scourge is
    weighed,
But never the offence. To bear all smooth and even,
This sudden sending him away must seem
Deliberate pause. Diseases desperate grown
By desperate appliance are relieved, 10
Or not at all.

Enter ROSENCRANTZ

        How now, what hath befallen?

ROSENCRANTZ Where the dead body is bestowed, my lord,
We cannot get from him.

KING   But where is he?

ROSENCRANTZ Without, my lord, guarded, to know your
    pleasure.

KING   Bring him before us. 15

ROSENCRANTZ Ho Guildenstern, bring in my lord.

Enter HAMLET *and* GUILDENSTERN

KING   Now Hamlet, where's Polonius?

HAMLET   At supper.

KING   At supper? Where?

HAMLET   Not where he eats, but where 'a is eaten; a 20
certain convocation of politic worms are e'en at
him. Your worm is your only emperor for diet; we

[handwritten annotations in margins: "NEEDS TO KILL HIM BUT THE PEOPLE LIKE HIM.", "DESPERATE ACTION", "HAMLET WON'T TELL THEM"]

Hamlet, again playing with words and ideas when Claudius is present, eventually hints at Polonius's whereabouts, and servants are sent to find the body. Claudius tells Hamlet he must leave immediately for England, suggesting that he has his reasons. Hamlet hints in return that he is aware of them.

25 variable service: different courses
32 progress: as in 'royal progress' – where the king or queen travels through the kingdom
35 seek him...yourself: a roundabout way of saying 'Go to hell'.
37 nose: smell
42 tender: care about
45 bark: ship
  at help: in the right quarter
46 associates tend: the escorts are waiting
  bent: set, ready to leave
52 I see...sees them: Hamlet manages to suggest not only that he suspects something of Claudius' purposes, but also that heaven has its eye on him, too.

> • *Should Claudius sense a threat to himself in Hamlet's word-play concerning maggots, kings and beggars?*

[handwritten margin notes: seems + maggot = evil corruption]

fat all creatures else to fat us, and we fat ourselves
for maggots; your fat king and your lean beggar is
but variable service, two dishes, but to one   25
table – that's the end.

KING   Alas, alas!

HAMLET   A man may fish with the worm that hath eat of a
king, and eat of the fish that hath fed of that worm.

KING   What dost thou mean by this?   30

HAMLET   Nothing but to show you how a king may go a
progress through the guts of a beggar.

KING   Where is Polonius?   *[handwritten: Heaven + hell.]*

HAMLET   In heaven. Send thither to see; if your messenger
[handwritten: evilness]   find him not there, seek him i' th' other place   35
yourself. But if indeed you find him not within this
month, you shall nose him as you go up the stairs
into the lobby.

KING   Go seek him there.   [*To some* ATTENDANTS

HAMLET   'A will stay till you come.   40
                                        [*Exeunt* ATTENDANTS

KING   Hamlet, this deed, for thine special safety –   *[handwritten: Hamlet]*
Which we do tender, as we dearly grieve   *[handwritten: must]*
For that which thou hast done – must send thee   *[handwritten: leave]*
    hence
With fiery quickness. Therefore prepare thyself.
The bark is ready, and the wind at help,   45
Th' associates tend, and every thing is bent
For England.

HAMLET   For England.

KING   Ay Hamlet.

HAMLET   Good.   50

KING   So is it if thou knew'st our purposes.

HAMLET   I see a cherub that sees them. But come, for
England. Farewell dear mother.

Claudius tries to ensure early departure for Hamlet. In a soliloquy he reveals his instructions for Hamlet's execution. Then he will be able to relax.

55 **My mother...my mother**: Hamlet says goodbye to his mother who is not present, not to Claudius, who is. Making use of the concept of man and woman in marriage as one flesh, he points up their crime.
58 **at foot**: close behind, close on his heels
60 **every thing...th' affair**: everything else that depends on this business has been completed
62 **England**: he is addressing the King of England
   if...aught: if you set any store by my good will
63 **As my...sword**: my power should make you see the sense of securing my goodwill, since your country still smarts from wounds inflicted by Denmark
64 **cicatrice**: scar
65 **free awe**: unforced reverence or respect
66 **coldly set...process**: look upon our royal mandate with indifference
67 **imports at full**: gives directions for
68 **congruing**: agreeing
69 **present**: immediate
70 **hectic**: fever
72 **haps**: fortunes

> • *Note the first mention of letters ordering Hamlet's death.*

Fortinbras and his army arrive, claiming the promised permission to march across Denmark.

2 **licence**: permission
3 **Craves the conveyance**: requests safe passage
6 **express...his eye**: pay our respects in his presence
7 **And...so**: please tell him this

> • *Once again we are reminded of the presence in the wings of Fortinbras..*

KING	Thy loving father, Hamlet.
HAMLET	My mother – father and mother is man and wife, 55
	man and wife is one flesh; and so, my mother.
	Come, for England. [*Exit*
KING	Follow him at foot, tempt him with speed
	aboard,
	Delay it not; I'll have him hence tonight.
	Away, for every thing is sealed and done 60
	That else leans on th' affair; pray you make haste.

      [*Exeunt* ROSENCRANTZ *and* GUILDENSTERN

And England, if my love thou hold'st at aught –
As my great power thereof may give thee sense,
Since yet thy cicatrice looks raw and red
After the Danish sword, and thy free awe   65
Pays homage to us – thou mayst not coldly set
Our sovereign process, which imports at full,
By letters congruing to that effect,
The present death of Hamlet. Do it, England,
For like the hectic in my blood he rages,   70
And thou must cure me. Till I know 'tis done,
Howe'er my haps, my joys were ne'er begun.

            [*Exit*

Scene 4

Enter FORTINBRAS, *with his army over the stage*

FORTINBRAS	Go captain, from me greet the Danish King;
	Tell him that by his licence Fortinbras
	Craves the conveyance of a promised march
	Over his kingdom. You know the rendezvous.
	If that his majesty would aught with us, 5
	We shall express our duty in his eye,
	And let him know so.
CAPTAIN	I will do't my lord.

Hamlet meets one of the Norwegian army captains. The army is on its way to do battle for a small patch of ground in Poland. Both the captain and Hamlet are cynical about the point of this. Rosencrantz tries to hurry Hamlet along, as instructed.

 8 **softly**: carefully
 9 **powers**: troops
11 **How purposed**: this has the force of both 'Where are they going?' and 'What are their intentions?'
15 **main**: whole country
17 **addition**: exaggeration
22 **ranker**: higher
   sold in fee: sold outright
26 **debate**: dispute, contest
   this straw: this worthless issue
27 **imposthume**: abcess.
32 **all occasions...against me**: everything that happens seems to point up my failings
34 **market of his time**: the use to which he puts his time

> • *Again we have a glimpse of what Hamlet might have been like as king. Would he have refused to fight pointless battles, or would he have been pushed into it by 'reasons of state', 'need to keep the army employed' etc, etc? Can a crown prince afford to think too much, to plan either his love life or his statecraft?*

FORTINBRAS	Go softly on. [*Exeunt* FORTINBRAS *and* SOLDIERS

Enter HAMLET, ROSENCRANTZ, GUILDENSTERN, *and others*

HAMLET	Good sir, whose powers are these?	
CAPTAIN	They are of Norway sir.	10
HAMLET	How purposed sir I pray you?	
CAPTAIN	Against some part of Poland.	
HAMLET	Who commands them sir?	
CAPTAIN	The nephew to old Norway, Fortinbras.	
HAMLET	Goes it against the main of Poland sir,	15
	Or for some frontier?	
CAPTAIN	Truly to speak, and with no addition,	
	We go to gain a little patch of ground	
	That hath in it no profit but the name.	
	To pay five ducats, five, I would not farm it;	20
	Nor will it yield to Norway or the Pole	
	A ranker rate, should it be sold in fee.	
HAMLET	Why then the Polack never will defend it.	
CAPTAIN	Yes, it is already garrisoned.	
HAMLET	Two thousand souls and twenty thousand ducats	25
	Will not debate the question of this straw.	
	This is th' imposthume of much wealth and peace,	
	That inward breaks, and shows no cause without	
	Why the man dies. I humbly thank you sir.	
CAPTAIN	God buy you sir.	
	[*Exit*	
ROSENCRANTZ	Will't please you go my lord?	30
HAMLET	I'll be with you straight, go a little before.	
	[*Exeunt all except* HAMLET	
	How all occasions do inform against me,	
	And spur my dull revenge! What is a man,	
	If his chief good and market of his time	
	Be but to sleep and feed? A beast, no more.	35

In a soliloquy, Hamlet considers again the possible reasons for his inaction in the task of vengeance. He looks at the army assembled to fight for nothing worth having – except the honour. He sees his shame, when with honour at stake he has done nothing. Again he promises bloody thoughts.

36 discourse: powers of reasoning
39 fust: go stale, moulder
40 bestial oblivion: the heedlessness of animals
　craven scruple: cowardly hesitation
41 the event: the outcome
45 Sith: since
46 gross: plain, obvious
47 this army...charge: this enormous and costly army
48 delicate and tender: sensitive, young
50 Makes mouths: pulls faces at, scorns
　invisible event: outcome which cannot yet be seen
53 Rightly...at the stake: it is true that to be great is not to
　avoid taking a stand when the quarrel is over something
　petty, but to enter a quarrel even for something
　insignificant when it is one's honour that is at stake
62 fight for...the slain?: fight for a small piece of land of an
　area scarcely large enough to contain the fighting-men or
　to accommodate the graves of all who are killed

- *As a man of action Fortinbras ('strong of arm') is an impossible role model for Hamlet. Hamlet much admires his ability not to have scruples about the outcome, but to act, when honour is at stake.*
- *Are we convinced by Hamlet's latest resolution (lines 65–66)? Is he?*

Sure he that made us with such large discourse,
Looking before and after, gave us not
That capability and god-like reason
To fust in us unused. Now whether it be
Bestial oblivion, or some craven scruple   40
Of thinking too precisely on the event –
A thought which quartered hath but one part
    wisdom,
And ever three parts coward – I do not know
Why yet I live to say 'This thing's to do',
Sith I have cause, and will, and strength, and
    means   45
To do 't. Examples gross as earth exhort me:
Witness this army of such mass and charge,
Led by a delicate and tender prince;
Whose spirit with divine ambition puffed
Makes mouths at the invisible event,   50
Exposing what is mortal, and unsure
To all that fortune, death, and danger dare,
Even for an egg-shell. Rightly to be great
Is not to stir without great argument,
But greatly to find quarrel in a straw   55
When honour's at the stake. How stand I then,
That have a father killed, a mother stained,
Excitements of my reason and my blood,
And let all sleep, while to my shame I see
The imminent death of twenty thousand men,   60
That for a fantasy and trick of fame
Go to their graves like beds, fight for a plot
Whereon the numbers cannot try the cause,
Which is not tomb enough and continent
To hide the slain? O from this time forth,   65
My thoughts be bloody, or be nothing worth. [*Exit*

It is clear that Ophelia has asked for an audience with the
Queen. Gertrude has refused but as a gentleman of the court
explains what a state of distress and near-madness Ophelia is
in, the Queen agrees to see her. This seems to her another
ominous development.

1 **importunate**: persistent
2 **distract**: mad
2 **Her mood...pitied**: her state of mind must give rise to pity
5 **hems**: clears her throat
6 **Spurns...straws**: spitefully rejects whatever is said to her,
   however unimportant *or* takes offence easily
   in doubt: where the meaning is not clear
7 **nothing**: nonsense
8 **Yet...collection**: but the very dislocated nature of it makes
   those who hear her want to piece it together
9 **they aim at it**: they guess at it
13 **unhappily**: too close for comfort
15 **conjectures**: suspicions
   ill-breeding minds: minds which ferment mischief
17 **as...is**: sin's true nature is that it is a sickness of the soul
18 **toy**: trifle, insignificant happening
   amiss: calamity
   artless: clumsy, foolish
19 **jealousy**: mistrust
20 **spills**: destroys

> • *Taking the Gentleman's observation of Ophelia as*
>   *accurate, make sure that – whatever performance or*
>   *video you may have seen – you have a clear picture*
>   from the text *of the change that has come over*
>   *Ophelia, before she enters.*

Scene **5**

handwritten annotation: REALITY OF OPHELIAS MADNESS TO COMPARE WITH ANTIC-DISPOSITION

Enter QUEEN, HORATIO, *and a* GENTLEMAN

QUEEN	I will not speak with her.

GENTLEMAN   She is importunate,
Indeed distract. Her mood will needs be pitied.

QUEEN   What would she have?

GENTLEMAN   She speaks much of her father, says she hears
There's tricks i' th' world, and hems, and beats her
    heart,   5
Spurns enviously at straws, speaks things in doubt
That carry but half sense. Her speech is nothing,
Yet the unshaped use of it doth move
The hearers to collection; they aim at it,
And botch the words up fit to their own
    thoughts,   10
Which as her winks, and nods, and gestures yield
    them,
Indeed would make one think there might be
    thought,
Though nothing sure, yet much unhappily.

handwritten annotation: SUM UP HER INSANITY

HORATIO   'Twere good she were spoken with, for she may
    strew
Dangerous conjectures in ill-breeding minds.   15

QUEEN   Let her come in.   [*Exit* GENTLEMAN
To my sick soul, as sin's true nature is,
Each toy seems prologue to some great amiss.
So full of artless jealousy is guilt,
It spills itself in fearing to be spilt.   20

Enter GENTLEMAN *with* OPHELIA

OPHELIA   Where is the beauteous majesty of Denmark?

QUEEN   How now Ophelia!

When Ophelia comes in she is distractedly singing snatches of songs about true love and death. These themes are so intermingled that they can be seen to refer to the loss of the man she loved, Hamlet, and her father's death and possibly, as the King enters, even to the death of Hamlet's father, for whom Gertrude hardly wept.

25 cockle hat: the original tradition was that a pilgrim to the shrine of St James at Compostella wore a scallop shell (not a cockle shell) on his hat. Scallop shells carved in stone also still decorate many of the churches on the pilgrim routes to Compostella.

26 shoon: shoes. Ophelia, in her mad unhappiness adapts the ballad form of the love song to her needs. The reference to a pilgrim recalls the famous Walsingham ballad where a pilgrim to the shrine at Walsingham is met by a lover enquiring for his 'true love'.

36 Larded: decorated, covered with. Larded is still used in the culinary sense, to put strips of fat in or over meat which is likely to be dry.

37 Which bewept...showers: '*not*' is likely to be a pointed alteration by Ophelia – it puts one syllable too many in the line. Neither her father nor Hamlet's was properly mourned.

40 God dild you: a corruption of 'God yield you (thanks)' – thank you
the owl was a baker's daughter: according to legend Christ went into a baker's shop to ask for something to eat. The baker's wife immediately put a cake into the oven for him, but her daughter said it was too large and reduced it by half. The dough, however, swelled to an enormous size, and the daughter cried out 'Heugh! heugh! heugh!' and was transformed into an owl.

43 Conceit upon: fanciful ideas about

51 dupped: ('dup' is a contraction of 'do up') here: opened

- *Compare what you have seen of Hamlet's madness and Ophelia's.*

Handwritten margin note (top): OPHELIAS MADNESS PROVIDES A COMPARISON FOR HAMLETS ANTIC DISPOSITION.

OPHELIA	[*Sings*] How should I your true love know
	From another one?
	By his cockle hat and staff, 25
	And his sandal shoon.
QUEEN	Alas sweet lady, what imports this song?
OPHELIA	Say you? Nay, pray you mark.
	[*Sings*] He is dead and gone lady,
	He is dead and gone, 30
	At his head a grass-green turf,
	At his heels a stone.
	Oho!
QUEEN	Nay but Ophelia, –
OPHELIA	Pray you mark.
	[*Sings*] White his shroud as the mountain snow –
	Enter KING
QUEEN	Alas, look here my lord. 35
OPHELIA	[*Sings*] Larded all with sweet flowers,
	Which bewept to the grave did not go
	With true-love showers.
KING	How do you pretty lady?
OPHELIA	Well, God dild you. They say the owl was a 40
	baker's daughter. Lord, we know what we are, but
	know not what we may be. God be at your table.
KING	Conceit upon her father.
OPHELIA	Pray let's have no words of this, but when they ask
	you what it means, say you this: 45
	[*Sings*] Tomorrow is Saint Valentine's day,
	All in the morning betime,
	And I a maid at your window,
	To be your Valentine.
	Then up he rose, and donned his clothes, 50
	And dupped the chamber door,
	Let in the maid, that out a maid,
	Never departed more.

Handwritten margin note (right): SONGS ARE RELEVANT TO WHAT HAS HAPPENED TO HER EMPHASISE LOSS OF HAMLET + POLONIUS

Handwritten margin note (left): CONTRAST WITH CHARACTER IN EARLIER SCENE

Soon Ophelia's singing is providing echoes of Hamlet's bawdy conversation with her and of her brother's and her father's warnings. Claudius, having sent Horatio to keep an eye on Ophelia, briefly interprets her madness as the result of grief. He then goes on to list the recent misfortunes and to regret that Polonius's burial was done in secret, as he fears the reaction.

56 Gis: Jesus
Saint Charity: not a real saint
58 do't: have sexual intercourse
59 By Cock: a common avoidance of the oath 'By God' but also with a sexual reference
60 tumbled me: lay with me, had intercourse with me
76 spies: scouts, reconnoitering ahead of the main army
79 muddied: agitated, stirred up like a muddy pool
81 greenly: foolishly (because of unripe, immature judgement)
82 hugger-mugger: secretly
83 Divided...mere beasts: a repetition of the idea that without reason human beings are no different from animals, mere figures
85 as much containing: as of much significance

> • *Claudius is again forced to consider the reasons for the madness of a young person at his court. How quickly does this turn to thoughts for himself?*

KING	Pretty Ophelia.
OPHELIA	Indeed without an oath I'll make an end on't. 55

[Sings

By Gis and by Saint Charity,
  Alack and fie for shame,
Young men will do't if they come to't,
  By Cock, they are to blame.
Quoth she, before you tumbled me, 60
  You promised me to wed.
He answers,
    So would I 'a done by yonder sun,
      An thou hadst not come to my bed.

KING	How long hath she been thus? 65
OPHELIA	I hope all will be well. We must be patient, but I

cannot choose but weep to think they should lay
him i' th' cold ground. My brother shall know of it,
and so I thank you for your good counsel. Come,
my coach. Good night ladies, good night, 70
sweet ladies, good night, good night. *[Exit*

KING   Follow her close; give her good watch I pray you.

[Exit HORATIO

O this is the poison of deep grief, it springs
All from her father's death. And now behold
O Gertrude, Gertrude, 75
When sorrows come, they come not single spies,
But in battalions. First her father slain,
Next, your son gone, and he most violent author
Of his own just remove, the people muddied,
Thick and unwholesome in their thoughts and
  whispers, 80
For good Polonius' death. And we have done but
  greenly
In hugger-mugger to inter him. Poor Ophelia
Divided from herself and her fair judgment,
Without the which we are pictures, or mere beasts.
Last, and as much containing as all these, 85

A further concern for Claudius is that Laertes has come back secretly from France. He, Claudius fears, will find it all too easy to blame him for his father's death and hasty burial. The angry Laertes and his armed followers, proposing Laertes for king, approach noisily and rush in.

87 **his wonder**: his bewilderment
   keeps himself in clouds: wraps himself in suspicion
88 **wants not buzzers**: does not lack tale-bearers
90 **Wherein necessity...and ear**: so that, lacking true facts, the need to find a scapegoat will stop at nothing to accuse me, first in one ear and then the other
93 **murdering-piece**: small cannon which fired a scattering charge: it was also called a 'murderer'
94 **superfluous**: because any one of the pieces of shot could have killed him
95 **Attend**: listen
96 **Switzers**: Swiss mercenaries were often employed as guards – and still do guard the Vatican
98 **overpeering of its list**: rising above its furthest limits
99 **flats**: mudflats, shallows
   impiteous: pitiless. Some editions prefer '*impetuous*', with the suggestion of violence.
100 **in a riotous head**: leading a rebellious force. This does also continue the metaphor of the ocean rushing in, '*riotous head*' suggesting a tumultuous head of water.
101 **O'erbears**: overwhelms
102 **as**: as if
103 **Antiquity forgot...every word**: precedent and custom both forgotten, which back up and support our every word
109 **counter**: in hunting, the hounds run counter when they trace the scent backwards, in the wrong direction.
112 **give me leave**: leave me

> • *Now Claudius has broken the expected succession to the throne, it is easier for people to put up any likely candidate as king.*

[handwritten margin note: ...ERTIS IS ...MING CLAUDIUS ...P. DEATH.]

Her brother is in secret come from France, *[handwritten: LAERTIS IS BACK —]*
Feeds on his wonder, keeps himself in clouds,
And wants not buzzers to infect his ear
With pestilent speeches of his father's death;
Wherein necessity, of matter beggared,   90
Will nothing stick our person to arraign.
In ear and ear. O my dear Gertrude, this *[handwritten: HIS OWN]*
Like to a murdering-piece in many places *[handwritten: POSITION IS]*
Gives me superfluous death.   [*A noise within* *[handwritten: INSECURE]*

[handwritten margin note: ...UESTIONS ...F HE IS SAFE.]

QUEEN   Alack, what noise is this?

KING   Attend.   95
Where are my Switzers? Let them guard the door.

Enter MESSENGER

What is the matter?

MESSENGER   Save yourself my lord:
The ocean overpeering of his list
Eats not the flats with more impiteous haste
Than young Laertes in a riotous head   100
O'erbears your officers. The rabble call him lord,
And as the world were now but to begin,
Antiquity forgot, custom not known,
The ratifiers and props of every word,
They cry 'Choose we! Laertes shall be king':   105
Caps, hands, and tongues applaud it to the clouds:
'Laertes shall be king, Laertes king.'

QUEEN   How cheerfully on the false trail they cry. *[handwritten: SUPPORTS HIM —]*
O this is counter, you false Danish dogs.

KING   The doors are broke. *[handwritten: CLOSE RELATION- SHIP.]*   110
                                [*Noise within*

Enter LAERTES *and other* DANES, *armed*

LAERTES   Where is this King? Sirs, stand you all without.

DANES   No let's come in.

LAERTES   I pray you give me leave.

Laertes, insisting that his followers stay outside, confronts the King. Gertrude tries to calm him. The King invokes the divinity of kingship and acts with some dignity. Laertes is furious over his father's death and wants to take revenge, even if his own damnation results.

114 Keep: guard

116 That drop…true mother: if a single drop of Laertes's blood remains calm, then it is to declare that his father was made unfaithful by his whore of a mother. (See note on branding prostitutes Act 3 scene 4 line 45.) Laertes is saying 'If I stay calm, then I am not my father's son'.

121 fear: fear for

122 There's such…will: kingship is so protected by its divine nature that treason scarcely dares attempt what it has in mind to do

131 grace: God's free gift to man, without which there is no salvation or heaven after death

132 To this point…for my father: I stick at this point, that both this world and the next can go hang, let happen whatever will happen, I will be thoroughly revenged for my father

136 My will…world's: (by) my will, not all the world's (will)

137 And for my means…little: however difficult it may appear, I'll find a way to do it

139 the certainty…father: the facts about your father's death

- *Compare Laertes's angry declaration of intent to avenge his father with those made by Hamlet.*

DANES	We will, we will. [*Exeunt* FOLLOWERS
LAERTES	I thank you. Keep the door. O thou vile King,
	Give me my father.
QUEEN	Calmly, good Laertes 115
LAERTES	That drop of blood that's calm proclaims me
	bastard,
	Cries cuckold to my father, brands the harlot
	Even here between the chaste unsmirched brows
	Of my true mother.
KING	What is the cause, Laertes,
	That thy rebellion looks so giant-like? 120
	Let him go Gertrude, do not fear our person.
	There's such divinity doth hedge a king,
	That treason can but peep to what it would,
	Acts little of his will. Tell me Laertes,
	Why thou art thus incensed – let him go
	Gertrude. 125
	Speak man.
LAERTES	Where is my father?
KING	Dead.
QUEEN	But not by him.
KING	Let him demand his fill.
LAERTES	How came he dead? I'll not be juggled with.
	To hell allegiance, vows to the blackest devil 130
	Conscience and grace to the profoundest pit!
	I dare damnation. To this point I stand,
	That both the worlds I give to negligence,
	Let come what comes, only I'll be revenged
	Most throughly for my father.
KING	Who shall stay you? 135
LAERTES	My will, not all the world's.
	And for my means, I'll husband them so well,
	They shall go far with little.
KING	Good Laertes,
	If you desire to know the certainty

Handwritten annotations: IMAGERY OF PASSION. IN ORDER TO SEEK REVENGE HE NEEDS A PASSIONATE RESPONSE. CONTRAST WITH HAMLET. playing for time. aware of what could happen. rude – -ve policeman. appears calm. overly defending Claudius. afraid of what Laertes might do. doesn't care for himself.

Claudius manages to calm Laertes a little, to the point where he is prepared to grant that the King may not be guilty of Polonius's death. At this Ophelia comes in. Laertes is both distressed and angry at the sight of what she has become. Ophelia sings about a funeral. Laertes claims that her madness moves him to revenge more than any persuasion would.

141 swoopstake: sweepstake. You will take all the stakes, ie you will be revenged on friend and foe alike

145 pelican: traditionally the pelican was supposed to peck its own breast to feed its young with blood

146 Repast: feed

149 most sensibly: with deep emotion

155 Burn out...mine eye: burn out the sensitivity and the function of my eye, ie destroy my sight

157 Till our scale turn the beam: till the weight on our side tilts the scales. The beam is the bar which links the two sides of old-style scales.

161 fine: sensitive. This sensitivity is so acute that human nature loses some part of itself to the loved one when he or she goes away. Ophelia's mind has gone, with her father's death and possibly with the loss of Hamlet.

164 They bore him...nonny: Ophelia sings lines from a ballad lamenting a death, but incongruously adds a cheerful chorus line, more suitable for a love-song.

> • *How does Claudius set about changing Laertes's angry and accusatory mood?*

Of your dear father, is't writ in your revenge,   140
That, swoopstake, you will draw both friend and
    foe,
Winner and loser?

LAERTES   None but his enemies.

KING   Will you know them then?

LAERTES   To his good friends thus wide I'll ope my arms,
And like the kind life-rendering pelican,   145
Repast them with my blood.

KING   Why now you speak
Like a good child, and a true gentleman.
That I am guiltless of your father's death,
And am most sensibly in grief for it,
It shall as level to your judgment 'pear   150
As day does to your eye.

DANES   [*Within*] Let her come in.

LAERTES   How now, what noise is that?

Enter OPHELIA

O heat, dry up my brains, tears seven times salt
Burn out the sense and virtue of mine eye.   155
By heaven, thy madness shall be paid with weight,
Till our scale turn the beam. O rose of May,
Dear maid, kind sister, sweet Ophelia –
O heavens, is't possible a young maid's wits
Should be as mortal as an old man's life?   160
Nature is fine in love, and where 'tis fine,
It sends some precious instance of itself
After the thing it loves.

OPHELIA   [*Sings*]
    They bore him barefaced on the bier;
    Hey non nonny, nonny, hey nonny,   165
    And in his grave rained many a tear –
Fare you well my dove.

LAERTES   Hadst thou thy wits, and didst persuade revenge,

Ophelia distributes wild flowers and herbs she has picked. Laertes, seized by grief, is persuaded by Claudius to go with him so that they may talk.

170 **A-down a-down**: a frequent refrain in country songs

171 **the wheel**: the wheel of Fortune; the spinning-wheel; a wheeling dance step, or 'wheel' used as a refrain. All would suggest the idea of a recurring pattern.

172 **the false...daughter**: no ballad or story can be found to fit, but there are many instances in the play of the betrayal of trust.

173 **This nothing's...matter**: this nonsense means more than a lot of 'sense'

174 **There's rosemary**: supposed to strengthen the memory, rosemary was also used both at weddings and funerals, and meant 'fidelity in love'. There are no stage directions indicating who should receive any of these flowers. It is assumed that rosemary and pansies are offered to Laertes, possibly with some confusion on Ophelia's part that he also represents her love for Hamlet.

175 **pansies**: in French 'pensée' means 'pansy' and 'thought'

177 **document**: lesson

179 **fennel** and **columbines**: 'flattery' and 'infidelity in marriage'

180 **rue**: a small greeny-grey evergreen shrub with bitter-tasting leaves. It stands for repentance and regret – 'rue'.

182 **a difference**: in heraldry a term used for a distinguishing mark on the arms adopted by a junior family member
daisy: symbol of changeable and inconstant love

183 **violets**: stand for faithfulness

185 **For...all my joy**: a line from a popular song on the subject of love and unfaithful love

186 **Thought**: sorrow
passion: suffering

187 **favour**: attraction

188 **And...come again**: a lament for her dead father, possibly mingling in her crazed grief with the loss of Hamlet's love

194 **All flaxen was his poll**: his hair was white

196 **we cast away moan**: we stop lamenting – it is pointless

200 **commune with**: talk to you about

It could not move thus.

OPHELIA   You must sing 'A-down a-down', an you call   170
           him a-down-a. O how the wheel becomes it! It is
           the false steward that stole his master's daughter.

LAERTES   This nothing's more than matter.

OPHELIA   There's rosemary, that's for remembrance –
           pray you love, remember – and there is pansies,   175
           that's for thoughts.

LAERTES   A document in madness, thoughts and
           remembrance fitted.

OPHELIA   There's fennel for you, and columbines. There's
           rue for you, and here's some for me; we may   180
           call it herb of grace a Sundays – o you must wear
           your rue with a difference. There's a daisy, I would
           give you some violets, but they withered all when
           my father died – they say 'a made a good end –
           [Sings] For bonny sweet Robin is all my joy.   185

LAERTES   Thought and affliction, passion, hell itself,
           She turns to favour and to prettiness.

OPHELIA   [Sings] And will 'a not come again?
               And will 'a not come again?
                   No, no, he is dead,   190
                   Go to thy death-bed,
               He never will come again.

               His beard was as white as snow,
                   All flaxen was his poll.
                   He is gone, he is gone,   195
                   And we cast away moan.
               God ha' mercy on his soul!
           And of all Christian souls I pray God. God buy you.
                                                      [Exit

LAERTES   Do you see this o God?

KING   Laertes, I must commune with your grief,   200
           Or you deny me right. Go but apart,
           Make choice of whom your wisest friends you will,

Claudius tells Laertes he may choose friends of his to judge where the blame for Polonius's death lies – if with him, he will offer full satisfaction. If the guilt is elsewhere, Claudius will join with Laertes for vengeance. Laertes agrees, mentioning again the hasty and secret nature of his father's funeral.

204 by direct...hand: if I am found to be involved directly or indirectly

209 we shall...content: I shall work with your deepest emotions to give you satisfaction

211 His means of death: the way he died

212 hatchment: coat of arms

213 ostentation: show, ceremony

Sailors come to Horatio with letters.

8 'A shall sir an't please him: he shall sir, if it please him

And they shall hear and judge 'twixt you and me:
If by direct or by collateral hand
They find us touched, we will our kingdom give, 205
Our crown, our life, all that we call ours
To you in satisfaction; but if not,
Be you content to lend your patience to us,
And we shall jointly labour with your soul
To give it due content.

HE SEES AN OPPORTUNITY.

LAERTES   Let this be so.   210
His means of death, his obscure funeral,
No trophy, sword, nor hatchment o'er his bones,
No noble rite nor formal ostentation,   *DIDN'T HAVE HONOURS DUE TO A NOBLE MAN.*
Cry to be heard as 'twere from heaven to earth,
That I must call 't in question.

KING   So you shall;   215
And where th' offence is let the great axe fall.
I pray you go with me.   [*Exeunt*

IS WILLING TO BE JUDGED

LAERTES IS NOT CONVINCED - DUE TO FAST FUNERAL

Scene 6

LETTER DELIVERED FROM HAMLET.

Enter HORATIO *and a* SERVANT

HORATIO   What are they that would speak with me?

SERVANT   Sea-faring men sir, they say they have letters for
               you.

HORATIO   Let them come in.   [*Exit* SERVANT
               I do not know from what part of the world
               I should be greeted, if not from Lord Hamlet.   5

Enter SAILORS

FIRST SAILOR God bless you sir.

HORATIO   Let him bless thee too.

FIRST SAILOR 'A shall sir an't please him. There's a letter for you
               sir, it comes from th' ambassador that was bound

FILLS IN WHAT WE DON'T SEE.

The letter to Horatio is from Hamlet. It tells him that their ship was attacked by pirates. When Hamlet boarded the pirate ship, it drew away, so that he became their only prisoner. Hamlet did a deal with them. He has been landed on Danish soil in exchange for favours to the pirates. Horatio will give the sailors access to the King and they will tell Horatio where to find Hamlet.

12 overlooked: scanned, read

13 means: access

17 the grapple: (now grapnel) as the ships closed, Hamlet's captain decided the only solution was the 'brave' one ('a compelled valour'). Grappling irons – like small anchors with several metal claws on them – were used to haul the ships close enough for the enemy ship to be boarded.

21 knew what they did: it was clear, from his dress and bearing, that Hamlet was an aristocratic and probably wealthy prize

23 repair thou to me: come to me

26 the bore of the matter: the bore refers to the diameter of a cannon. Hamlet is saying that his words are (necessarily, in a letter which might be intercepted) far too insignificant for the important subject he needs to tell him about, as small shot would be to a great cannon.

Claudius and Laertes have spoken and Laertes, while allowing that Hamlet may have tried to kill Claudius, asks why no action was taken against him.

1 my acquittance seal: release me from any suggestion of guilt

3 knowing: understanding

> • *Laertes is coming closer and closer to siding with Claudius. What does this tell us about Claudius?*

for England, if your name be Horatio, as I am let 10
to know it is.

HORATIO   [*Reads*] 'Horatio, when thou shalt have overlooked
this, give these fellows some means to the King,
they have letters for him. Ere we were two days old
at sea, a pirate of very warlike appointment gave   15
us chase. Finding ourselves too slow of sail, we put
on a compelled valour, <u>and in the grapple I
boarded them,</u> on the instant they got clear of our
ship, so I alone became their prisoner. They have
dealt with me like thieves of mercy, but they   20
knew what they did, I am to do a good turn for
them. Let the King have the letters I have sent, and
repair thou to me with as much speed as thou
wouldst fly death. I have words to speak in thine
ear will make thee dumb, yet are they much too   25
light for the bore of the matter. These good fellows
will bring thee where I am. Rosencrantz and
Guildenstern hold their course for England, of
them I have much to tell thee. Farewell.

         He that thou knowest thine,   30

                        HAMLET.'

Come, I will give you way for these your letters,
And do't the speedier that you may direct me
To him from whom you brought them.   [*Exeunt*

Scene 7

Enter KING *and* LAERTES

KING   Now must your conscience my acquittance seal,
And you must put me in your heart for friend,
Sith you have heard, and with a knowing ear,
That he which hath your noble father slain
Pursued my life.

LAERTES   It well appears. But tell me   5
Why you proceeded not against these feats,

Handwritten annotations:
we see the man of action; his own accord
impressive account of how he was.
Hamlets trust in Horatio
foregoing
their relationship.
he isn't guilty Hamlet to
Hamlet kill Polonius + threatened Claudius' life too

Claudius has to explain to Laertes why, if he knew that
Hamlet meant to kill him, he has taken no action against
him. He cites Gertrude's love for Hamlet, his own love for
his wife, and Hamlet's popularity with the general public.
Laertes has to comfort himself with the thought that he will
avenge his father's death and Ophelia's madness.

7 **capital**: punishable by death
10 **unsinewed**: feeble
12 **Lives...looks**: lives for the sight of him
13 **My virtue...either which**: be it good or bad, whichever
14 **so conjunctive**: so closely joined
15 **moves not but in his sphere**: can only move in its
appointed orbit
sphere: astronomers believed that concentric hollow globes
(spheres) revolved round the earth, carrying the various
heavenly bodies (sun, moon, planet and fixed stars)
16 **I could...by her**: I could only exist by her side
17 **count**: legal indictment
18 **general gender**: common people
20 **Would...stone**: there are natural springs which in time will
coat objects left in their flow with a deposit like stone
21 **gyves**: fetters, and so the offences which caused a man to
be put in chains
graces: virtues
22 **Too slightly timbered**: made of too light a wood
23 **reverted**: turned back
27 **go back again**: go back to earlier days
28 **Stood challenger...perfections**: such were her qualities
that on a peak of perfection she stood above all others of
her time
29 **Break not your sleeps for that**: do not lose any sleep over
that
31 **flat**: spiritless
32 **with danger**: with what threatens danger

- *The Queen his mother lives almost by his looks'. If this
is true, and there are other indications that it is, what
light does this throw on the 'closet' scene?*

handwritten margin note: WHY HAS NO ACTION BEEN TAKEN

So criminal and so capital in nature,
As by your safety, greatness, wisdom, all things else,
You mainly were stirred up.

KING   O for two special reasons,
Which may to you perhaps seem much
    unsinewed,   10
But yet to me th' are strong. The Queen his
    mother

handwritten margin note: PERSONAL + POLITICAL REASONS

handwritten margin note: GERTRUDE'S LOVE FOR HER SON

Lives almost by his looks, and for myself –
My virtue or my plague, be it either which –
She is so conjunctive to my life and soul,
That as the star moves not but in his sphere,   15
I could not but by her. The other motive,
Why to a public count I might not go,
Is the great love the general gender bear him;

handwritten margin note: CLAUDIUS' LOVE FOR GERTRUDE

handwritten margin note: THE PEOPLE LIKE HIM

Who dipping all his faults in their affection,
Would like the spring that turneth wood to
    stone   20
Convert his gyves to graces, so that my arrows,
Too slightly timbered for so loud a wind,
Would have reverted to my bow again,
And not where I had aimed them.

handwritten margin note: IMAGERY OF ARROW

handwritten margin note: HAMLET – HERO CLAUDIUS – ENEMY

LAERTES   And so have I a noble father lost,   25
A sister driven into desperate terms,
Whose worth, if praises may go back again,
Stood challenger on mount of all the age
For her perfections. But my revenge will come.

handwritten margin note: NOBLE FATHER OPHELIAS PERFECTION DESTROYED

KING   Break not your sleeps for that; you must not
    think   30
That we are made of stuff so flat and dull,
That we can let our beard be shook with danger,
And think it pastime. You shortly shall hear more.
I loved your father, and we love ourself,
And that I hope will teach you to imagine –   35

Enter a MESSENGER

How now, what news?

The messenger hands over Hamlet's letters to the King, one
for him and one for Gertrude. Hamlet reveals that he is back
in the country. Laertes is glad that he will be able to tax him
with the murder of Polonius. The King makes it clear that he
too has plans, if Hamlet will not go to England.

44 naked: destitute, stripped of everything he had
50 abuse: deception
　　no such thing: nothing of the sort has really happened
51 hand: handwriting
　　character: handwriting
54 devise me: work it out for me
58 Thus didst thou: some editions emend *'didst'* to *'diest'*
　　and those advocating *'didst'* want a mimed sword thrust to
　　accompany *'Thus'*. However, *'Thus didst thou'* seems
　　sufficient, without any decoration. An essential part of
　　revenge is to make sure the offender knows that you know
　　his offence, and face to face (*'to his teeth'*) to watch him
　　understand that you know, before the vengeance is carried
　　out.
63 checking: whether borrowed from falconry or
　　horsemanship, it means balking suddenly or shying, in mid-
　　flight, mid-gallop
65 ripe in my device: just come to completion, to fruition, in
　　my mind

MESSENGER	Letters my lord, from Hamlet
	This to your majesty; this to the Queen.
KING	From Hamlet? Who brought them?
MESSENGER	Sailors my lord they say, I saw them not;
	They were given me by Claudio, he received
	them 40
	Of him that brought them.
KING	Laertes, you shall hear them.

Leave us.   [*Exit* MESSENGER

[*Reads*] 'High and mighty, you shall know I am set
naked on your kingdom. Tomorrow shall I beg
leave to see your kingly eyes, when I shall, first   45
asking your pardon thereunto, recount the occasion
of my sudden and more strange return.

HAMLET.'

What should this mean? Are all the rest
come back?
Or is it some abuse, and no such thing?   50

| LAERTES | Know you the hand? |
| KING | 'Tis Hamlet's character. |

'Naked?'
And in a postscript here, he says 'alone'.
Can you devise me?

LAERTES	I'm lost in it my lord. But let him come; 55
	It warms the very sickness in my heart,
	That I shall live and tell him to his teeth,
	'Thus didst thou'.
KING	If it be so Laertes –
	As how should it be so? How otherwise? –
	Will you be ruled by me?
LAERTES	Ay my lord, 60
	So you will not o'errule me to a peace.
KING	To thine own peace. If he be now returned,
	As checking at his voyage, and that he means
	No more to undertake it, I will work him
	To an exploit, now ripe in my device, 65

Laertes asks to be the means of bringing revenge on Hamlet.
Claudius has heard from a Norman acquaintance of Laertes
who has visited the court that Laertes is a most accomplished
swordsman. When Hamlet had heard this he had been full of
envy. The Norman was a brilliant rider and Laertes identifies
him as Lamord.

66 shall not choose: cannot help

68 uncharge the practice: acquit the stratagem of any guilt

71 organ: perpetrator, the doer of the deed

77 the unworthiest siege: of the least significance

78 very riband: mere ribbon

79 for youth...graveness: the light and careless fashions are
no less suitable for youth than furs and garments for
mature age, indicating a concern for well-being and for
dignity

85 can well: are very skilful

88 incorpsed and demi-natured with: of one body and half
the nature of, like the centaurs of Greek mythology who
were half-man, half-horse. Wise, strong and gifted, they
brought up and trained many of the Greek heroes of myth
and fable.

89 So far he...thought: he exceeded so far what I had
imagined to be possible

90 in forgery...tricks: in conceiving displays and feats of
horsemanship

93 Lamord: if names are in fact significant, then Lamord is
very close to French 'la mort' (death) and Lamord's
remarks have suggested to Claudius the means of Hamlet's
death

94 the brooch...gem: the very ornament, the jewel

> • *Claudius has brought matters so far, that instead of
> blaming him for Polonius's death, Laertes is now his
> eager accomplice and instrument for revenge on
> Hamlet. What has precipitated Claudius's plans for
> vengeance?*

[margin notes, handwritten: INVOLW DOESN'T UNDERSTAND WHY HAMLET SAID HE'S COMING.]

Under the which he shall not choose but fall.
And for his death no wind of blame shall
    breathe
But even his mother shall uncharge the practice,
And call it accident.

[margin note, handwritten: VOLUNTEER.]

LAERTES   My lord, I will be ruled,
    The rather if you could devise it so   70
    That I might be the organ.

KING   It falls right.

[margin note, handwritten: SAYING LAERTES SKILL HAMLETS JEALOUSY.]

    You have been talked of since your travel much.
    And that in Hamlet's hearing, for a quality
    Wherein they say you shine. Your sum of parts
    Did not together pluck such envy from him   75
    As did that one, and that in my regard
    Of the unworthiest siege.

LAERTES   What part is that my lord?

KING   A very riband in the cap of youth,
    Yet needful too, for youth no less becomes
    The light and careless livery that it wears   80
    Than settled age his sables and his weeds
    Importing health and graveness. Two months
    since, Here was a gentleman of Normandy –
    I have seen myself, and served against the French,
    And they can well on horseback, but this gallant   85
    Had witchcraft in 't, he grew unto his seat,
    And to such wondrous doing brought his horse,
    As had he been incorpsed and demi-natured
    With the brave beast. So far he topped my thought,
    That I in forgery of shapes and tricks   90
    Come short of what he did.

LAERTES   A Norman was't?

KING   A Norman.

LAERTES   Upon my life, Lamord.

KING   The very same.

LAERTES   I know him well, he is the brooch indeed
    And gem of all the nation.   95

Hamlet had said he would like to try his duelling skills with Laertes. Claudius tries to make sure that Laertes has the will to avenge his father.

96 **He made...you**: he declared your skill
98 **For art and exercise**: of your brilliant accomplishments
101 **The scrimers**: the master fencers
102 **He swore...eye**: he claimed he had no skill in movement, guarding nor quickness of eye
104 **envenom**: literally 'poison' – foreshadowing Act 5
112 **love is begun by time**: there is a moment which triggers the beginnings of love
113 **passages of proof**: examples which prove this
114 **qualifies**: lessens, diminishes
115 **There lives...abate**: love contains within itself the seeds of its own decay
116 **snuff**: the part of the wick already burnt
117 **And nothing...still**: and nothing remains in a similar state of goodness all the time
118 **For goodness...too much**: love, in excess, consumes itself (*'too much'* is here used as a noun meaning 'excess') **plurisy**: (1) excess (2) a disease involving inflammation of membranes around the lungs, believed in Shakespeare's time to be caused by excess of humours
119 **That we would...delays**: something which we have the will to do, we ought to carry out while the will is still strong, for the intention changes and is subject to being diminished and delayed
122 **tongues, hands, accidents**: all ways in which the intention can be brought to nothing
123 **spendthrift's sigh**: it was believed that each sigh cost a loss of blood from the heart. A spendthrift wastes money on extravagance. Claudius suggests that if we don't act promptly, the duty becomes painful, as breathing is to someone with pleurisy.
124 **to the quick of th' ulcer**: to the heart of the trouble.

- *Claudius's remarks about the will to action growing cold is an interesting, if unwitting comment on Hamlet.*

KING	He made confession of you,
	And gave you such a masterly report
	For art and exercise in your defence,
	And for your rapier most especial,
	That he cried out, 't would be a sight indeed 100
	If one could match you. The scrimers of their nation
	He swore had neither motion, guard, nor eye,
	If you opposed them. Sir, this report of his
	Did Hamlet so envenom with his envy,
	That he could nothing do but wish and beg 105
	Your sudden coming o'er to play with him.
	Now, out of this –
LAERTES	What out of this my lord?
KING	Laertes, was your father dear to you?
	Or are you like the painting of a sorrow,
	A face without a heart?
LAERTES	Why ask you this? 110
KING	Not that I think you did not love your father,
	But that I know love is begun by time,
	And that I see in passages of proof,
	Time qualifies the spark and fire of it.
	There lives within the very flame of love 115
	A kind of wick or snuff that will abate it,
	And nothing is at a like goodness still;
	For goodness growing to a plurisy
	Dies in his own too much. That we would do
	We should do when we would, for this 'would' changes, 120
	And hath abatements and delays as many
	As there are tongues, are hands, are accidents;
	And then this 'should' is like a spendthrift's sigh,
	That hurts by easing. But to the quick of th' ulcer –
	Hamlet comes back, what would you undertake 125
	To show yourself in deed your father's son
	More than in words?

Handwritten annotations: LAERTES SKILLS. · TRIES TO GET LAERTES TO FOCUS. · BY DOING IT, OUT OF HATRED, WITH REDOUCE OR BE DESTROY · ACT NOW IRONIC WHAT HAMLET WASN'T DOING

Claudius suggests a match with foils, where Laertes's rapier, instead of being blunt, for a bout of skill, shall be sharp enough to kill Hamlet. In addition this foil will be smeared with a poison for which there is no antidote. Claudius then gives the scheme another twist.

128 **sanctuarize**: give sanctuary. Fugitives would seek sanctuary in a church, safe from pursuit. Claudius agrees that this thinking should not apply to Hamlet.

130 **Will you do this**: if you mean to do this

132 **We'll put on those**: we'll arrange for some

133 **set a double varnish**: give an extra gloss to

134 **in fine**: in conclusion

135 **remiss**: lax

136 **all contriving**: any idea of plots

137 **peruse**: study

138 **shuffling**: sleight-of-hand

139 **unbated**: unblunted – in a match for show, as a test of skill, 'hits' would be counted but there would be no intention to hurt or kill
pass of practice: either a practice bout – *or* sword-thrust; *or* a bout involving trickery

140 **Requite him**: pay him back

142 **unction**: ointment
mountebank: travelling salesman of medicines and remedies

144 **cataplasm**: plaster, poultice

145 **simples**: herbs

146 **Under the moon**: herbs collected at night were supposed to have more power, *'virtue'*

148 **contagion**: (here) poison
gall: injure

151 **shape**: role

152 **drift**: intentions
look through: can be guessed at as a result of

153 **assayed**: attempted

155 **blast in proof**: fall apart when put to the test

156 **your cunnings**: the skill of you both

157 **ha 't**: have it

158 **in your motion**: as a result of your exercise

PASSIONATE REPLY

LAERTES	To cut his throat i' th' church. — *NORMAL SANCTUARY*
KING	No place indeed should murder sanctuarize;

L. SKILL

Revenge should have no bounds. But good Laertes,
Will you do this, keep close within your chamber. 130
Hamlet returned shall know you are come home;
We'll put on those shall praise your excellence,

A BET WILL BE PLACED — THE BEST SWORD MAN (PLAN)

And set a double varnish on the fame
The Frenchman gave you, bring you in fine together,
And wager on your heads; he being remiss,   135
Most generous, and free from all contriving,
Will not peruse the foils, so that with ease,
Or with a little shuffling, you may choose
A sword unbated, and in a pass of practice
Requite him for your father.

LAERTES	I will do 't. 140

And for that purpose I'll anoint my sword.
I bought an unction of a mountebank,

THIS PLAN SHOULD BE REPUGNANT TO AN HONOURABLE MAN.

So mortal, that but dip a knife in it,
Where it draws blood no cataplasm so rare,
Collected from all simples that have virtue   145
Under the moon, can save the thing from death
That is but scratched withal. I'll touch my point
With this contagion, that if I gall him slightly,
It may be death.

KING	Let's further think of this,

Weigh what convenience both of time and
      means   150
May fit us to our shape. If this should fail,
And that our drift look through our bad
      performance,
'Twere better not assayed; therefore this project
Should have a back or second, that might hold
If this did blast in proof. Soft, let me see –   155
We'll make a solemn wager on your cunnings –
I ha 't!
When in your motion you are hot and dry,
As make your bouts more violent to that end.

When Hamlet is hot and thirsty from the fencing, there will
be a poisoned drink already prepared, in case the poisoned
foil does not kill him. At this point Gertrude comes in to tell
them that Ophelia has drowned. The account she gives is
that Ophelia fell while climbing up to hang a garland on a
willow tree. The water weighed down her clothes and she
drowned.

160 **I'll...him**: I'll have him offered
161 **for the nonce**: for this particular occasion
162 **stuck**: sword-thrust
168 **askant**: aslant, slanting over
169 **hoar**: grey-white
170 **Therewith**: with these ie. with pliable twigs of willow
171 **crowflowers**: ragged robin
      nettles: presumably the white or yellow flowers of the
      'dead' nettle which does not sting
      long purples: a kind of wild orchis, with long purple
      flowers and with roots like blanched fingers. The *'grosser
      name'* alluded to, is prompted by the suggestion that the
      roots spread from a tuberous mass which looks like
      testicles.
172 **liberal**: (here) free-spoken
173 **cold**: (here) modest
174 **pendent**: hanging
      crownet weeds: coronets of wild flowers
175 **envious sliver**: spiteful, malicious slender branch. The
      word *'sliver'* normally refers to a piece which has already
      been cut or split off.
176 **trophies**: usually weapons, helmets etc. captured by the
      victorious army and hung on a memorial
180 **incapable of**: not realizing
181 **a creature...element**: an aquatic creature, fitted for living
      in water
184 **melodious lay**: tuneful song

> • *If all these details are known about Ophelia's death,
> why didn't anybody rescue her?*

(handwritten note: EXTENDS THE PLOT NECESSARY FOR PLOT.)

(handwritten note: BACK-UP, PLAN.)

And that he calls for drink, I'll have preferred
    him   160
A chalice for the nonce, whereon but sipping,
If he by chance escape your venomed stuck,
Our purpose may hold there. But stay, what noise?

Enter QUEEN

How sweet Queen!

QUEEN   One woe doth tread upon another's heel,   165
So fast they follow: your sister's drowned,
    Laertes.

LAERTES   Drowned! O where?

QUEEN   There is a willow grows askant the brook,
That shows his hoar leaves in the glassy stream;
Therewith fantastic garlands did she make,   170
Of crowflowers, nettles, daisies, and long
    purples
That liberal shepherds give a grosser name,
But our cold maids do dead men's fingers call them.
There on the pendent boughs her crownet weeds
Clamb'ring to hang, an envious sliver broke,   175
When down her weedy trophies and herself
Fell in the weeping brook. Her clothes spread
wide, And mermaid-like awhile they bore her up,
Which time she chanted snatches of old tunes,
As one incapable of her own distress,   180
Or like a creature native and indued
Unto that element; but long it could not be
Till that her garments, heavy with their drink,
Pulled the poor wretch from her melodious lay
To muddy death.

(handwritten notes in left margin: Says she feel in. Is she ensuring Ophelia gets a proper burial or just a fanciful account)

(handwritten note in right margin: If Gertrude saw this why did no-one help.)

LAERTES   Alas, then she is drowned?   185

QUEEN   Drowned, drowned.

LAERTES   Too much of water has thou poor Ophelia,
And therefore I forbid my tears, but yet

Laertes cannot help his tears at Ophelia's death, but underneath, his anger blazes. When Laertes has left, Claudius tells Gertrude he is afraid that this news has undone all the calming effect he has had on Laertes.

189 It is our trick: it is the way with us
191 The woman will be out: the female element in my nature will be played out
193 this folly: his tears

- *What does Claudius fear after this news?*

It is our trick, nature her custom holds,
Let shame say what it will; when these are
    gone,   190
The woman will be out. Adieu my lord.
I have a speech of fire that fain would blaze,
But that this folly drowns it.   [*Exit*

KING   Let's follow, Gertrude.
How much I had to do to calm his rage!   A LIE WE KNOW
Now fear I this will give it start again,   195 IT'S NOT TRUE
Therefore let's follow.
                         [*Exeunt*

DRAMATIC PICTURE OF OPHELIA'S
DEATH.
ONE STEP CLOSER TO THE FINAL
  TRAGEDY.

Keeping track

Scene 1

1 The scene opens with Gertrude in some distress and Claudius anxious to know what has happened in her encounter with Hamlet. How accurate is Gertrude's account of the killing of Polonius?
2 What conclusions do you draw from her behaviour here?
3 How does Claudius react to the death of Polonius?
4 Why is he so anxious now to remove Hamlet from Elsinore?

Scene 2

This short scene has a narrative function in that we see Hamlet being summoned into the presence of Claudius. However, it also reinforces our understanding of Hamlet's thoughts and feelings about his 'friends', Rosencrantz and Guildenstern.
1 What are his thoughts and feelings about them?
2 Do you agree with him?

Scene 3

1 What 'reasons' does Claudius give for sending Hamlet away rather than allowing the *'strong law'* to apprehend him?
2 What do you think are his real 'reasons'?
3 When Hamlet enters he has slipped once more into his *'antic disposition'*. Why do you think he has done this?
4 What do his words reveal about his attitude towards Polonius?
5 How does he behave towards Claudius?
6 What does Claudius's short soliloquy at the end of the scene reveal about his plan to deal with the problem of Hamlet for once and for all?
7 What is the role of Rosencrantz and Guildenstern in this plot?

Scene 4

1 As Hamlet prepares to leave for England he encounters Fortinbras and his army returning to do battle for *'a little patch of ground'*. What is Hamlet's conclusion about this military action?
2 Hamlet's soliloquy (lines 31–66) is prompted by the sight of so many men prepared to risk their lives for no obvious reason or reward. What

accusations does Hamlet make at himself in this speech? In what ways does this speech echo the *'To be, or not to be'* soliloquy?

Scene 5

1 Why do you think Gertrude is unwilling to see Ophelia at first and why does she eventually agree to admit her?
2 What does Gertrude's aside (lines 17–20) reveal about her? Do you find your attitude towards her changing?
3 Ophelia's songs show her madness. Can you detect any underlying themes in her words? How do you react to the sight of Ophelia like this?
4 How does Claudius react to the situation?
5 The entrance of Laertes shows another reaction to the killing of a father. In what ways does he form a contrast with Hamlet? What effect does his arrival have on Ophelia?

Scene 6

1 What is the purpose of this short scene?
2 What questions does this scene leave unanswered?
3 Why do you think Hamlet has written to Claudius?

Scene 7

1 At the beginning of this scene Claudius has succeeded in directing Laertes's fury towards Hamlet. How do you think he did this?
2 How does Laertes react to Hamlet's letter?
3 What is the plan agreed between Claudius and Laertes?
4 Gertrude enters this scene bringing news of Ophelia's death. How does she describe her death?
5 How does Laertes respond to the news of Ophelia's death?
6 What do you make of Claudius's reaction?

Drama

1 • Rehearse Act 4 scene 3 lines 17–57. Think about how Claudius deals with this situation which is potentially damaging to his position: a royal member of the family has apparently murdered a loyal Councillor in the Queen's bedchamber – on top of which, Hamlet now seems to be completely mad. Work at the moves and gestures which will show the tension in Claudius.
   • Work with a partner: one of you, as a royal spokesperson, tells the other, a cynical reporter, what happened to Polonius in the palace that day.

2 Look at Claudius's speech in Act 4 scene 5 lines 75–94. What is Gertrude doing? In pairs, work out how Gertrude deals with this speech, after what happened between her and Hamlet. Does Claudius realize anything has changed? How does she hide her feelings?

3 Use FORUM THEATRE to explore the moment when Gertrude comes in on Claudius with Laertes in Act 4 scene 7 line 164 'How sweet Queen!'. Consider the contrast between their secret plotting and the Queen's news. Neither party knows what the other knows. What does Gertrude think is going on? Do they think she has overheard them? How can she tell Laertes the news?

Key elements

In Act 4 these are:
- Hamlet's soliloquy: *'How all occasions do inform against me'*
- Ophelia's madness and death
- Laertes's revenge plot.

The key scene

Claudius and Laertes: Act 4 scene 7.

Keying it in

Laertes returns to the play in Act 4 scene 5.
- What is his mood?
- How does he form a contrast with Hamlet?
- Who is the object of his desire for revenge?
- In what way is this ironic?
- How does he justify his demand for blood?
- What are your thoughts and feelings about Laertes up to this point in the play?

The scene itself

1 At the beginning of the scene Claudius has apparently succeeded in persuading Laertes that he is not guilty of Polonius's death.
- What else has he suggested to Laertes?
- How has he persuaded Laertes?
- In what ways is this clever?

- Is it typical of Claudius? How?
2 Look at lines 5–24.
   - Laertes asks an obvious and reasonable question. What is it?
   - What answers does Claudius give?
   - Do you believe him?
3 Look at lines 25–35.

   Laertes seems to accept what Claudius has said but he is still determined to have his revenge.
   - What is Claudius's intention now?
   - Do you think he sees an opportunity to solve his problems?
   - What do you think he is about to tell Laertes when he is interrupted by the messenger?
4 Look at lines 36–60.
   - Why is Claudius so shocked to receive a letter from Hamlet?
   - How does he react to the content of the letter?
   - What is Laertes's response to this unexpected development?
   - Claudius is quick to seize the initiative here. When he says *'Will you be ruled by me?'* he obviously intends to use Laertes for his own purposes.
5 Look at lines 62–107.
   - What is Claudius suggesting here?
   - How does Laertes react?
6 Look at lines 108–163.

   Claudius changes his approach at this point as he lures Laertes into his plan.
   - Why does he ask *'was your father dear to you?'*
   - What is he suggesting in the speech from lines 111–127?
   - What effect does this have on Laertes?
   - What does Laertes's claim that he would *'cut his throat i' th' church'* reveal about his mood and character?
   - Claudius says, *'Revenge should have no bounds.'* (line 129) Do you agree with him?
   - Does the fact that it is Claudius who says this affect your reaction? He also describes Hamlet as *'Most generous and free from all contriving'*.
   - Is this an accurate description?
   - Do you find it ironic that Claudius should say this?

   Laertes's approach to revenge has changed under the influence of Claudius.
   - How has it changed?
   - What does he suggest in lines 140–149?
   - How does Claudius respond to the suggestion?
   - Do you find their plan ironic, or perhaps typical?

Overview

In this scene, Claudius is desperately, and perhaps skilfully, trying to contain a dangerous situation which threatens his security. He manipulates the enraged Laertes and draws him into his own devious scheme.

However, the 'corrupting' of Laertes sheds some interesting light on the whole issue of revenge and acts as a prompt to the audience to consider their attitude to revenge.

Think about the implications of these quotations:

'I dare damnation.'

'To cut his throat i' th' church.

No place indeed should murder sanctuarize;

Revenge should have no bounds.'

Close study

Act 4 scene 2 lines 6–31

* When Hamlet mentions Polonius's body, what is his tone?
* What does this reveal about his attitude to the killing?
* Do you approve of Hamlet's behaviour?
* What does the word *'sponge'* reveal about Hamlet's attitude to Rosencrantz?
* What warning does he give Rosencrantz in these lines?
  Look at Act 3 scene 2 lines 342–369.
* What similarities can you find in these exchanges?
* Do you admire Hamlet's handling of his spying 'friends'?

Hamlet and revenge

After the success of the inner play in Act 3, Hamlet did perform *'bitter business'*, but it was directed against Polonius and his mother. In Act 4, the rage appears to have subsided once more and he confronts Claudius more in a mood of scornful contempt than violent outrage.

The encounter with Fortinbras and his army forces Hamlet to explore, yet again, the issue of revenge and his own failure to take direct action. It is entirely possible that an audience could see Fortinbras's expedition as a form of senseless bravado, an example of masculine pride posing as 'honour'. However, Hamlet sees it as courage and a damning indictment of his own cowardice. Not for the first time in the play, Hamlet reproaches himself with failure to act like a man because of '*Bestial oblivion*' or *'thinking too precisely'*. To have 'scruples' is to be *'craven'* and this speech echoes the *'To be, or not to be'* soliloquy.

The reactions of Ophelia and Laertes to the violent death of Polonius are also illuminating. Ophelia is driven to madness and suicide as the 'violence' of grief goes inward and destroys her; Laertes is driven to treachery and damnation as his violence lashes outward. In a way, they enact the alternatives in responding to such powerful emotion. You might like to think about the parallels between Hamlet and Laertes and Ophelia. The 'violence' in Hamlet seems to go both inward and outward at different times.

Assignments

Essays

1 Look at the two soliloquies *'To be, or not to be'* and *'How all occasions do inform against me'*. How do these speeches develop your understanding of Hamlet's difficulties as a revenger?
2 Compare the reactions of Laertes and Ophelia to the death of Polonius. In what ways do they illuminate Hamlet's situation?

The sexton and his mate are discussing the fact that the coroner at the inquest has said Ophelia is to be allowed a Christian burial, when as far as they know, she committed suicide. They discuss what constitutes deliberate drowning and come to the conclusion that if she had not been a lady of the court she would not have been buried in sacred ground.

1 **christian burial**: Christians would normally be buried in sanctified ground, usually a churchyard. If a person had committed suicide the burial would take place outside consecrated ground, sometimes at a crossroads and with a stake through the body.

4 **straight**: straightaway
crowner: coroner

6 **in her own defence**: this would have been, and still is, a plea in a murder case, likely if proved, to reduce the sentence. Since suicide was regarded by the church as self-murder, there is a certain logic attaching to it in the speaker's mind.

8 **found**: decided in court

9 **se offendendo**: a mistake for 'se defendendo' (in self-defence), or possibly a deliberate coining of a pseudo-Latin phrase, since his argument has been throughout that she killed herself knowingly

11 **wittingly**: knowingly – possibly why Gertrude has made the point that Ophelia did not realize the danger she was in
three branches: a reference to the legal argument used in a real court case over a suicide

12 **argal**: mistake for 'ergo' Latin for 'therefore'

14 **goodman delver**: master digger

23 **quest**: inquest

26 **out**: outside, without

> - *The 'ordinary people' in Shakespeare's plays are often credited merely with producing 'comic relief' to lighten the tragic proceedings. Look carefully at what the two grave-diggers say and do. What kind of people are they? What effect do they seem to you to have?*

CHARACTERS OUTSIDE CASTLE

Act five

LIGHT RELIEF FROM RECENT NEWS.

Scene (1)

FINALITY + PERMANENCE a DEATH.

Enter two CLOWNS, _the_ SEXTON, _and his_ MATE

COUNTRY FOLK

1ST CLOWN   Is she to be buried in christian burial when
she wilfully seeks her own salvation?

DID SHE COMMIT SUICIDE?

2ND CLOWN   I tell thee she is, and therefore make her grave
straight. The crowner hath sat on her, and finds it
christian burial.   5

1ST CLOWN   How can that be, unless she drowned herself in
her own defence?

2ND CLOWN   Why, 'tis found so.

IF THEY HAD COMMITED

1ST CLOWN   It must be 'se offendendo', it cannot be else.
For here lies the point, if I drown myself   10
(_CLASS_) wittingly, it argues an act, and an act hath three
branches; it is to act, to do, and to perform: argal
she drowned herself wittingly.

SUICIDE THEY WOULD NOT BE BURIED ON CHRISTIAN GROUND

2ND CLOWN   Nay, but hear you goodman delver –

1ST CLOWN   Give me leave. Here lies the water – good.   15
Here stands the man – good. If the man go to this
water and drown himself, it is, will he, nill he, he
goes, mark you that. But if the water come to him,
and drown him, he drowns not himself; argal, he
that is not guilty of his own death, shortens not   20
his own life.

2ND CLOWN   But is this law?

1ST CLOWN   Ay marry is 't, crowner's quest law.

2ND CLOWN   Will you ha' the truth on 't? If this had not
been a gentlewoman, she would have been   25
buried out a christian burial.

_SUPERFICIALLY SIMPLY WALL a SPEAKING
YET IS PERTINANT TO PLAY._

The two men consider that it is unfair that a suicide from the court circle should still be entitled to a Christian burial. They have a jokey conversation about digging and then about grave-digging. Horatio and Hamlet are seen in the distance.

28 countenance: permission
29 even-christian: fellow-Christians
30 ancient: traditional, from earliest times
34 bore arms: usually 'had a coat of arms' but here used punningly, as line 38 will reveal
40 confess thyself: 'and be hanged' completes the proverb
44 frame: structure
53 unyoke: unyoke the oxen from the plough, come to the end of the day's work
57 Cudgel: beat
58 mend his pace: speed up

ONE OF THE MOST IMPORTANT THEMES IN HAMLET.
DEFINES PHILOSOPHICAL CONTEXT IN WHICH THE WHOLE
TRAGEDY TAKES PLACE.
SHAKESPEARE DID NOT INVENT THE MEMENTO MORI BUT
GAVE IT POWERFUL EXPRESSION.
SINGING GRAVE-MAKER HAS PROFOUND IMPACT; HAPPILY
SINGING, SO FULL OF LIFE WHILST SO NEAR DEATH.
AMUSING + TERRIFYING.
WHAT HE DOES TAKES US INTO THE NEXT WORLD.
PRESENTED AS ORDINARY FALLIBLE HUMAN BEING + ALSO THE
SUPERHUMAN GRAVE DIGGER FOR WHOLE WORLD. HE WAS THERE
+ CONTINUE TO BE THERE LONG AFTER BRIEF ENTRANCES + EXITS.
HIS CAREER BEGAN WHEN HAMLET WAS BORN ∴ WILL TAKE CARE OF
HIM WHEN HE DIES.
THE SKULL SHOWS HOW ALL THE FRIVOLITY + VITALITY SOON SUCCOMBS
TO NOTHING (194) H. SEES THE INSIGNIFICANCE OF MAN WHO
AT THE BEGINNING HE COMPARES TO GOD. Pg 255.

| 1ST CLOWN | Why, there thou say'st, and the more pity that great folk should have countenance in this world to drown or hang themselves, more than their even-christian. Come my spade. There is no ancient gentlemen but gardeners, ditchers, and grave-makers, they hold up Adam's profession. | 30 |

CLASS (handwritten annotation)

| 2ND CLOWN | Was he a gentleman? |
| 1ST CLOWN | 'A was the first that ever bore arms. |

PUNNING – ADDS TO WIT (handwritten annotation)

2ND CLOWN	Why he had none.	35
1ST CLOWN	What, art a heathen? How dost thou understand the Scripture? The Scripture says 'Adam digged'. Could he dig without arms? I'll put another question to thee; if thou answerest me not to the purpose, confess thyself –	40
2ND CLOWN	Go to.
1ST CLOWN	What is he that builds stronger than either the mason, the shipwright, or the carpenter?
2ND CLOWN	The gallows-maker, for that frame outlives a thousand tenants.	45
1ST CLOWN	I like thy wit well in good faith; the gallows does well, but how does it well? It does well to those who do ill; now thou dost ill to say the gallows is built stronger than the church; argal, the gallows may do well to thee. To 't again, come.	50
2ND CLOWN	'Who builds stronger than a mason, a shipwright, or a carpenter?'

COMPARED WITH SONGS OPHELIA USED (handwritten annotation)

1ST CLOWN	Ay, tell me that and unyoke.
2ND CLOWN	Marry now I can tell.
1ST CLOWN	To 't.	55
2ND CLOWN	Mass I cannot tell.

Enter HAMLET *and* HORATIO *afar off*

| 1ST CLOWN | Cudgel thy brains no more about it, for your dull ass will not mend his pace with beating; and, when |

While one of the men goes off to fetch a drink the other
starts to sing as he digs the grave. As he digs, he uncovers a
skull and throws it out. Hamlet considers whose head this
might have been in life.

61 Yaughan: Johann, John
62 stoup: jar (a measure containing approximately two litres)
63 In youth...meet: the grave-digger's version of a popular
   song, turned into the rhythm of a work-song, while he digs
65 contract-a...behove: to pass the time to my advantage
66 meet: so fitting, suitable
69 Custom...easiness: he is so used to digging graves that the
   thought of why he is digging does not bother him at all
70 the hand...daintier sense: someone who has a good deal
   of leisure can afford more delicate feelings
77 jowls: knocks
78 Cain's jawbone: again a reminder of the theme of
   fratricide
79 pate: head
80 o'er-reaches: takes advantage of
   circumvent: get the better of
89 chopless: without the lower jaw
90 mazzard: head

> • *To Hamlet's introspection is now added a physical
> realization of mortality. How does this affect him?*

you are asked this question next, say 'a grave-
maker', the houses that he makes last till   60
doomsday. Go, get thee to Yaughan: fetch me a
stoup of liquor.

> [*Exit* 2ND CLOWN
> [*He digs, and sings*

In youth when I did love, did love,
    Methought it was very sweet,
To contract-a the time, for-a my behove,   65
    O methought there-a was nothing-a meet.

HAMLET   Has this fellow no feeling of his business, that 'a
sings at grave-making?   IT'S WRONG -

HORATIO   Custom hath made it in him a property of easiness.

HAMLET   'Tis e'en so, the hand of little employment hath   70
the daintier sense.

1ST CLOWN   [*Sings*]
But age with his stealing steps
    Hath clawed me in his clutch,
And hath shipped me into the land,
    As if I had never been such.   75

> [*Throws up a skull*

HAMLET   That skull had a tongue in it, and could sing once,
DEATH HAS
NO RESPECT
FOR CLASS
etc.
    PEOPLE
how the knave jowls it to the ground, as if 'twere
Cain's jawbone, that did the first murder. This
might be the pate of a politician, which this ass now
o'er-reaches; one that would circumvent God,   80
might it not?   LIFE IS INSIGNIFICANT -
ALL END UP THE
SAME.

HORATIO   It might my lord.

HAMLET   Or of a courtier, which could say 'Good morrow
sweet lord, how dost thou good lord?' This might
be my lord such-a-one, that praised my lord -   85
sucha-one's horse when 'a meant to beg it,
might it not?

HORATIO   Ay my lord.

HAMLET   Why e'en so, and now my Lady Worm's; chopless,
and knocked about the mazzard with a sexton's   90

Hamlet broods on the thought that everyone, however clever, wealthy, busy or pompous, comes to this end.

92 Did these bones...with them?: was the creation and raising of these people of so little importance that their bones should be used to play games?

93 loggats: a game where wooden clubs were thrown at a stake fixed in the ground. The nearest was the winner.

99 Why: not a question-word, but an exclamation

100 quiddities, quillities: quibbling, fussy legal arguments

101 tenure: the legal title by which property is held

103 sconce: (here) head, a jokey use

104 action of battery: a legal term 'action for assault'

106 statutes...recoveries: jargon used in land deals; 'statute' bond which secured for the creditor the mortgaged land and goods if the debtor could not pay; *'recognizances'* the bonds acknowledging the debt; *'double vouchers'* a voucher was the person called upon to warrant a tenant's title – two warrantors made the process even more secure

106 his fines...his recoveries: fine and recovery – the method by which the entail on an estate, which prevented the current owner disposing of it as he wished, could be converted into outright ownership

107 fine: final result – play on the word *'fine'*, as also in:

108 fine pate: clever head

109 fine dirt: well-sifted soil

110 purchases: the obtaining of property other than by inheritance; acquisition

111 pair of indentures: an agreement between two or more parties of which two or more copies were made. Originally they were written on one large sheet and separated by the cutting of a zig-zag line. They should thus fit together exactly, making forgery difficult.

113 inheritor: the man who has acquired, not inherited, the land. Now in his coffin, he occupies no more space than the documents.

118 They are...in that: only fools would assume that any document would be 'proof' against death
assurance: legal proof

120 sirrah: form of address to servants, etc

spade; here's fine revolution an we had the trick
to see 't. Did these bones cost no more the
breeding, but to play at loggats with them? Mine
ache to think on 't.

1ST CLOWN [*Sings*]
 A pick axe, and a spade, a spade,   95
  For and – a shrouding sheet,
 O a pit of clay for to be made
  For such a guest is meet.
        [*Throws up another skull*

HAMLET There's another. Why may not that be the skull
of a lawyer? Where be his quiddities now, his 100
quillities, his cases, his tenures, and his tricks? Why
does he suffer this rude knave now to knock him
about the sconce with a dirty shovel, and will not
tell him of his action of battery? Hum! This fellow
might be in 's time a great buyer of land, with 105
his statutes, his recognizances, his fines, his double
vouchers, his recoveries. Is this the fine of his fines,
and the recovery of his recoveries, to have his fine
pate full of fine dirt? Will his vouchers vouch him
no more of his purchases, and double ones 110
too, than the length and breadth of a pair of
indentures? The very conveyances of his lands will
scarcely lie in this box; and must the inheritor
himself have no more, ha?

HORATIO Not a jot more my lord.   115

HAMLET Is not parchment made of sheep-skins?

HORATIO Ay my lord, and of calves' skins too.

HAMLET They are sheep and calves which seek out assurance
in that. I will speak to this fellow. Whose grave's
this sirrah?   120

1ST CLOWN Mine sir.
 [*Sings*] O a pit of clay for to be made
   For such a guest is meet.

Hamlet asks for whom the grave is being dug. The grave-digger proves very pedantic in his answers, but Hamlet learns that a woman is to be buried. The man does not recognize Hamlet, but tells him he has been a grave-digger since Hamlet's birth. Hamlet, he says, has gone mad and been sent to England.

124 thou liest: the first of the *puns* (see GLOSSARY page 328) on telling lies and lying

129 the quick: the living

140 absolute: exact

by the card: accurately, according to precise rules; the compass card, on which the 32 points of the compass are marked, used for accurate naval navigation

141 equivocation: the using of a word in more than one sense and the ambiguity that may thus come about

143 picked: finicky, fussy

145 galls his kibe: rubs his chilblain. The lower orders are treading so close on the heels of the aristocracy in manners, that there will soon be little to choose between them.

> • *What do you notice about Hamlet's duel of words with the grave-digger, compared with those he tries to start at court?*

HAMLET	I think it be thine indeed, for thou liest in 't.
1ST CLOWN	You lie out on 't sir, and therefore 'tis not 125 yours; for my part I do not lie in 't, yet it is mine.
HAMLET	Thou dost lie in 't, to be in 't and say it is thine. 'Tis for the dead, not for the quick; therefore thou liest. 130
1ST CLOWN	'Tis a quick lie sir, 'twill away again from me to you.
HAMLET	What man dost thou dig it for?
1ST CLOWN	For no man sir.
HAMLET	What woman then? 135
1ST CLOWN	For none neither.
HAMLET	Who is to be buried in 't?
1ST CLOWN	One that was a woman sir, but rest her soul she's dead.
HAMLET	How absolute the knave is! We must speak by 140 the card, or equivocation will undo us. By the Lord, Horatio, these three years I have took note of it – the age is grown so picked, that the toe of the peasant comes so near the heel of the courtier he galls his kibe. How long hast thou been grave- 145 maker?
1ST CLOWN	Of all the days i' th' year I came to 't that day that our last King Hamlet overcame Fortinbras.
HAMLET	How long is that since?
1ST CLOWN	Cannot you tell that? Every fool can tell that; 150 it was that very day that young Hamlet was born – he that is mad and sent into England.
HAMLET	Ay marry, why was he sent into England?
1ST CLOWN	Why because 'a was mad. 'A shall recover his wits there, or if 'a do not, 'tis no great matter there. 155
HAMLET	Why?

According to the sexton, Hamlet's madness will not be noticed in England, where everyone is mad. The sexton has been doing his job for thirty years, he says. Hamlet asks how long a body may lie in the ground before it decomposes. Picking up a skull the sexton says it has been in the earth for 23 years. It was the skull of Yorick, the King's jester. As a child Hamlet had known him and enjoyed his company.

165 thirty years: this seems to put Hamlet's age at thirty, or it may just mean 'many, many years'

168 pocky: infected with the pox, usually referring to the venereal disease syphilis

hold the laying in: last through until the burial

174 whoreson: (here) wretched – used to indicate a jokey familiarity

1ST CLOWN	'Twill not be seen in him there, there the men are as mad as he.
HAMLET	How came he mad?
1ST CLOWN	Very strangely they say. 160
HAMLET	How strangely?
1ST CLOWN	Faith e'en with losing his wits.
HAMLET	Upon what ground?
1ST CLOWN	Why here in Denmark. I have been sexton here man and boy thirty years. 165
HAMLET	How long will a man lie i' the earth ere he rot?
1ST CLOWN	Faith if 'a be not rotten before 'a die, as we have many pocky corses nowadays that will scarce hold the laying in, he will last you some eight year, or nine year. A tanner will last you nine year. 170
HAMLET	Why he more than another?
1ST CLOWN	Why sir, his hide is so tanned with his trade that 'a will keep out water a great while; and your water is a sore decayer of your whoreson dead body. Here's a skull now hath lien you i' th' earth three and 175 twenty years.
HAMLET	Whose was it?
1ST CLOWN	A whoreson mad fellow's it was, whose do you think it was?
HAMLET	Nay I know not. 180
1ST CLOWN	A pestilence on him for a mad rogue, 'a poured a flagon of Rhenish on my head once; this same skull sir, was sir, Yorick's skull, the King's jester.
HAMLET	This?
1ST CLOWN	E'en that. 185
	[*Takes the skull*
HAMLET	Let me see. Alas poor Yorick! I knew him Horatio, a fellow of infinite jest, of most excellent fancy; he hath borne me on his back a thousand

Handwritten annotations:
SCROLL TO REMIND HAMLET WAS LITTLE IS LEFT IN LIFE +

DESTINY OF ALL IS DEATH

Hamlet is fascinated and horrified by the thought that when flesh covered Yorick's skull he knew the man, and as a child was carried on his shoulder, kissed him and laughed at his jokes. His mother, however thickly she may paint her face, must come to this state. Even the greatest men, Alexander and Caesar, came to dust at last. Ophelia's funeral procession enters.

189 abhorred: it is a terrible thought that he once rode on the back of what is now a heap of bones

190 my gorge rises: I feel like retching

195 chop-fallen: dispirited, crestfallen. Also (here) literally with the lower jaw hanging loose, or missing

207 bung-hole: the hole in a barrel which is tapped for the beer to be drawn

208 too curiously: too closely

210 modesty: moderation
likelihood to lead it: the likelihood of what will be found leads the expectation on

213 loam: a clayey earth made into a kind of mortar by the addition of sand and straw

218 flaw: squall

> • *Why does the knowledge that he is handling Yorick's skull provoke more horror in Hamlet than the other deaths?*

times, and now how abhorred in my imagination it
is – my gorge rises at it. Here hung those lips   190
that I have kissed I know not how oft. Where be
your gibes now? Your gambols, your songs, your
flashes of merriment, that were wont to set the
table on a roar? Not one now to mock your own
grinning? Quite chop-fallen? Now get you to   195
my lady's chamber, and tell her, let her paint an
inch thick, to this favour she must come. Make her
laugh at that. Prithee Horatio tell me one thing.

HORATIO   What's that my lord?

HAMLET   Dost thou think Alexander looked a this   200
fashion i' th' earth?

HORATIO   E'en so.

HAMLET   And smelt so? Pah!   [*Puts down the skull*

HORATIO   E'en so my lord.

HAMLET   To what base uses we may return, Horatio!   205
Why may not imagination trace the noble dust of
Alexander, till 'a find it stopping a bung-hole?

HORATIO   'Twere to consider too curiously to consider so.

HAMLET   No faith, not a jot, but to follow him thither with
modesty enough, and likelihood to lead it;   210
as thus – Alexander died, Alexander was buried,
Alexander returneth to dust, the dust is earth, of
earth we make loam, and why of that loam whereto
he was converted might they not stop a beer barrel?
Imperious Cæsar, dead and turned to clay,   215
Might stop a hole to keep the wind away.
O that that earth which kept the world in awe
Should patch a wall t' expel the winter's flaw!
But soft, but soft awhile – here comes the King,

Enter the KING, QUEEN, LAERTES *in funeral procession
following the corpse of* OPHELIA, *then the* DOCTOR *of*
DIVINITY *and* LORDS

Hamlet and Horatio move aside as the funeral procession approaches. From the lack of full ceremony, Hamlet deduces that it is the funeral of a suicide of some rank. He recognizes Laertes to whom the priest explains that even this ceremonial and the burial in sanctified ground is an exception. Laertes angrily refers to his sister as an angel and Hamlet realizes whose funeral this is. The Queen says farewell to the girl who might have become her son's wife.

221 **maimed**: incomplete
223 **Fordo**: do away with
   estate: rank
224 **Couch we awhile**: let's stay hidden. Couch usually means 'lie'.
228 **obsequies...warranty**: the arrangements for her funeral have been made as extensive as we have been allowed
229 **warranty**: permission, authorization
   Her death: the way she met her death
230 **great command**: the permission of our superiors
   the order: the normal practice
232 **For**: instead of
233 **Shards**: broken pieces of pottery
234 **virgin crants**: garlands or wreaths carried in front of a virgin's coffin and then hung up in the church
235 **strewments**: flowers strewn on her coffin
   bringing home of bell and burial: bringing to her last resting-place with the sound of church bells and with a proper funeral
238 **profane the service of the dead**: desecrate the burial service
239 **sage requiem**: solemn funeral hymns
241 **unpolluted**: chaste
244 **When...howling**: in his anger and hurt Laertes suggests that while Ophelia will become an angel of Heaven, the priest will be suffering the torments of Hell
245 **Sweets**: sweet-smelling flowers

> • *We have heard Hamlet theorizing about suicide, now we learn about the Church's strictures from a priest. Is Laertes a consistent character in his reactions to perceived wrongs?*

[Handwritten margin note: FIRST OBSERVATION IS IT'S NOT A FULL CHRISTIAN BURIAL]

The Queen, the courtiers. Who is this they
follow? 220
And with such maimed rites? This doth
betoken,
The corse they follow did with desperate hand *[IRONIC]*
Fordo it own life. 'Twas of some estate. *[IT'S OPHELIA]*
Couch we awhile and mark.   [*Retires with* HORATIO

LAERTES	What ceremony else? *[ALSO QUESTIONING THE BURIAL]* 225
HAMLET	That is Laertes, a very noble youth. Mark.
LAERTES	What ceremony else?
DOCTOR *[PRIEST]*	Her obsequies have been as far enlarged *[CREATES SYMPATHY]*
	As we have warranty. Her death was doubtful,
	And but that great command o'ersways the order, 230
	She should in ground unsanctified been lodged
	Till the last trumpet. For charitable prayers,
	Shards, flints, and pebbles should be thrown on her;
	Yet here she is allowed her virgin crants,
	Her maiden strewments, and the bringing home 235
	Of bell and burial.
LAERTES	Must there no more be done? *[STILL CONDEMNING OPHELIA]*
DOCTOR	No more be done.
	We should profane the service of the dead,
	To sing sage requiem and such rest to her
	As to peace-parted souls.
LAERTES	Lay her i' th' earth: 240
	And from her fair and unpolluted flesh
	May violets spring. I tell thee churlish priest,
	A minist'ring angel shall my sister be
	When thou liest howling.
HAMLET	What, the fair Ophelia!
QUEEN	Sweets to the sweet. Farewell. [*Scatters flowers* 245
	I hoped thou shouldst have been my Hamlet's wife.

[Handwritten margin note: LAERTES PASSION →]

Laertes, in his grief, curses Hamlet for killing Polonius and thus driving Ophelia mad. He leaps into the grave and tells them to bury him alive with his dead sister. Hamlet find this grief excessive in a brother and they struggle. They are parted and Hamlet declares how he had loved Ophelia.

250 thy most ingenious sense: your sensitivity of mind, your precious reason
254 flat: level ground, plain
255 Pelion: a mountain in Thessaly, Greece
256 Olympus: the mountain in Thessaly where the Greek gods lived
257 emphasis: intensity of feeling
phrase: phraseology, expression
258 wandering stars: planets
259 wonder-wounded: transfixed with astonishment, astounded
263 splenitive: quick to anger, irascible
269 wag: move, blink

> • *Laertes has cursed a priest; a lover and a brother fight each other physically and with words at Ophelia's funeral. What atmosphere might we expect this to project over the rest of the play?*

I thought thy bride-bed to have decked, sweet
   maid,
And not have strewed thy grave.

LAERTES   O treble woe
Fall ten times treble on that cursed head,   *HATRED of*
Whose wicked deed thy most ingenious sense   250 *HAMLET*
Deprived thee of! Hold off the earth awhile,
Till I have caught her once more in mine arms;
                      [*Leaps into the grave*

OUR SYMPATHY IS DISPULED

Now pile your dust upon the quick and dead,
Till of this flat a mountain you have made,
T'o'ertop old Pelion or the skyish head   255
Of blue Olympus.

HAMLET   [*Advancing*]   What is he whose grief   *HE HAS AS MUCH RIGHT*
Bears such an emphasis, whose phrase of sorrow *AS*
Conjures the wandering stars, and makes them *LAERTES TO*
   stand   *FEEL PAIN of*
Like wonder-wounded hearers? This is I,   *HER DEATH*
Hamlet the Dane.   260
                      [*Leaps into the grave*

ACTS AS LAERTES

LAERTES   The devil take thy soul.
                      [*Grapples with him*

HAMLET   Thou pray'st not well.   *THE*
I prithee take thy fingers from my throat,   *PRINCE*
For, though I am not splenitive and rash, *CELEBRATES HIS*
Yet have I something in me dangerous,   *EMANCIPATION*
Which let thy wisdom fear. Hold off thy hand.   265 *BY*

KING   Pluck them asunder.   *ANNOUNC-*

QUEEN   Hamlet, Hamlet!   *ING --*

ALL   Gentlemen, –

HORATIO   Good my lord, be quiet.
              [*The* ATTENDANTS *part them, and*
                    they come out of the grave

HAMLET   Why, I will fight with him upon this theme
Until my eyelids will no longer wag.

Hamlet challenges a brother's love for Ophelia with his own, which sounds extreme. The Queen explains this excess as one of his mad fits, giving him time to calm down and leave. At the King's request Horatio goes after Hamlet. Claudius reminds Laertes of their earlier talk and urges patience.

275 forbear him: leave him be
276 thou 't: thou wilt – you will
    woo't: wilt thou – will you
278 eisel: vinegar
284 the burning zone: the path of the sun between the tropics of Cancer and Capricorn
285 Ossa: another mountain in Thessaly. When, in Greek mythology the giants tried to climb into heaven, they piled Pelion (see note on line 255) on Ossa, in the hope of reaching high enough.
289 golden couplets are disclosed: the dove lays two eggs, out of which golden yellow chicks hatch
290 His silence...drooping: he will be quiet again with head bowed like the dove over her chicks
293 Let Hercules...day: *either*: 'even Hercules (a mythical Greek hero of great strength and cleverness) would not be able to stop you, cats and dogs must act according to their nature' *or*: whatever Laertes, in the pretended guise of a Hercules does, my day will come
297 present push: immediate action
299 living: lasting, enduring – possibly also a reference to the death of Hamlet, already arranged between them

> • *How did Hamlet treat Ophelia the last time he was with her? How can you square this with his declarations of love now?*

QUEEN	O my son, what theme?	270
HAMLET	I loved Ophelia, forty thousand brothers	*His love is better.*
	Could not, with all their quantity of love,	
	Make up my sum – what wilt thou do for her?	
KING	O he is mad, Laertes.	
QUEEN	For love of God forbear him.	275
HAMLET	'Swounds, show me what thou 't do.	
	Woo't weep, woo't fight, woo't fast, woo't tear	
	thyself?	
	Woo't drink up eisel, eat a crocodile?	
	I'll do't. Dost come here to whine,	
	To outface me with leaping in her grave?	280
	Be buried quick with her, and so will I.	
	And if thou prate of mountains, let them throw	
	Millions of acres on us, till our ground,	
	Singeing his pate against the burning zone,	
	Make Ossa like a wart. Nay an thou'lt mouth,	285
	I'll rant as well as thou.	
QUEEN	*Trying to protect her son* This is mere madness,	
	And thus awhile the fit will work on him;	*Madness will pass.*
	Anon as patient as the female dove	
	When that her golden couplets are disclosed,	
	His silence will sit drooping.	
HAMLET	Hear you sir,	290
	What is the reason that you use me thus?	
	I loved you ever – but it is no matter.	
	Let Hercules himself so what he may,	*Foreboding –*
	The cat will mew, and dog will have his day.	*Revenge will take place*
	[*Exit*	
KING	I pray thee, good Horatio, wait upon him.	295
	[*Exit* HORATIO	
	[*To Laertes*] Strengthen your patience in our last	
	night's speech,	
This is not the plan he has in store	We'll put the matter to the present push.	
	Good Gertrude, set some watch over your son.	
	This grave shall have a living monument.	*Reference to H.*

Alone with Horatio, Hamlet tells him about the events on board ship. Unable to sleep, Hamlet put on his coat and went to the cabin of Rosencrantz and Guildenstern. He found and took away their sealed instructions from Claudius. These, giving reasons of state and the danger of Hamlet's continued existence, ordered that he should be beheaded. Hamlet shows the commission to the astonished Horatio.

2 circumstance: details
6 mutines in the bilboes: mutineers in their chains
   bilbo: a long iron bar, with sliding shackles to confine the ankles of prisoners, and a lock by which one end of the bar could be fixed to the floor or the ground
   Rashly: suddenly (cf modern German 'rasch' – quickly, swiftly) or recklessly. Either 'on a sudden impulse' or 'recklessly' would fit here. He was after all going to burgle the cabin of his two gaolers while they were asleep.
7 let us know...pall: let us acknowledge that our impetuousity sometimes does us a good turn when the careful plots we have laid grow stale
9 learn: teach (cf modern French 'apprendre', which can mean either 'learn' or 'teach')
10 There's a divinity...how we will: there's a divine power which directs our destiny – however we may start shaping it ourselves
13 My sea-gown scarfed about me: my sea-going coat over my shoulders
15 Fingered: stole
   in fine: in conclusion
20 Larded: see note to Act 4 scene 5 line 36
21 Importing: concerning
22 bugs: bogeys, terrifying creatures
23 on the...bated: having read this, without delay ('*supervise*' is the Latin-based version of 'o'erlook')
24 stay: wait for

His plan will go ahead.

An hour of quiet shortly shall we see,   300
Till then in patience our proceeding be.   [*Exeunt*

Scene 2

Importance of scene (278)

Enter HAMLET and HORATIO

HAMLET	So much for this sir, now shall you see the other –
	You do remember all the circumstance?
HORATIO	Remember it my lord!
HAMLET	Sir, in my heart there was a kind of fighting,
	That would not let me sleep; methought I lay 5

Significant move for Hamlet

	Worse than the mutines in the bilboes. Rashly –
	And praised be rashness for it; let us know,
	Our indiscretion sometimes serves us well
	When our deep plots do pall: and that should
	learn us
	There's a divinity that shapes our ends, 10
	Rough-hew them how we will –

Now believes that rash acts turn out better.

HORATIO	That is most certain.
HAMLET	Up from my cabin,
	My sea-gown scarfed about me, in the dark
	Groped I to find out them, had my desire,
	Fingered their packet, and in fine withdrew 15
	To mine own room again; making so bold,
	My fears forgetting manners, to unseal
	Their grand commission; where I found, Horatio –
	O royal knavery – an exact command,
	Larded with many several sorts of reasons, 20
	Importing Denmark's health, and England's too,
	With ho, such bugs and goblins in my life,
	That on the supervise, no leisure bated,
	No not to stay the grinding of the axe,
	My head should be struck off.
HORATIO	Is 't possible? 25

Hamlet rewrote the commission from Claudius, with his minders as the victims, resealing the letter with his father's seal. The next day the pirates struck.

29 **be-netted round**: snared, trapped
30 **Ere...the play**: before I could instruct my brains about the prologue (a speech or poem used as an introduction to a play) they were working on the play itself
33 **statists**: statesmen
34 **A baseness**: beneath my dignity
36 **yeoman's**: a faithful servant's
38 **earnest conjuration**: solemn appeal
39 **tributary**: he paid him tribute (the Danegeld of Act 3 scene 1 line 173)
41 **wheaten garland**: peace traditionally wore a garland of full ears of wheat, to stand for the plenty she would bring
42 **And stand...amities**: just as the comma is the punctuation which offers least pause, so are their nations as close as can be, without being joined
43 **And...charge**: Hamlet has enjoyed writing in a style which he despises
   As'es: a possible pun on 'asses'
47 **Not shriving time allowed**: with no time allowed for confession and absolution
48 **even in that...ordinant**: even here Heaven directed the course of events
49 **signet**: a stone with his father's crest engraved on it, or the same, set in a ring. Seals were used to make an impression in soft sealing-wax across the join of a folded letter. This then hardened and it was clear (1) who the letter came from (2) that it had not been tampered with.
50 **the model of**: exactly like
52 **Subscribed**: signed
53 **changeling**: usually a baby or child substituted by the fairies for the human child they have stolen
56 **go to 't**: are going to their deaths

> • *Hamlet answers Horatio's implied reproach (l.56)*
> *with 'They are not near my conscience'. Why not?*

HAMLET ACTS QUICKLY

HAMLET	Here's the commission; read it at more leisure.
	But wilt thou hear now how I did proceed?
HORATIO	I beseech you.
HAMLET	Being thus be-netted round with villanies –
	Ere I could make a prologue to my brains, 30
	They had begun the play – I sat me down,
	Devised a new commission, wrote it fair –
	I once did hold it as our statists do,
	A baseness to write fair, and laboured much
	How to forget that learning, but, sir, now 35
	It did me yeoman's service – wilt thou know
	Th' effect of what I wrote?
HORATIO	Ay, good my lord.
HAMLET	An earnest conjuration from the King,
	As England was his faithful tributary,
	As love between them like the palm might
	flourish, 40
	As peace should still her wheaten garland wear
	And stand a comma 'tween their amities,
	And many such-like 'As'es' of great charge,
	That on the view and knowing of these contents,
	Without debatement further more or less, 45
	He should the bearers put to sudden death,
	Not shriving time allowed.
HORATIO	How was this sealed?
HAMLET	Why even in that was heaven ordinant.
	I had my father's signet in my purse,
	Which was the model of that Danish seal; 50
	Folded the writ up in form of th' other,
	Subscribed it, gave 't the impression, placed it
	safely,
	The changeling never known. Now the next day
	Was our sea-fight, and what to this was sequent
	Thou knowest already. 55
HORATIO	So Guildenstern and Rosencrantz go to 't.

HAMLET TELLS HORATIO HE USED HIS JOINENCE HIS COUNT AT SEA. DISCOVERING THE ORDER FOR HIS EXECUTION

HE SENT ORDER TO EXECUTE R+G WHICH HE SEALED WITH HIS FATHERS RING

FIRST BENEIT HE THIS ON JOINED A KING HIS FATHERS SON.

Horatio, shaken by proof of Claudius's attempt on Hamlet's life, points out that news will soon come from England of its failure. Hamlet regrets his behaviour with Laertes, now seeing similarities in their fate.

57 they did...employment: they were happy to be used

58 defeat: destruction, ruin

59 by their own insinuation grow: the fact that they insinuated themselves into the King's favour helped bring about their destruction

60 'Tis dangerous...baser nature: it is not a good idea for insignificant people to come between the angry sword thrusts of great opponents

63 Does it not...now upon: does it not now rest on me

65 Popped in...my hopes: come between the election (of the new king) and my hopes

66 Thrown out...proper life: cast his fishing line to catch my own life

67 cozenage: deception

68 quit: repay

69 canker: (here) cancer, disease
   come In: engage in, enter upon

73 interim: the period until that time

74 And a man's...say 'One': a man's life is over in the time it takes to count 'One'

77 by the image...his: Hamlet sees his state of mind and circumstances reflected in Laertes. They have both had a father murdered and have both lost Ophelia.

79 bravery: spectacular demonstration

82 water-fly: fly that hovers over water, without any obvious direction, or possibly the water-boatman, a fly that skates aimlessly around on the surface

84 gracious: blessed

> • *Hamlet seems to have reasoned himself into an acceptance that his conscience should also approve the killing of Claudius (lines 63-70). He is relying on Horatio for a reassuring answer. Does he get it?*

HAMLET	Why man, they did make love to this employment.
	They are not near my conscience, their defeat
	Does by their own insinuation grow.
	'Tis dangerous when the baser nature comes 60
	Between the pass and fell incensed points
	Of mighty opposites.

They brought it on themselves

| HORATIO | Why, what a King is this! |

HAMLET	Does it not, think thee, stand me now upon –
	He that hath killed my king, and whored my
	mother; *Sexual*
	Popped in between the election and my hopes, 65
	Thrown out his angle for my proper life,
	And with such cozenage – is 't not perfect
	conscience
	To quit him with this arm? And is 't not to be
	damned,
	To let this canker of our nature come
	In further evil? 70

Justification for revenge on Claudius

Inclination of Hamlet wanting to be next King

| HORATIO | It must be shortly known to him from England |
| | What is the issue of the business there. |

HAMLET	It will be short; the interim is mine,
	And a man's life's no more than to say 'One'.
	But I am very sorry, good Horatio, 75
	That to Laertes I forgot myself;
	For by the image of my cause, I see
	The portraiture of his; I'll court his favours.
	But sure the bravery of his grief did put me
	Into a towering passion.

Determined & focusing on destroying Claudius

| HORATIO | Peace, who comes here?   80 |

Enter OSRIC   *Provides light relief before ultimate tragedy & death.*

| OSRIC | Your lordship is right welcome back to Denmark. |

| HAMLET | I humbly thank you sir. Dost know this water-fly? |

| HORATIO | No my good lord. |

| HAMLET | Thy state is the more gracious, for 'tis a vice to |
| | know him. He hath much land, and fertile.   85 |

Osric, long-winded and affected, anxious to please, tells Hamlet of the wager Claudius has laid on a duel with Laertes. Hamlet finds Osric ridiculous and enjoys using similar language to him.

86 **Let a beast...mess**: as long as an animal owns many other animals, his manger will stand beside the King's table
   crib: the manger from which farm animals eat

87 **chough**: either a bird of the crow family, and therefore talkative or (usual spelling 'chuff') a boorish fellow. The word 'chuff' could also mean buttocks or arse.
   spacious in the possession of dirt: the bird would have plenty of dirt to scratch around in; the boor might boast of owning much land, or (see the note on 'chuff' above) 'talking a lot of shit'

92 **bonnet**: hat or cap

95 **indifferent**: fairly

97 **complexion**: constitution

103 **for my ease**: Osric politely insists on keeping his hat off

105 **excellent differences**: accomplishments quite out of the ordinary

106 **of very soft society**: well-mannered
   great showing: distinguished appearance

107 **card or calendar**: map or directory

108 **you shall find...would see**: he contains in himself all the attributes a gentleman could wish to find

110 **his definement**: the definition of the qualities you offer
   perdition: loss (cf modern French 'perdre'– to lose)

111 **to divide him inventorially**: to make a list (an inventory) of his qualities, one by one, to catalogue

112 **dozy**: make dizzy, confuse
   and yet...sail: it's no good going off at a tangent to try and get close to him because he is so far ahead
   yaw: divert from a straight course

113 **in the verity of extolment**: to speak truth in praising him

114 **of great article**: with many items

115 **his infusion...rareness**: his essence of such rare value

116 **as...true diction of him**: to speak the truth about
   his semblable...umbrage: the only one like him is his mirror image; only his shadow can follow at his heels

	Let a beast be lord of beasts, and his crib shall stand at the king's mess. 'Tis a chough, but as I say, spacious in the possession of dirt.
OSRIC	Sweet lord, if your lordship were at leisure, I should impart a thing to you from his majesty. 90
HAMLET	I will receive it sir, with all diligence of spirit. Put your bonnet to his right use, 'tis for the head.
OSRIC	I thank your lordship, it is very hot.
HAMLET	No believe me, 'tis very cold, the wind is northerly.
OSRIC	It is indifferent cold my lord, indeed. 95
HAMLET	But yet methinks it is very sultry, and hot for my complexion.
OSRIC	Exceedingly my lord, it is very sultry – as 'twere – I cannot tell how. But my lord, his majesty bade me signify to you that 'a has laid a great wager on 100 your head. Sir, this is the matter –
HAMLET	I beseech you remember –

[HAMLET *moves him to put on his hat*

| OSRIC | Nay good my lord, for my ease in good faith. Sir, here is newly come to court Laertes; believe me an absolute gentleman, full of most excellent 105 differences, of very soft society and great showing; indeed to speak feelingly of him, he is the card or calendar of gentry, for you shall find in him the continent of what part a gentleman would see. |
| HAMLET | Sir, his definement suffers no perdition in you, 110 though I know to divide him inventorially would dozy th' arithmetic of memory, and yet but yaw neither, in respect of his quick sail. But in the verity of extolment, I take him to be a soul of great article, and his infusion of such dearth and 115 rareness, as to make true diction of him, his semblable is his mirror, and who else would trace him, his umbrage, nothing more. |

deliberate complicated sentences

Hamlet showing how good he is at mocking Claudius' courtiers.

Osric seems rather taken aback by Hamlet's parodying of
him and in much briefer exchanges Hamlet learns what the
wager is – six Barbary horses against six French rapiers and
daggers and all the pieces of equipment belonging to them.

120 concernancy: how does this concern us?
  Why...breath?: why are we talking about this gentleman?
123 Is 't...sir really: is it not possible to understand in a
  different language? You will get there in the end.
125 nomination: naming
127 His purse...spent: taking Osric's *'golden words'* as coins
  in a purse – he has run out of currency
131 it would not much approve me: it would not say much
  for me
134 I dare not...himself: Hamlet suggests that to recognize
  excellence in another person, you must be capable of that
  excellence yourself – so in a sense you would be boasting
  of your own qualities
137 but...unfellowed: (with this punctuation) according to
  what those in his service say about him, he's unmatched;
  (with the comma after *'them'*) according to what they say
  about him, in excellence he is unmatched
140 Rapier and dagger: this was two-handed fighting, with
  the dagger (poniard) in the left hand warding off the
  opponent's rapier thrusts, while attempting to make hits
  with one's own rapier
142 Barbary: Arab
143 he has imponed: placed a bet
145 assigns: appurtenances, attachments
  girdle: sword-belt
  hangers: straps from which the rapier hung on the
  sword-belt
  and so: and so on
146 carriages: another word for 'hangers' based on the
  original sense of 'gun carriages'
  very dear to fancy...liberal conceit: matching the hilts,
  finely and imaginatively crafted
150 I knew...had done: I knew you'd need an explanation in
  the margin

OSRIC	Your lordship speaks most infallibly of him.
HAMLET	The concernancy sir? Why do we wrap the gentleman in our more rawer breath?
OSRIC	Sir?
HORATIO	Is 't not possible to understand in another tongue? You will do 't sir really.
HAMLET	What imports the nomination of this gentleman?
OSRIC	Of Laertes?
HORATIO	His purse is empty already, all's golden words are spent.
HAMLET	Of him sir.
OSRIC	I know you are not ignorant –
HAMLET	I would you did sir, yet in faith if you did, it would not much approve me. Well sir?
OSRIC	You are not ignorant of what excellence Laertes is –
HAMLET	I dare not confess that, lest I should compare with him in excellence; but, to know a man well, were to know himself.
OSRIC	I mean sir for his weapon, but in the imputation laid on him by them in his meed, he's unfellowed.
HAMLET	What's his weapon?
OSRIC	Rapier and dagger.
HAMLET	That's two of his weapons – but well.
OSRIC	The King sir, hath wagered with him six Barbary horses, against the which he has imponed, as I take it, six French rapiers and poniards, with their assigns, as girdle, hangers, and so. Three of the carriages in faith are very dear to fancy, very responsive to the hilts, most delicate carriages, and of very liberal conceit.
HAMLET	What call you the carriages?
HORATIO	I knew you must be edified by the margent ere you had done.

Line numbers: 120, 125, 130, 135, 140, 145, 150

Handwritten note: OSRIC GIVES DETAIL OF THE DUAL.

The wager is that in a duel of twelve bouts, Laertes will not
score three more hits than Hamlet. Hamlet replies that he
will win for the King if he can. Osric leaves to convey this
message to the King, and Hamlet and Horatio again amuse
themselves at his expense.

153 german: (or 'germane') relevant

154 cannon: a reference to note on line 146

160 The King...twelve for nine: a wager against Laertes
scoring more than three hits over Hamlet is easy to
understand – but the additional arithmetic in this speech
makes the details obscure. Of course, the King and
Laertes know that the match will never go the full length,
and Hamlet seems casually concerned merely to do
whatever is required of him.

169 breathing time: time for exercise

174 re-deliver you e'en so?: take this back as your answer?

175 after what...will: with whatever embellishment your
nature will allow

177 I commend...lordship: leave–taking phrase

179 commend: Hamlet chooses to take *'commend'* in the set
phrase as 'recommend' 'advocate' and goes on to say that
no one else is likely to do so.

181 This lapwing...its head: lapwings nest on the ground,
often in exposed positions and just a few hours after
hatching, the young are led away to safety. They are used
here as a *metaphor* (see GLOSSARY page 328) for young
people who are quick off the mark.

shell on his head: so recently hatched that a piece of shell
still sticks to its head

183 'A did...his dug: he used to flatter his mother's (or more
likely his wet-nurse's) teat

185 drossy age: frivolous times

got the tune of the time: only learnt to parrot the
prevailing tune. Hamlet is commenting on people like
Osric who take for themselves other people's thoughts
and opinions and ape their behaviour. When they are
really put to the test their trivial nature is revealed.

186 outward habit of encounter: external appearance of
behaviour

OSRIC	The carriages sir, are the hangers.
HAMLET	The phrase would be more german to the matter, if we could carry cannon by our sides; I would it might be hangers till then. But on – six 155 Barbary horses against six French swords, their assigns, and three liberal-conceited carriages; that's the French bet against the Danish. Why is this 'imponed', as you call it?
OSRIC	The King sir, hath laid sir, that in a dozen 160 passes between yourself and him, he shall not exceed you three hits; he hath laid on twelve for nine; and it would come to immediate trial, if your lordship would vouchsafe the answer.
HAMLET	How if I answer 'no'? 165
OSRIC	I mean, my lord, the opposition of your person in trial.
HAMLET	Sir, I will walk here in the hall. If it please his majesty, it is the breathing time of day with me; let the foils be brought, the gentleman willing, and 170 the King hold his purpose, I will win for him an I can; if not, I will gain nothing but my shame and the odd hits.
OSRIC	Shall I re-deliver you e'en so?
HAMLET	To this effect sir, after what flourish your 175 nature will.
OSRIC	I commend my duty to your lordship.
HAMLET	Yours, yours. [*Exit* OSRIC] He does well to commend it himself, there are no tongues else for 's turn. 180
HORATIO	This lapwing runs away with the shell on his head.
HAMLET	'A did comply with his dug, before 'a sucked it. Thus has he, and many more of the same breed that I know the drossy age dotes on, only got 185 the tune of the time, and outward habit of

(handwritten margin notes:) LAERTES VERSUS 3 +HITS ON HAMLET

(handwritten bottom notes:) PEOPLE LIKE OSRIC COPY OTHER PEOPLES OPINIONS (- + R+G, POLONIUS ETC)

A courtier comes to enquire whether Hamlet accepts the duel and to announce that the King and Queen and the court are coming down. Horatio warns Hamlet that he will lose the wager and Hamlet, although he thinks he can win, admits to some foreboding. Horatio offers to help him withdraw, but Hamlet insists that fate will take its course.

187 **yeasty collection**: superficial bunch – the image is of frothy bubbles of yeast once they start working

189 **winnowed**: sifted and sorted out
do but...trial: once they are put to the test – once you blow at the bubbles, they disappear

191 **commended him to you**: sent his compliments

196 **I...purposes**: I stand by what I say I'll do

197 **If...ready**: whatever time is convenient for him, it will be so for me

200 **In happy time**: at an appropriate moment

201 **use some gentle entertainment**: receive with courtesy

211 **gain-giving**: misgiving, ominous feeling

213 **forestall their repair hither**: stop their coming here

214 **we defy augury**: Hamlet rejects his feeling of foreboding. An *'augury'* is the interpretation of signs which seem to foretell what is to come.
there is...a sparrow: a reference to the *Bible* (*Matthew 10.29*). God has charge of everything that happens, so that even a sparrow's death is taken account of.

215 **it**: death. In these lines Hamlet sets out the inevitability of fate.

- *How would you describe Hamlet's mood at this stage?*
- *How does Shakespeare increase the tension before the duel?*

HE CONFESSES MISGIVINGS ABOUT THE CONTEST BUT REFUSES TO POSTPONE IT. DEATH COMES TO US ALL ALL THAT MATTERS IS BEING READY FOR IT.

encounter, a kind of yeasty collection, which carries
them through and through the most profound
and winnowed opinions; and do but blow them
to their trial, the bubbles are out.   190

Enter a LORD

LORD   My lord, his majesty commended him to you by
            young Osric, who brings back to him, that you
            attend him in the hall. He sends to know if your
            pleasure hold to play with Laertes, or that you will
            take longer time.   195

HAMLET   I am constant to my purposes. They follow the
            King's pleasure. If his fitness speaks, mine is ready;
            now or whensoever, provided I be so able as now.

LORD   The King and Queen and all are coming down.

HAMLET   In happy time.   200

LORD   The Queen desires you to use some gentle
            entertainment to Laertes before you fall to play.

HAMLET   She well instructs me.   [*Exit* LORD

HORATIO   You will lose this wager my lord.

HAMLET   I do not think so. Since he went into France,   205
            I have been in continual practice; I shall win at the
            odds. But thou wouldst not think how ill all 's
            here about my heart – but it is no matter.

HORATIO   Nay my good lord, –

HAMLET   It is but foolery, but it is such a kind of   210
            gain-giving as would perhaps trouble a woman.

HORATIO   If your mind dislike any thing, obey it. I will
            forestall their repair hither, and say you are not fit.

HAMLET   Not a whit, we defy augury; there is special
            providence in the fall of a sparrow. If it be now, 215
            'tis not to come; if it be not to come, it will be
            now; if it be not now, yet it will come – the

The audience, consisting of the King, Queen and court
enters with Laertes. The King gets Hamlet and Laertes to
shake hands and Hamlet excuses himself to Laertes for
killing Polonius, saying it was his madness. Laertes answers
politely.

218 readiness is all: the most important thing is to be
prepared
Since...betimes: since no one knows what life would have
held, if he'd lived, it is no hardship to die early
223 presence: those assembled here
225 a sore distraction: madness which is hard to bear
226 exception: dislike
229 If Hamlet...denies it: if Hamlet is not himself, because
he has lost his mind, and in this state wrongs Laertes,
then it is not really Hamlet who does the wrong and he
denies responsibility for it.
ta'en: taken
233 faction: party
236 Let my...evil: let my assertion that I meant no wrong
239 in nature: as far as my natural feelings go
240 Whose motive...revenge: and it is those which in the
present circumstance should most move me to revenge
241 in my...honour: as far as the question of honour goes
242 I stand...ungored: I will keep myself at a distance and
reject any reconciliation until from some elders, seen as
men of honour, I may have a judgement and precedent
for reconciliation to keep my name undamaged
247 And will not wrong it: Hamlet has not told Laertes how
Polonius came to die. Laertes is not being frank with
Hamlet now.

> • *Compare Hamlet's and Laertes's public reconciliation.*
> *Who is the more honest?*

THE APOLOGY MANY COMMENTATORS HAVE
BEEN UNHAPPY ABOUT THIS. HAMLET LAYS THE
BLAME ON HIS "MADNESS". WHICH WE KNOW
HAS BEEN A CONVENIENT FICTION. SHAKESPEARE
SURELY INTENDS HAMLET TO APPEAR SINCERE. THE TO
OF THE FINAL LINES IS MOVING IT IS THE REASON
WHICH IS UNSATISFACTORY.

ATMOSPHERE – MORE INTENSE –
FULL OF ANTICIPATION.

readiness is all. Since no man knows aught of what
he leaves, what is 't to leave betimes? Let be.

A table prepared, Trumpets, Drums, and OFFICERS
with Cushions. KING, QUEEN, *and all the state, foils,*
daggers, and LAERTES

KING

PROSE
END.

Come Hamlet, come and take this hand from
me.   220

[*The* KING *puts* LAERTES' *hand into* HAMLET'S

HAMLET

GENUINE
APOLOGY
TO
LAERTES

Give me your pardon sir, I've done you wrong;
But pardon 't as you are a gentleman.
This presence knows,
And you must needs have heard, how I am
    punished
With a sore distraction. What I have done   225
That might your nature, honour, and exception
Roughly awake, I here proclaim was madness.
Was 't Hamlet wronged Laertes? Never Hamlet.
If Hamlet from himself be ta'en away,
And when he's not himself does wrong Laertes, 230
Then Hamlet does it not, Hamlet denies it.   *WAS*
Who does it then? His madness. If 't be so,   *PASSION,*
Hamlet is of the faction that is wronged,   *FURY + RAGE.*
His madness is poor Hamlet's enemy.   *IN THIS WAY*
Sir, in this audience,   235
Let my disclaiming from a purposed evil   *HE ACTED*
Free me so far in your most generous thoughts,   *MADLY*
That I have shot my arrow o'er the house,
And hurt my brother.   *ACCIDENT – NOT WHAT*

IT WASN'T
HIM, IT WAS
HIS ANTIC
DISPOSITION.

LAERTES

GOES
SOME
EXTENT HE
CONCEDES
IT

                    I am satisfied in nature,   *HE*
Whose motive in this case should stir me most   240 *WANTED.*
To my revenge; but in my terms of honour
I stand aloof, and will no reconcilement
Till by some elder masters of known honour
I have a voice and precedent of peace,
To keep my name ungored. But till that time   245
I do receive your offered love like love,
And will not wrong it.   *THERE IS A CODE OF*
                          HONOUR AT STAKE.

SEE'S HE IS
GENUINE – CHANGE FOR
                DUEL.

IMPACT OF C. BEING ISOLATED AS THE SINGLE VILLA[IN]

Hamlet and Laertes seem reconciled for the moment, but Laertes is still very touchy. Osric fetches the foils and Laertes rejects the first one offered to him and chooses another. Hamlet is satisfied with his. The King orders goblets of wine to be set ready. At Hamlet's success the cannon shall sound, and he will drink to Hamlet's health and throw a rich pearl into Hamlet's cup. He orders the match to begin.

248 frankly: freely, with an open mind
250 foil: (here) setting for a jewel and a pun on the foils they will fight with
252 Stick fiery off: blaze out
256 laid the odds: laid your bet
258 but since...therefore odds: but since he is generally considered to be the better, we have the advantage of the handicap
262 stoups: drinking-vessels, cups, flaggons, tankards
264 Or quit...exchange: makes a convincing comeback in the third bout
266 better breath: staying power
267 union: rich pearl
270 kettle: kettledrum

HAMLET WHO HAS RETURNED TO DENMARK HAS A NEW STRENGTH. THE PROSE TO HORATIO IS CONCERNANT (CHANGE) HE NOW BECOMES AWARE OF HIS OWN SITUATION + THE WORLD. REACHED A NEW MORAL POSITION. SHAKESPEARE (Pg 27[ ] DOES THIS TO PREPARE US FOR THE GRIEF OF LOSING H. HE EXPRESSES HIS FAITH IN GOD, Pg 275. IMPORTANT THING IS BEING PREPARED FOR THE NEXT WORLD. SHAKESPEARE GENERATES GREAT PATHOS BY HAMLET NOT KNOWING (TOTAL INNOCENCE UNTIL LAERTES TELLS HIM) RATHER THAN HIM KNOWING + SWOPING THE SWORDS.
GERTRUDE IS RESTORED TO HAMLETS LOVING MOTHER BY DEFYING CLAUDIUS + DRINKING THE WINE. THIS ALLOWS CLAUDIUS TO BE ISOLATED AS SINGLE VILLAIN.
HORATIO'S FAREWELL EXPRESSES THE AUDIENCES FEELINGS. FORTINBRAS SPEECH GIVES THE TRAGEDY A DIGNIFIED END. COME FULL CIRCLE AS HE REGAINS THE LAND OLD HAMLET TOOK FROM HIS FATHER.

HAMLET	I embrace it freely, And will this brother's wager frankly play. Give us the foils. Come on.
LAERTES	Come, one for me.
HAMLET	I'll be your foil Laertes, in mine ignorance 250 Your skill shall like astar i' th' darkest night Stick fiery off indeed.
LAERTES	You mock me sir.
HAMLET	No by this hand.
KING	Give them the foils, young Osric. Cousin Hamlet, You know the wager?
HAMLET	Very well, my lord. 255 Your grace hath laid the odds a th' weaker side.
KING	I do not fear it, I have seen you both; But since he is bettered, we have therefore odds.
LAERTES	This is too heavy. Let me see another.
HAMLET	This likes me well. These foils have all a length? 260 *[They prepare to play*
OSRIC	Ay my good lord.
KING	Set me the stoups of wine upon that table. If Hamlet give the first or second hit, Or quit in answer of the third exchange, Let all the battlements their ordnance fire. 265 The King shall drink to Hamlet's better breath, And in the cup an union shall he throw, Richer than that which four successive kings In Denmark's crown have worn. Give me the cups, And let the kettle to the trumpet speak, 270 The trumpet to the cannoneer without, The cannons to the heavens, the heaven to earth, 'Now the King drinks to Hamlet'. Come, begin; And you the judges bear a wary eye. *[Trumpets the while*
HAMLET	Come on sir. 275

(Handwritten annotations:)

ORIC VERBAI ATTECTION + MISPRISIONS SPARK HAMLET INTO HIS WITTIEST MOMEMENTS

IRONY - CLAUDIUS KILLS HIS WIFE LAERTES IS STRUCK WITH POISONED SWORD.

Hamlet scores two hits and at the second the trumpets give
the signal for the cannons to sound. The King drinks to
Hamlet, at the same time putting the pearl in a cup and
offering it to Hamlet, who refuses to drink yet. Gertrude
drinks to Hamlet from this poisoned cup before Claudius
can stop her. Laertes is about to wound Hamlet – though his
conscience protests. Hamlet challenges him to play more
decisively.

280 palpable: evident, obvious
287 fat: sweaty *or* out of condition. From internal evidence –
  'take my napkin, rub thy brows' the former seems more
  likely. Also Hamlet has claimed (line 206) that he has
  been practising.
288 napkin: handkerchief
289 carouses: drinks a health
297 you but dally: you are only playing about
298 pass: thrust
299 you make a wanton of me: you are treating me like a
  spoilt child
302 Have at you now! : the challenge preceding a fresh
  thrust

- *Why is Claudius unable to prevent Gertrude drinking
  from the poisoned cup? How would you stage this?*
- *Is Laertes having second thoughts?*

THE DRAMATIC QUALITIES OF THE FENCING
MATCH ARE NOT APPARENT. TAKES A FEW
SECONDS TO READ WHILST SEVERAL SECONDS ON
STAGE.
SOME PRODUCTIONS SHOW HAMLET REALISING
HE HAS BEEN WOUNDED + DELIBERATELY
CHANGING FOILS. THIS IS NOT SUPPORTED
BY THE TEXT WHICH SHOWS LAERTES HAMLET
TOTALLY INNOCENT, UNTILL LAERTES TELLS
HIM.

LAERTES	Come my lord.	[*They play*
HAMLET	One.	
LAERTES	No.	
HAMLET	Judgment.	
OSRIC	A hit, a very palpable hit.	280
LAERTES	Well, again.	
KING	Stay, give me drink. Hamlet, this pearl is thine, Here's to thy health.	

[*Trumpets sound, and cannon shot off within*
Give him the cup.

HAMLET	I'll play this bout first, set it by awhile. Come – another hit. What say you?	285
LAERTES	A touch, a touch, I do confess 't.	
KING	Our son shall win.	
QUEEN	He's fat and scant of breath. Here Hamlet, take my napkin, rub thy brows. The Queen carouses to thy fortune, Hamlet.	
HAMLET	Good madam.	
KING	Gertrude do not drink.	290
QUEEN	I will my lord, I pray you pardon me.	
KING	[*Aside*] It is the poisoned cup; it is too late.	
HAMLET	I dare not drink yet madam – by and by.	
QUEEN	Come, let me wipe thy face.	
LAERTES	My lord, I'll hit him now.	
KING	I do not think 't.	295
LAERTES	[*Aside*] And yet 'tis almost against my conscience.	
HAMLET	Come, for the third Laertes, you but dally. I pray you pass with your best violence; I am afeared you make a wanton of me.	
LAERTES	Say you so, come on.	[*They play* 300
OSRIC	Nothing neither way.	
LAERTES	Have at you now!	

Laertes wounds Hamlet and in the ensuing scuffle they exchange rapiers and Laertes is hurt with the poisoned foil. The Queen dies, a victim of the poisoned wine she has drunk. Hamlet orders the doors to be locked and the perpetrator found. Laertes confesses to the poisoned rapier and blames the King for Gertrude's death. Having learnt about the poisoned weapon, Hamlet stabs the King and then forces him to drink the poison. Claudius dies. Laertes suggests that he and Hamlet forgive one another.

303 incensed: furiously angry

308 as a...springe: like a woodcock caught in my own snare

310 swounds: faints

319 envenomed: poisoned

323 The point envenomed too!: Hamlet has already learnt the foil is unbated, since he has been wounded

325 Treason, treason!: anyone laying hand on the King would be guilty of treason. Of those present (and still alive) only Hamlet and Horatio know the whole story of the King's wickedness; Laertes knows only the latest manifestation of it. Of these three, two are as good as dead.

328 union: double meaning – the pearl/poison capsule and the 'incestuous' and ill–fated union with his mother

330 tempered: compounded, mixed

> • *With the deaths of the main characters achieved or imminent, a different concern will take centre stage, triggered by the bystanders' cry of 'Treason'. What is it?*

✗ STRENGTHS

THE TRUTH PREVAILS.

HAMLET BELIEVES DEATH COMES TO US ALL
IT'S BEING READY FOR IT WHAT COUNTS.

CHAIN REACTION OF EVIL PRODUCING EVIL

[LAERTES *wounds* HAMLET; *then, in scuffling, they
change rapiers, and* HAMLET *wounds* LAERTES

KING	Part them, they are incensed.
HAMLET	Nay come, again. [*The* QUEEN *falls*
OSRIC	Look to the Queen there, ho! 305
HORATIO	They bleed on both sides. How is it my lord?
OSRIC	How is 't Laertes?
LAERTES	Why as a woodcock to mine own springe, Osric.
	I am justly killed with mine own treachery.
HAMLET	How does the Queen?
KING	She swounds to see them
	bleed. 310
QUEEN	No, no, the drink, the drink – o my dear Hamlet –
	The drink, the drink! I am poisoned. [*Dies*
HAMLET	O villany! Ho, let the door be locked. Treachery!
	Seek it out.
LAERTES	It is here, Hamlet. Hamlet, thou art slain. 315
	No medicine in the world can do thee good,
	In thee there is not half an hour of life.
	The treacherous instrument is in thy hand, *INEVITABLE*
	Unbated and envenomed. The foul practice *CONSEQUENCE*
	Hath turned itself on me; lo here I lie, 320 *OF*
	Never to rise again. Thy mother's poisoned – *EVIL*
	I can no more – the King, the King's to blame.
HAMLET	The point envenomed too!
	Then, venom, to thy work. [*Stabs the* KING
ALL	Treason, treason! 325
KING	O yet defend me friends, I am but hurt.
HAMLET	Here, thou incestuous, murderous, damned Dane,
	Drink off this potion. Is thy union here?
	Follow my mother. [KING *dies*
LAERTES	He is justly served,
	It is a poison tempered by himself. 330
	Exchange forgiveness with me noble Hamlet.

Laertes dies as he expresses the hope of mutual forgiveness, which Hamlet grants, as he asks Horatio to report the true motives behind these deaths. Horatio protests that he will follow Hamlet into death by drinking the remaining poison. Hamlet begs him to restore honour to his name by telling the true story. There are sounds of an army approaching. Fortinbras is coming. Hamlet is dying but gives Fortinbras his vote in the election to King of Denmark.

337 mutes: characters in a play without speaking parts. Hamlet has shown before that he considers he could be an actor. Now that his revenge has come out of the darkness of his troubled thoughts and has been enacted before the whole court, it must seem as real/unreal to him as if it were a play. He also now needs Horatio to perform the functions of chorus (see note Act 3 scene 2 line 245) and epilogue (a speech or short poem delivered by one of the actors to the spectators after a play is over).

338 fell: cruel

sergeant: sheriff's officer; an officer of the court with powers of arrest

342 the unsatisfied: those who need a satisfactory explanation of Hamlet's strange conduct

343 more an antique Roman: more inclined to regard suicide in such a case as a noble act, worthy of admiration, rather than inviting shame and damnation

349 Absent thee from felicity awhile: put off for a while the happiness death brings

355 o'er-crows: triumphs over, crows over – as the winning cock in a cockfight

359 th' occurrents more or less: all the happenings, important and unimportant

---

- *What is it that persuades Horatio not to follow Hamlet immediately into death?*
- *Why, in spite of all his previous reservations about death, does Hamlet now call it 'felicity'?*

IT WAS CLAUDIUS' NOT THEIR FAULT

Mine and my father's death come not upon thee,
Nor thine on me.   [*Dies*

HAMLET   Heaven make thee free of it. I follow thee.
            I am dead, Horatio. Wretched Queen, adieu.   335
            You that look pale and tremble at this chance,
            That are but mutes or audience to this act,
            Had I but time, as this fell sergeant death
            Is strict in his arrest, o I could tell you –
            But let it be. Horatio, I am dead,   340
            Thou livest; report me and my cause aright
            To the unsatisfied.

HORATIO   Never believe it;
            I am more an antique Roman than a Dane.
            Here's yet some liquor left.

HAMLET   As thou 'rt a man,
            Give me the cup – let go, by heaven I'll ha't.   345
            O God, Horatio, what a wounded name,
            Things standing thus unknown, shall leave
                behind me!
            If thou didst ever hold me in thy heart,
            Absent thee from felicity awhile,
            And in this harsh world draw thy breath in pain, 350
            To tell my story.   [*March afar off, and shot within*
                              What warlike noise is this?

            Enter OSRIC

OSRIC   Young Fortinbras, with conquest come from
                Poland,
            To th' ambassadors of England gives
            This warlike volley.

HAMLET   O I die Horatio,
            The potent poison quite o'er-crows my spirit.   355
            I cannot live to hear the news from England,
            But I do prophesy the election lights
            On Fortinbras, he has my dying voice;
            So tell him, with th' occurrents more and less

LAERTES + HAMLET EACH FORGIVE EACH OTHER

BEGS HORATIO NOT TO COMMIT SUICIDE AS HE MUST TELL THE STORY.

CONCERNED FOR HIS HONOUR

HE WANTS HORATIO TO TELL HAMLETS STORY SO HE DOESN'T LOOK BAD.

Hamlet dies. Fortinbras, accompanied by martial music and the English ambassadors, enters. He has heard of the deaths. The English ambassadors expect thanks for achieving the deaths of Rosencrantz and Guildenstern and learn that it was not Claudius who gave the order. Horatio asks for the bodies to be placed on view while he tells the assembled company the background to what has happened.

360 have solicited: have caused (this result)

366 quarry: heap of the dead – normally the 'bag' after a hunt
havoc: originally in the call 'Havoc!' an incitement to a victorious army to pillage. Here, wholesale destruction or slaughter.

367 feast: the idea that Death will feast on the dead bodies
toward: being planned
eternal: sometimes used, as here, for 'infernal', 'damned'

377 jump: immediately
question: strife

383 Of carnal...inventors' heads: this is a catalogue, a trail, for the story Hamlet has asked Horatio to tell. While many of the items in the list can be applied to more than one death, some of the applications may be as follows: *'carnal'* refers to the 'incestuous' marriage, which was itself possibly one of the motives for the *'unnatural'* killing of a brother; *'accidental judgments'* – sentences apparently carried out by accident, as that on Gertrude; *'casual slaughters'* – chance killings – Polonius and possibly Ophelia, Laertes; deaths *'put on by cunning and forced cause'* – Hamlet's intended execution in England and the actual deaths there of Rosencrantz and Guildenstern, and Hamlet's own death.

385 put on: set up
forced cause: contrivance

386 in this upshot: in this event – the upshot was the final shot in an archery match
purposes mistook...heads: methods of carrying out their intentions which misfired and destroyed those who had thought them up

Which have solicited. The rest is silence.   360

[*Dies*

HORATIO   Now cracks a noble heart. Good night sweet
              prince,
            And flights of angels sing thee to thy rest.
            Why does the drum come hither?

Enter FORTINBRAS *with Drum and colours, the*
ENGLISH AMBASSADORS, *and others*

FORTINBRAS Where is this sight?

HORATIO   What is it ye would see?
            If aught of woe or wonder, cease your search.   365

FORTINBRAS This quarry cries on havoc. O proud death,
            What feast is toward in thine eternal cell,
            That thou so many princes at a shot
            So bloodily hast struck?

FIRST
AMBASSADOR   The sight is dismal,
            And our affairs from England come too late.   370
            The ears are senseless that should give us hearing,
            To tell him his commandment is fulfilled,
            That Rosencrantz and Guildenstern are dead.
            Where should we have our thanks?

HORATIO   Not from his mouth
            Had it th' ability of life to thank you;   375
            He never gave commandment for their death.
            But since, so jump upon this bloody question,
            You from the Polack wars, and you from England,
            Are here arrived, give order that these bodies
            High on a stage be placed to the view,   380
            And let me speak to the yet unknowing world
            How these things came about; so shall you hear
            Of carnal, bloody, and unnatural acts,
            Of accidental judgments, casual slaughters,
            Of deaths put on by cunning and forced cause,   385
            And, in this upshot, purposes mistook

HE HAS GRASPED NOT ONLY HIS OWN SITUATION BUT ALSO OF THE UNIVERSE IN WHICH HE OPERATES.

Horatio finishes sketching out what he will have to tell and Fortinbras takes control, while Horatio points out that Fortinbras has Hamlet's vote, which will attract that of others. Fortinbras orders Hamlet's body to be placed by four captains on a raised platform and speaks of the potential he seemed to have as the future king. The other bodies too are carried up, and cannons are fired.

391 rights of memory: possibly a reference to the claims of Fortinbras in Act 1 scene 1, which were threatening to cause a war

392 my vantage: the advantage I now have

394 whose voice will draw on more: Hamlet's dying declaration for the election of Fortinbras will influence others

396 wild: in disarray

397 On: on top of

399 had he been put on: ie if he had been made king

400 passage: passing from this world

401 rite of war: martial ceremonies

404 Becomes the field: is fitting for the battlefield

- *'Something is rotten in the state of Denmark'. Has this rottenness now been purged, in preparation for a fresh start?*
- *What might Hamlet's dying hopes for Denmark have been in his choice of Fortinbras for king?*

- *Estimate the importance of Horatio's role in the play.*
- *Fortinbras makes a judgement about Hamlet's potential as king. What is yours?*

+ HAMLET HAD NO MISGIVINGS ABOUT SENDING 2 MEN TO DEATH, SINCE THEY MADE ACE TO THIS ENTRAPMENT.

HIS FORWARD NOW BECAME CLEAR + HIS SCRUPLES ABOUT KILLING, C. ARE GONE. NOW MATTER OF OPPORTUNITY "THE INTERIMS MINE"

Fall'n on the inventors' heads. All this can I
Truly deliver.

FORTINBRAS   Let us haste to hear it,
And call the noblest to the audience.
For me, with sorrow I embrace my fortune.   390
I have some rights of memory in this kingdom,
Which now to claim my vantage doth invite me.

HORATIO   Of that I shall have also cause to speak,
And from his mouth whose voice will draw on
    more.
But let this same be presently performed,   395
Even while men's minds are wild, lest more
    mischance
On plots and errors happen.

FORTINBRAS   Let four captains
Bear Hamlet like a soldier to the stage,
For he was likely, had he been put on,
To have proved most royal: and for his passage,   400
The soldiers' music and the rite of war
Speak loudly for him.
Take up the bodies – such a sight as this
Becomes the field, but here shows much amiss.
Go bid the soldiers shoot.   405
    [*Exeunt marching, after which a peal of ordnance is*
                                              shot off

Handwritten annotations:

(left margin, beside line 398): HE REPRESENTS NATURAL ORDER OF DENMARK BEING RESTORED

(right margin, beside lines 397–404): HE IS THE FUTURE OF DENM- ARK / STATE FUNERAL ETC. / HOW SIGNIFICANT HE IS, HIS HONOUR.

(bottom): CONTRAST WITH HIM, HAMLET, LAERTES. OUTSIDE BREAKING THROUGH TO INSIDE WORLD.

ACTIVITIES

Keeping track

Scene 1

1 The scene begins with the 'humorous' discussion between the grave-diggers on the subject of whether or not Ophelia is entitled to a 'Christian burial'. What is the attitude of the grave-diggers to the death of Ophelia?

2 Why do you think Shakespeare introduces these 'comic' figures? Is it simply a matter of 'light relief'?

3 What is Hamlet's reaction to the grave-diggers' behaviour as he and Horatio enter?

4 As the skulls are casually thrown out of the ground, Hamlet is forced to confront the stark reality of death. What are his thoughts and feelings at this point?

5 What is Hamlet's reaction to the discovery that the skull is that of Yorick?

6 Hamlet observes the *'maimed rites'* which accompany the funeral of Ophelia. How does Laertes respond to the lack of ceremony? What explanation does the priest give?

7 Why does Hamlet disrupt the funeral?

8 How do Gertrude and Claudius react?

Scene 2

1 What are Hamlet and Horatio discussing as the scene opens?

2 What do we learn of Claudius's plot against Hamlet's life?

3 Hamlet says, *'There's a divinity that shapes our ends'*. Is this an important line: has Hamlet changed?

4 What has happened to Rosencrantz and Guildenstern and how does Hamlet feel about it?

5 What reasons does Hamlet give for arguing that it would be *'perfect conscience'* to kill Claudius?

6 How does Hamlet treat Osric when he arrives, and why does he behave like this?

7 Why do you think Hamlet is so willing to accept the challenge proposed by Claudius?

8 How does Hamlet behave towards Laertes when he appears?

9 What exactly happens in the duel?

10 How is Gertrude killed, and how does Hamlet react to her death?

11 What finally pushes Hamlet to kill Claudius?

12 What news do the ambassadors bring from England?
13 How does Fortinbras respond to Hamlet's death?

Drama

1 Consider the arrival of the funeral party at the graveside. Using members of the class, arrange the characters as if they were in a photograph. (See PHOTOGRAPHS on page 298.) Concentrate on the line 'What ceremony else?'

How do the different people feel about the death of Ophelia? Examine the arguments put forward by the two grave-diggers earlier in the scene to see how complicated the issue of suicide was for Elizabethans. How does this argument impinge on the various characters present? Is Claudius bothered? What effect has it had on Laertes? Has Gertrude considered taking her own life?

When you have arranged the photograph ask each character to say aloud what they are thinking. Consider what difference there might be between the thoughts they might share with others and their innermost thoughts.

2 Use FORUM THEATRE (see page 299) to explore the moment when Hamlet leaps into the grave 'This is I, Hamlet the Dane.' How does everyone react to such a sacrilegious act?

3 Osric
   • Osric is an example of Shakespeare's skill in producing humour at the blackest moments. As costume and prop designers, how would you deal with this character? Create some designs and ask one of your group to act as a model so that you can develop some mannerisms as well.
   • In threes, improvise Osric reporting back to Claudius and Laertes after his encounter with Hamlet and Horatio. Does he keep up the pretentious manner or is it just an act? What is he really like? How does he feel about his treatment by Hamlet?

4 After the tragedy
   • Hold a series of television news conferences with the survivors – including Horatio, Osric, attendants, grave-diggers and Fortinbras.
   • Produce a variety of articles and reports written in different styles. This could include Horatio's statement to the police, the post-mortem documents, newspaper headlines and obituaries.

Key elements

In Act 5 these are:
• the graveyard scene
• the duel scene.

Key Scene

The duel scene: Act 5 scene 2 lines 262–363

Keying it in

This scene is the violent climax of the play.
- How does Hamlet behave to Laertes as they prepare for their duel?
- How does he try to excuse his past actions?
- How does Laertes respond to Hamlet's apology?
- Is he sincere?
- Is Hamlet a guilty man at this stage of the play?

The scene itself

1 As Hamlet and Laertes prepare to play, Claudius asks for wine to be put on the table.
   - What appearance is Claudius trying to give here?
   - What are his real hopes and intentions?
2 Hamlet wins the first bout of fencing.
   - How does Claudius react to this?
   - Why does Gertrude drink from the poisoned cup?
   - Why is Claudius unable to prevent her from drinking?
3 The fight becomes more intense and both Hamlet and Laertes are wounded with the poisoned rapier.
   - Why do you think Laertes says he is 'justly killed'?
   - Do you agree with him?
   - Does the fate of Laertes affect your response to Hamlet himself?
4 Laertes condemns Claudius for the deaths of himself, Hamlet and Gertrude.
   - What do you think is the importance of this public accusation?
   - How does Hamlet react?
   - What does he achieve in this moment of violence? Is it revenge or justice? Look at Laertes's dying words.
5 Horatio pays tribute to the dead prince (lines 361–363).
   - How do you react to his words?
   - Do you agree with his sentiments?

Close study

Act 5 scene 1 lines 186–219
- What was Hamlet's relationship with Yorick?
- How does he react to the realization that this is Yorick's skull?
- What effect does this have on Hamlet?
- How does the language of these lines stress the horror of death?
- What conclusions does Hamlet draw from what he has just seen?
- How would you describe his feelings and attitudes?

Hamlet and revenge

In Act 5, Hamlet is drawn into the conspiracy planned by Claudius and Laertes. It is interesting to note that Hamlet himself makes no active attempt to plot against the life of Claudius.

In the graveyard scene, Hamlet is brought face to face with the gruesome realities of death. At first, he seems to feel a mixture of shock, horror and revulsion and yet, also, a kind of grim satisfaction in the recognition that all is vanity, and that the pretensions of human existence simply end in the grave. However, death is made unbearable by the sight of Ophelia's body, and Hamlet is forced to abandon the theory in favour of a passionate, but tragically belated, declaration of love.

After the graveyard scene he does seem calmer, more at peace with himself. He seems more prepared to accept that there is *a divinity that shapes our ends*' and less frantic in his pursuit of revenge. Perhaps the assertion of love for Ophelia has purged some of the *'evil'* from his consciousness. Whether his mood is now one of spiritual enlightenment, fatalism or weary resignation is not easy to determine, but Hamlet seems to come to terms with death and the possibility of death. As he says – *'the readiness is all'*.

In the duel scene, Hamlet achieves his revenge, but it is at a terrible cost and it is the result of unpremeditated action. It is perhaps worth asking the question: when Hamlet does finally kill Claudius, whom exactly is he avenging?

When he kills Claudius it is not a secret murder and it perhaps looks more like an act of public justice than private revenge.

Assignments

Essays

1 Look at the graveyard scene. What is the dramatic significance of this scene?
2 Some critics have observed that Hamlet is a changed man in Act 5. How far do you agree with this observation?
3 Do you think that the duel scene brings the play to a satisfactory conclusion?

POLONIUS,

ACT 1-3 MANY DRAMATIC PURPOSES, ACT 5 TAKEN OUT BY OSR

DESIRE TO SERVE KING,

FOR OWN VANINITY + IMPORTANCE.

LIKE GHOST, DEMANDS OBEDIENCE FROM KIDS.

AUTHORITARIAN.

"FISHMONGER" PIMP.

NO INTEREST IN KIDS VIEW.

GIVE LAERTES "LEAVE TO GO".

BLESSING + MORAL INSTRUCTIONS.

LATER SENDS A SPY TO PARIS.

INITIATES SURVEILLENCE.

EAVESDROPPING COSTS HIM HIS LIFE.

COMIC → GETS LOST IN TEDIOUS ELABORATIONS.

FIRST SPEECH (19)

SIMILAR TO HAMLET.

P IS LIKE H GONE SENILE.

Explorations

A question of approach

When you study a play, you need to be able to see it from two different perspectives simultaneously. You need to be able to imagine and experience the text line by line, sharing the thoughts and feelings of the characters as they go through the events of the play, but at the same time you need to be able to 'look down on' the play as a whole and see the patterns of character and relationship, of language and imagery, of themes and issues.

A play is essentially an audio-visual experience. No two members of the audience see quite the same 'play' and no two performances are ever exactly the same. Two important lessons should be learned from this. The first is that the printed text is not the play; the play is what you see when you go to the theatre. The text is a set of instructions to be interpreted by the director and the actors, artists and technicians. The second lesson is that there is no one 'right answer' to the play, only a range of possible interpretations. Your view can be just as valid as any one else's, but only if you can present it clearly and support it by valid arguments derived from the text. For this purpose you need, again, to see it as a whole and as a set of details.

Thinking about the play

By the time you have discussed the text carefully you should be beginning to clarify and organize your response to the play as a whole. Most examination questions concentrate on content and form, and these are useful terms which offer you an approach and a framework within which you can prepare to write successfully.

Your first task is to establish clearly in your mind the broad issues raised by the text and the possible areas for discussion, including major characters. You need to consider and discuss some of the possible views and interpretations of these issues and lay down a sensible framework within which personal response can be convincing and well–considered. You also need to get close to the text and identify the key incidents, scenes or even quotations which will form the basis of any essay. When you come to write essays on the whole text, or even a specified passage, the appropriate textual evidence and illustrations should be noted and easily available.

Drama activities

Most of these activities can be done in small groups or by the class as a whole. They work by slowing down the action of the play and helping you focus on a small section of it – so that you can think more deeply about characters, plot and themes.

Hotseating

Hotseating means putting one of the characters 'under the microscope' at a particular point in the play. This is how it works.

1 Begin by choosing a particular character and a particular moment in the play. For example you might choose Ophelia after Polonius has given her his lecture.
2 One person (student or teacher) is selected to be the chosen character.
3 That person sits 'in the hotseat', with the rest of the group arranged round in a semi-circle, or a circle.
4 The rest then ask questions about how the character feels, why s/he has acted in that way, and so on. Try to keep the questions going and not to give the person in the hotseat too much time to think.

Variations

1 The questioners themselves take on roles. (In the example above they could be Laertes, Gertrude, and Hamlet.)
2 Characters can be hotseated at a series of key moments in a scene to see how their opinions and attitudes change.
3 The questioners can take different attitudes to the character, for example:
   • aggressive
   • sympathetic
   • disbelieving.

Freeze!

It is very useful to 'stop the action' and concentrate on a single moment in the play. You can do this in a number of ways.

Photographs

Imagine that someone has taken a photograph of a particular moment (eg just as Hamlet and Laertes have exchanged blows with the poisoned foil), or that – as if it were a film or video – the action has been frozen. Once you have chosen the moment, you can work in a number of different ways.

- Act that part of the scene and then 'Freeze!' – you will probably find it easier if you have a 'director' standing outside the scene to shout 'Freeze!'
- Discuss what the photograph should look like and then arrange yourselves into the photograph.
- One at a time, place yourselves in the photograph; each person 'entering' it must take notice of what is there already.
- Once you have arranged the photograph, take it in turns to come out of it and comment on it, with suggestions for improvements.

There are a number of ways in which you can develop your photograph:

- Each person takes it in turn to speak his/her thoughts at that moment in the scene.
- The photograph is given a caption.
- Some members of the group do not take part in the photograph. Instead they provide a sound track of speech or sound effects, or both.

Statues/Paintings

Make a statue or a painting like this.

1 Select a moment in the play, or a title from the play (eg '*I'll cross it though it blast me.*').

2 Choose one member of the group to be the sculptor/painter. That person then arranges the rest of the group, one at a time, to make the statue or painting. Statues and paintings are different from photographs in two important ways:
   • they are made up by an 'artist' and tell us about the artist's view of the person or event
   • if they talk, they tell us about what they can 'see', for example how people react when they see the statue or painting for the first time.

Forum theatre

In FORUM THEATRE, one or two people take on roles and the rest of the group are 'directors'. It works like this.
1 Select a moment in the play. (For example, the moment when Claudius rises and leaves the play.)
2 Select a member of the group to be Claudius.
3 Organize your working area, so that everyone knows where the other characters are, where characters make entrances and exits, and so on.
4 Begin by asking Claudius to offer his own first thoughts about position, gesture, and movement.
5 The directors then experiment with different ways of presenting that moment. They can:
   • ask Claudius to take up a particular position, use a particular gesture, move in a certain way
   • ask him to speak in a particular way
   • discuss with Claudius how he might move or speak and why – for example, to communicate a certain set of thoughts and feelings.
6 The short sequence can be repeated a number of times, until the directors have used up all their ideas about their interpretation.

Character

Questions about character are common in A-level examinations, although they very rarely invite a simple 'character-sketch'. Usually you will be asked to explore the 'importance' or 'dramatic function' of a character or to give your personal evaluation and response.

Judging a character is not simply a matter of accumulating the evidence of the written word and drawing conclusions. It is more complicated, and requires some selection and evaluation to allow you to reach a coherent response to the character.

The evidence 1

Characters are revealed by:
- what they say
- what they do.

Problems

1 Unfortunately (for examination purposes) characters are not always consistent. Major characters are subject to change because the events on which the action is based are significant enough to affect the main protagonists: the more important the character, the closer to the action and the greater the reaction to events.

   You must always be aware of how, and why, characters are developing and be prepared to explain and trace the changes.

2 Characters might say or do things for effect. They might be seeking to impress or mislead someone else and not mean what they say at all.

   You must always consider whether the character is being sincere or if s/he has an ulterior motive.

The evidence 2

Characters are also revealed by:
- what others say about them
- how others behave towards them.

Problems

As in life, whether you accept A's opinion of B depends on how you feel about A. If you believe that A is untrustworthy or has a perverted sense of justice, then A's criticism of B might be interpreted as a glowing character reference! Alternatively, an opinion might be based on false information or might be deliberately misleading.

It is essential that you do not simply accept one character's opinion of another at face value.

The evidence 3

Characters are also revealed by:
- soliloquies
- asides.

These are often the most reliable evidence on which to assess a character since s/he is sharing his/her thoughts with the audience. All pretence is dropped because the soliloquy and the aside are devices which allow characters to express their thoughts and feelings directly, and solely, to the audience.

Critical moments

At critical moments in the play you can begin to gain a better insight into a character by seeking answers to certain questions. Sadly, there is no formula which will apply to every situation, but you need to identify the key scenes and speeches which relate to a particular character and then ask these questions to start you off and perhaps prompt questions of your own.
- What has the character said or done here?
- Why has the character said or done this?
- What will happen as a result of this speech or action?
- How do you feel about the consequences of this speech or action?
- What does this incident tell us about the character?
- How does the character change or develop as a result of it?

The CRITICAL MOMENTS' approach can be used to highlight key points in the development of a character. For example, it is possible to do this with Hamlet himself.

1   Ophelia refers to Hamlet before the drama itself, to the young man she loved whom we never see:
    '*Th' expectancy and rose of the fair state*'
    (Act 3 scene 1)

2   However, our first glimpse of the prince reveals bitterness and hostility:
    '*A little more than kin, and less than kind.*'
    (Act 1 scene 2)
    '*I have that within which passes show*'
    (Act 1 scene 2)

3   In soliloquy, Hamlet reveals profound despair and disillusion:
    '*How weary, stale and unprofitable*
    Seem to me all the uses of this world!'
    (Act 1 scene 2)

4   He denounces his mother, and women in general:
    '*O most wicked speed, to post*
    With such dexterity to incestuous sheets.'
    '*frailty, thy name is woman.*'
    (Act 1 scene 2)

5   The Ghost's revelations produce a surge of passion and violence, as Hamlet is called upon to take action in the name of revenge:
    '*Haste me to know't, that I with wings as swift*
    As meditation or the thoughts of love,
    May sweep to my revenge.'
    (Act 1 scene 5)

6   However, there are signs of misgivings or self-doubt:
    '*And shall I couple hell?*'
    '*O cursed spite,*
    That ever I was born to set it right.'
    (Act 1 scene 5)

7 Hamlet then finds himself baffled, confused and distracted:
   the world is '*a foul and pestilent congregation of vapours.*'
   man is '*this quintessence of dust?*'
   (Act 2 scene 2)

8 He reproaches himself for his inaction:
   '*O what a rogue and peasant slave am I!*'
   '*I am pigeon-livered and lack gall*'
   (Act 2 scene 2)

9 He improvises a plan, using the arrival of the Players to his
   advantage:
   '*the play's the thing*
   Wherein I'll catch the conscience of the king.'
   (Act 2 scene 2)

10 However, Hamlet is still subject to violent swings of mood
   and preoccupied with death and life's futility:
   '*To die, to sleep... 'tis a consummation devoutly to be
   wished*'
   '*conscience does make cowards of us all*'
   '*the native hue of resolution*
   Is sicklied o'er by the pale cast of thought'
   (Act 3 scene 1)

11 He is also distracted by his feelings about women and sex:
   '*why wouldst thou be a breeder of sinners?*'
   '*I have heard of your paintings, too*'
   '*To a nunnery go.*'

12 The inner play brings proof of Claudius's guilt, and elation
   for Hamlet:
   '*I'll take the ghost's word for a thousand pound.*'
   '*Now could I drink hot blood*'
   (Act 3 scene 2)

13 However, he is frustrated in his desire for revenge as he
   encounters Claudius at prayer:
   '*this is hire and salary, not revenge.*'
   '*This physic but prolongs thy sickly days.*'
   (Act 3 scene 3)

14 In the closet scene Hamlet seems to release some of the
emotional pressure inside him as he finally confronts his
mother:
'You cannot call it love, for at your age
The hey-day of the blood is tame'
'To live In the rank sweat of an enseamed bed
Stewed in corruption, honeying and making love
Over the nasty sty.'
'go not to my uncle's bed,
Assume a virtue if you have it not.'
'I essentially am not in madness,
But mad in craft.'
''Tis sport to have the engineer
Hoist with his own petar.'
(Act 3 scene 4)

15 Hamlet prepares to depart for England but the meeting
with Fortinbras's army reminds him that his task is not
complete:
'How all occasions do inform against me,
And spur my dull revenge!'
'O from this time forth,
My thoughts be bloody or be nothing worth.'
(Act 4 scene 4)

16 On his return to Denmark, Hamlet is again confronted by
death:
'Now get you to my lady's chamber, and tell her, let her
paint an inch thick, to this favour she must come.'
'I loved Ophelia, forty thousand brothers
Could not, with all their quantity of love,
Make up my sum –.'
'I'll rant as well as thou.'
(Act 5 scene 1)

17 Hamlet seems less tortured at this stage of the play.
Perhaps he is more balanced emotionally, more resigned to
life and destiny or perhaps simply weary of the struggle:
'There's a divinity that shapes our ends'
'the readiness is all'
(Act 5 scene 2)

18 At the end he does kill Claudius but it costs his own life:

'I am dead, Horatio.
Thou livest; report me and my cause aright
To the unsatisfied.'
'But I do prophesy the election lights
On Fortinbras, he has my dying voice;'
'The rest is silence.'

(Act 5 scene 2)

There will be other events and other quotations to which you will wish to refer but this process of pursuing character development through the whole play is an invaluable exercise.

Claudius

See how many 'critical moments' you can find to illustrate the following characteristics in Claudius:

- charm
- cunning
- hypocrisy
- ruthlessness.

Relationships

You can use the same approach to explore the relationships
between characters. The quotations below are all concerned
with the relation between Hamlet and Ophelia and they are
presented in chronological order. Consider what you think
each of them reveals about their relationship and what stage
each of them marks in the development of that relationship.

1 *'For Hamlet and the trifling of his favour,*
  Hold it a fashion and a toy in blood.'
  LAERTES (Act 1 scene 3)

2 *'He hath my lord of late made many tenders*
  Of his affection to me.'
  OPHELIA (Act 1 scene 3)

3 *'I would not in plain terms from this time forth*
  Have you so slander any moment leisure
  As to give words to talk with the Lord
  Hamlet.'
  POLONIUS (Act 1 scene 3)

4 *'Yea, from the table of my memory*
  I'll wipe away all trivial fond records'
  HAMLET (Act 1 scene 5)

5 *'He took me by the wrist, and held me hard;*
  Then he goes to the length of all his arm,
  And with his other hand thus o'er his brow,
  He falls to such perusal of my face
  As a would draw it.'
  OPHELIA (Act 2 scene 1)

6 *'Or if thou wilt needs marry, marry a fool for wise men know*
  well enough what monsters you make of them.'
  HAMLET (Act 3 scene 1)

7 *'And I of ladies most deject and wretched,*
  That sucked the honey of his music vows'
  OPHELIA (Act 3 scene 1)

8 *'Lady, shall I lie in your lap?'*
  'Do you think I meant country matters?'
  'It would cost you a groaning to take off mine edge.'
  HAMLET (Act 3, scene 2)

9 '*I hoped thou shouldst have been my Hamlet's wife.*'
   GERTRUDE (Act 5 scene 1)
10 '*I loved Ophelia*'
   HAMLET (Act 5 scene 1)

It is possible to build a coherent, methodical approach to characters and the relationships between them by making selections of significant quotations and using them as a kind of 'skeleton' structure on which you can build an essay.

HORATIO.

2:2 "ONE MAN PICKED ----"

HONEST
AUDIENCE CAN TRUST.
REFLECT CHORUS
RESEMBLES HAMLETS FATHER.
SETS POLITICAL SCENE.
DEPENDABLE
WELL EDUCATED.
STOICAL.
DEVOUT.
REMAINS UNCONTAMINATED.
NOT TOUCHED BY CORRUPTION.
HAMLET ELECTS HIM.
RELATIONSHIP CONTRASTS WITH OPHELIA + R + G WHO ALL
   BETRAY HAMLET.

FEW WORDS
RITT EFFECT.

TALKING TO UNTRUTH 1:2 M + B CAN'T EXAGGERATES
HOW LONG GHOST VISITED FOR.
WORDS ARE NEUTRAL
TALKS OF KING "I DID VERY WELL NOT HIM"
REFUSE → JOIN PRINCE IN DEATH.
FAITH IN GOD 1:4.
ENOBLES QUALITIES H. NOMIRES.
HOW H IS QUIET + REFLECTIVE HE CELEBRATES
HORATIOS QUALITIES.

Some issues and themes

It is possible to explore the particular issues and themes across the whole play, and the sections on revenge have been an attempt to show how this might be done by pursuing a single line of enquiry through the text. As is so often the case, this is really a matter of sifting and selecting the evidence, spotting what is relevant and shaping the material into a coherent argument.

However, there are a number of themes and issues, other than revenge, which are developed in Hamlet. Inevitably, in such a complex, rather sprawling play there will be some overlap in dealing with themes which are interwoven and interrelated.

It is also worth noting those points or passages of text which seem to come up under almost every angle of approach. They are clearly important!

'Seems, madam?' – appearance and reality

The problem of deciding what is real is particularly acute in this play, both for the characters and the audience. Few things are as they 'seem' and almost every character in the play is acting a part.

1 The Ghost
- What views are expressed about the nature of the Ghost?
- Which view do you finally accept, and why?
- Why do you think Gertrude cannot see it?

2 The court of Elsinore
- What image of the court is presented in Act 1 scene 2?
- What evidence can you find to suggest that the reality of the life at court is very different?

3 Claudius
- Claudius presents an image of personal charm and political competence. How does he do this?
- What image does Claudius present when he is praying?

- How is the 'reality' of Claudius revealed to Hamlet and to the audience?

4 Ophelia

Ophelia presents many 'faces' to the characters in the play. How is she 'seen' by each of the following:
- Polonius
- Laertes
- Gertrude
- Claudius
- Hamlet?

How do their views of Ophelia change, and why?

What is your view of the 'real' Ophelia?

Make sure that you can point to the textual evidence to support all of these viewpoints.

5 Gertrude

- How does Claudius see Gertrude? Look carefully at Act 1 scene 2 and at the 'prayer scene' in Act 3 scene 3.
- How does Gertrude see herself?
- Does her self-image change in the course of the play?
- What does Hamlet believe is the 'truth' about his mother?
- Do you share Hamlet's view of his mother?

6 Polonius

Polonius appears to be a wise and trusted counsellor and a caring father.
- What evidence can you find to support this view?
- How does Hamlet see Polonius?
- What do you think are Polonius's motives for his actions in the play?

7 Rosencrantz and Guildenstern

- What 'appearance' do they attempt to present to Hamlet?
- Is it possible that they are sincere?
- Are they really 'adders'?

8 Hamlet

The prince is perhaps the most elusive character of them all.

- How does Hamlet 'seem' to Gertrude? to Polonius? to Claudius?
- What evidence can you find that Laertes does not trust Hamlet's 'appearance'?
- At what points in the play is Hamlet 'acting' a role?
- How does Hamlet 'appear' to Ophelia at various stages in the play?

You can add to this list of 'seemers' but it is worth thinking about this issue as Hamlet in particular is faced with the difficulty of deciding what is 'real' and what 'passes show'. One way of making sense of his confusion and uncertainty is to see him as a young man grappling with things and people who are not what they 'seem'.

'Frailty, thy name is woman.' – women and sex

Attitudes to women and sexuality are expressed frequently in the play and there are some key speeches dealing with this theme. It is also worth noting the close association of lust and murder in the play.

1 Look at the Ghost's speech to Hamlet in Act 1 scene 5.
   - What is his attitude to Gertrude's sexual conduct?
   - How do language and imagery convey his attitude?
   - What exactly is her 'crime' in the Ghost's opinion?

2 Look at the speeches of Laertes and Polonius in Act 1 scene 3.
   - What attitudes to women are implied or stated here?
   - What do they suggest about masculine sexuality?
   - What effect do they have on the relationship between Hamlet and Ophelia?

3 Look at the following speeches by Hamlet:
   Act 1 scene 2 – the soliloquy beginning *'O that this too too solid flesh would melt'*
   Act 2 scene 1 – the 'nunnery' speeches to Ophelia
   Act 3 scene 2 – the obscene comments to Ophelia
   Act 4 scene 4 – the 'closet' scene

Act 5 scene 1 – the 'graveyard' scene.
- What attitudes to women and sexuality does Hamlet express in these speeches?
- Are his attitudes consistent or do they change?
- Why does Hamlet feel the way he does about sex and women?
- Do you think he has justification for his views?
- What are the consequences of his attitudes and words?
- Identify particular examples of imagery and use of language which convey Hamlet's feelings about women and sex.

4 Look at Ophelia's 'mad' speeches in Act 4 scene 5.
- What attitudes to sexual relationships can you detect in these lines?
- What is the effect of Ophelia's comments on your view of both her and Hamlet?

The conventional view of Ophelia as innocent and naive and of Gertrude as simply lustful and treacherous has been challenged by some recent criticism. For example, some 'feminist' critics have suggested that attitudes to Gertrude, notably those of Hamlet and the Ghost, are a reflection of the male desire to control women and their sexuality and that their hysterical reactions to Gertrude's sexuality reveal more about them than they do about her. Of course, this situation is mirrored in the attempts by Polonius, and even Laertes, to force Ophelia into the role of the submissive, dutiful daughter. It is outside the scope of this volume to engage in a detailed consideration of this issue but it does raise some interesting questions.

- What exactly has Gertrude done to attract such a denunciation?
- Is she guilty of incest or adultery?
- In Act I scene 2 how does she behave towards her son?
- What evidence can you find about her relationship with Claudius?
- How do you react to Hamlet's view that she should apparently refrain from all sexual activity?

- Does her reaction to Hamlet's attack on her in the closet scene affect your opinion of Gertrude?
- How does she behave after the closet scene?

'The Undiscovered Country' – Hamlet and death

Death is a major preoccupation in the play and Hamlet in particular returns again and again to the subject. He expresses a variety of attitudes to death and at different times in the play his moods range from intense fear of the unknown to seeing death as a welcome release from the agonies and injustice of life. Once again, the most helpful approach here is to identify the key speeches on which you can base further thought and discussion.

1 Look at the Ghost's speech in Act 1 scene 5.
- How does he present the experience of death and purgatory?
- What is the effect of this description of the after–life?
- How does imagery convey and reinforce his view?

2 Look at Hamlet's first soliloquy in Act 1 scene 2.
- What is his attitude towards death?
- Why does he feel this way?

3 Look at Hamlet's soliloquy in Act 2 scene 1, and compare it with his first soliloquy.
- In what ways has Hamlet changed his views on death?
- In what ways has he remained constant in his views?
- What is the consequence, according to Hamlet, of the 'dread of something after death'?

4 Look at Act 5 scene 1.
- How do the grave-diggers react to death?
- How does Hamlet react to them?
- Do you detect any change in Hamlet's views from his earlier speeches?
- Does the arrival of Ophelia's body produce any change in Hamlet's attitudes to life and death?

5 Look at Act 5 scene 2.
- What is Hamlet's mood as he prepares for the duel with Laertes?
- Do you sense any change in his feelings about the possibility of death?

It is possible to argue that Hamlet's brooding on death, and indeed his fear of death, contribute to his problems with revenge and cause him to delay. On the other hand, his disgust and disillusion with life at times tempt him towards suicide and escape from the heartache of existence.

The afterlife in *Hamlet*

When Hamlet speaks of '*the dread of something after death*' he is not merely making excuses for his inaction. When he refuses to kill Claudius because he is at prayer, possibly in the act of confessing his sins and being forgiven, Hamlet is not just putting off the moment when he will commit a crime. The idea of a continuum of existence before and after death was very real. The body would die, but the soul was immortal and would exist for ever. 'For ever' is in itself a frightening thought and one that is very difficult for us to grasp, since everything we do is finite, and eternity is infinite. The horror really begins, however, with the contemplation of an eternity of punishment. Christopher Marlowe, a playwright contemporary with Shakespeare, expresses this horror in *Dr Faustus*. Dr Faustus is a scholar who has practised magic and has sold his soul to the devil in exchange for knowledge and power. As he has to face the moment when the devil will claim his soul and it will be condemned to eternity in hell, he cries:

'*O God,*
If thou wilt not have mercy on my soul,
Yet for Christ's sake, whose blood hath ransom'd me,
Impose some end to my incessant pain;
Let Faustus live in hell a thousand years,
A hundred thousand, and at last be sav'd.
O no end is limited to damned souls.'

Hamlet has been made aware of some of the consequences of the soul's torment in his father's experience. He is not in hell, but in purgatory, which is not eternal but is still unimaginably terrible, precisely because his father is forbidden to describe it.

Centuries of discussion have taken place over the true nature of the soul. Most world religions feel that in every human being there is something – soul or spirit – which cannot be accounted for by our physical existence alone, and which seems to recognize some absolute or divinity outside itself. We find it difficult to understand how a disembodied soul can suffer torments in purgatory. Horatio, the soldiers and Hamlet see the Ghost as he was in life. Because Hamlet's father was murdered '*in the blossoms of my sins*' he had not confessed his sins and had them forgiven, nor had he been given the penance to do which would have purged them – hence his sufferings in purgatory, which sooner or later will come to an end. When he is finally admitted to heaven he will see and be with God, which those condemned to hell never will. Hamlet's reluctance to kill Claudius springs from the assumption – incorrect as we later discover – that Claudius has made his peace with God, and will not have to suffer as Hamlet's father suffers.

Shakespeare wrote *Hamlet* at the end of the sixteenth century. A few decades earlier it would have been difficult for a character to imagine, as Hamlet did, that a man could confess his sins directly to God, without the intervention of a priest and the sacrament of confession, and in effect negotiate his own salvation. There had been great upheavals in religious beliefs and in religious observance since Henry VIII in 1534 had broken with the Church of Rome, denied the Pope's supremacy and declared himself 'supreme head of the church and clergy in England'. At about the same time, in Germany, Martin Luther was challenging the sale of 'indulgences'. Those who made a contribution to church funds could receive a plenary indulgence, which was seen as a kind of spiritual credit balance which they could set against their sins in 'God's bank'. Luther saw this practice as essentially corrupt and set out to formulate a view of religion based on personal faith. Hostility to the priesthood was widespread. As Ophelia's funeral progresses with the barest ceremony, hard-won from the Church's 'rules' for a presumed suicide, Laertes's resentment against church orthodoxy boils over against the priest himself, and threatens him ('*when thou liest howling*') with hell.

Preparing for an examination

You will be expected to have a detailed and accurate knowledge of your set texts. You must have read your set texts several times and you need to know the sequence of events and the narrative of a text. The plot summaries in this edition should help you with this. It may seem rather unfair but you will get little credit in the final examination for merely 'telling the story', and simply 'going through' the narrative is seen as particularly worthless in an open-book examination. However, you will be in no position to argue a convincing case or develop a deep understanding unless you have this detailed knowledge.

The questions

A-level questions are demanding but they should always be accessible and central, a fair test of your knowledge and understanding. They are rarely obscure or marginal. There is actually a relatively small number of questions which can be asked on any text, even though the ways in which they can be worded are almost infinite. They tend to fall into quite straightforward categories or types, as outlined below.

Character

You may be asked to discuss your response to a particular character, to consider the function or presentation of a character or perhaps to compare and contrast characters.

Society

You may be asked to consider the kind of society depicted by the text or perhaps the way in which individuals relate to that society.

Themes

You may be asked to discuss the ideas and underlying issues which are explored by a text, and what are the author's concerns and interests.

Attitudes

You may be asked to consider what views or values are revealed by the text, what is valued and what is attacked.

Style or technique

You may be asked to look at the methods a writer uses to achieve particular effects. In essence, you are being asked to examine 'how' a text achieves its effects and you need to consider such matters as diction, imagery, tone and structure.

Personal response

You may be asked to give your own view of the text but this must be more than just unsupported assertion. You need to move beyond 'I think...' to a well-considered evaluation based on close reading and textual evidence. It is worth remembering that there is not an infinity of sensible responses to a text.

'Whole text' questions

These questions require you to consider the text as a whole. You need a coherent overview of the text and the ability to select appropriate detail and evidence.

'Specific' passages

These questions require close reading and analysis but sometimes the specific passage has to be related to another passage or perhaps to the whole text.

By the time you have discussed the text carefully you should be beginning to clarify and organize your response to the text as a whole. As you will have gathered from the list of types of question, most A-level questions concentrate on content and form and these are useful terms which offer you an approach and a framework within which you can prepare to write successfully.

Your first task is to establish clearly in your mind the broad issues raised by the text and the possible areas for discussion, including major characters. You need to consider and discuss some of the possible views and interpretations of these issues and lay down a sensible framework within which personal response can be convincing and well-considered. You also need to get close to the text and identify the key incidents, scenes or even quotations which will form the basis of any essay. When you come to write essays on the whole text, or even a specified passage, the appropriate textual evidence and illustrations should be noted and easily available.

A critical essay attempts to construct a clear argument based on the evidence of the text. It needs a clear sense of direction and purpose and it is better to start with a simple, coherent attitude than to ramble aimlessly or produce a shapeless answer which never gets into focus. Each paragraph should be a step in a developing argument and should engage in analysis of textual detail which is relevant to the question. You must answer the question set – as opposed to the question you wanted to be set – and you must be prepared to discuss a specific aspect of the text or approach it from a slightly new or unexpected angle. You will need to be selective and choose the material which is appropriate to the actual question. An essay which deals only in sweeping generalizations may be judged to lack detail and substance while one which gets too involved in minor details may lack direction and a conceptual framework. The ideal balance is achieved when overview and detailed knowledge combine to allow easy movement from the general to the particular, and back again.

Although different examination boards and syllabuses have their own ways of expressing them, there are basically three criteria against which your work will be judged. They are:
• knowledge and understanding
• answering the question relevantly
• written expression.

The example and commentary which follow have been designed to help you in your exploration of the text and your preparation for the examination.

Writing an essay

There is rarely a single 'right' answer to an A-level essay question, but there is not an infinite range of sensible responses to a text and any interpretation must be clearly based on close reading and supporting evidence.

This is a fairly typical A-level question:

'*Consider Laertes's contribution to the theme of revenge.*'

The first task is to establish an overview of your broad response to the question and to get clear in your own mind a line of argument which engages with the question set. This question specifically links Laertes to the wider theme of revenge. It is not asking for a character-sketch, nor is it asking for an account of every appearance made by Laertes in the play. Time is short in examinations and you will need to be carefully selective and give your essay a sharp focus on the question.

The second task is to identify where the relevant material is to be found. Laertes appears in Act 1 of the play, but is absent for the whole of Acts 2 and 3. However, when he returns to the dramatic action in Acts 4 and 5, he emerges as a major character who makes a significant contribution to the play, particularly to the theme of revenge.

This is an answer to the question, written by an A-level student. It is not the only, nor indeed the 'perfect', answer, but it is very good and it may help you to identify some of the qualities which contribute to a good essay.

'Consider Laertes's contribution to the theme of revenge.' — HAMLET

Of the various parallels between characters in 'Hamlet', perhaps that between Hamlet and Laertes is one of the most telling. From the beginning of the play we see the two in comparable situations, each young men of the court, each seeking permission to leave Elsinore and go back to

university, each spied on by Polonius, each
(it would appear) loving Ophelia, in
different ways. Therefore, when Laertes
finds himself in Hamlet's position of having
a father murdered, the audience watches with
interest to see how he will react, and how
this will compare with Hamlet's behaviour in
the same situation.

In fact, although Hamlet points out that:
'by the image of my cause I see
The portraiture of his'
Laertes's reaction to the murder of his
father is very different from Hamlet's, and
indeed he is everything which Hamlet rebukes
himself for failing to be. He forms the very
epitome of a traditional revenger, and
almost everything he does forms a contrast
with what Hamlet does not do.

Immediately as he learns of Polonius's
death, believing his murderer to be
Claudius, he returns to the court *'in a*
riotous head', having recruited *'a rabble'*,
to aid him in his revenge. Thus we see that
he finds both opportunity and means to
destroy his father's supposed murderer as
soon as he possibly can. It is sometimes
argued that Hamlet has little opportunity,
during the first two acts of the play, at
least, to confront Claudius and exact his
revenge. However, it is clear that —
particularly since he is *'loved by the*
distracted multitude' — Hamlet might have
actively created such an opportunity for
himself, just as Laertes does.

Furthermore Laertes is determined that he
will *'dare damnation'* in order to revenge
his father. This is very important when
considered in comparison with Hamlet's

soliloquy beginning, *'To be, or not to be'*, in which he confesses that *'the dread of something after death'* is, in part, what makes him *'lose the name of action'*, for again we see Hamlet's attitude to his task differs radically from that of a traditional revenger.

This is also apparent when Laertes says that he would *'cut [Hamlet's] throat I' th' church!'*, since we are immediately reminded that Hamlet refused to kill Claudius, when given the perfect opportunity, because he was in prayer. Hamlet's refusal to kill Claudius at this time (because his prayers make him *'fit and seasoned'* to go to heaven — which is hardly a fitting revenge for a man who has sent his brother to be judged with *'his crimes broad blown'*) may — if we decide that they are more than just another rationalization (an entirely debatable point in itself) — prove that Hamlet reflects more carefully than Laertes on the business of revenge and that he is more caught up in the need for a perfect and fitting revenge. Nevertheless Laertes's clear opinion that *'Revenge should have no bounds'*, and his immediate and unhesitating action, in comparison with Hamlet's continual prevarication, persuade us that he is the more effective revenger.

Laertes falls into the same category as Fortinbras, who with his *'unimproved mettle hot and full'* seeks revenge on Denmark for winning and taking control of what had been his father's lands, and Pyrrhus, who brutally kills an old and defenceless man in the name of revenge. All these characters' unhesitating and decisive action, and what seems to be their lack of fear at the consequences, throw Hamlet's indecisiveness very much into relief, for whilst he can only *'unpack [his] heart with words'*, they can *'sweep...to revenge'* as he longs to.

However, it is Claudius, not Laertes, who actually states that *'Revenge should have no bounds'*, which is not only ironic, since it is Hamlet's hesitation alone which has saved him so far, but — I feel — also has sinister undertones, since one would hardly have put such words into the mouth of the clearest villain of the play without implying that this sentiment is also, somehow, villainous. Of course, as Claudius is here manipulating Laertes's strong desire for revenge, it would be unwise to attach too much importance to this point, but it is nevertheless interesting to examine our attitude to Laertes's attitude towards revenge as opposed to Hamlet's. After all, the impetuous approach of the former allows him to believe:

> *'The people muddied,*
> *Thick and unwholesome in their thoughts and*
> *whispers.'*

Thus he promptly accuses the wrong man (Claudius, rather than Hamlet) of killing his father. Compare this with Hamlet — well aware that all is not necessarily what it seems in Denmark — who creates an elaborate plan to 'catch the conscience of the king' before he proceeds. It might also appear to the audience that Laertes's defiance of damnation is more to do with a lack of reflection on *'The undiscovered country'* than courage in facing it. After all, as Hamlet points out:

> '*the native hue of resolution*
> *Is sicklied o'er with the pale cast of*
> *thought*'

Laertes is all 'resolution', untroubled by the words and thoughts which impede Hamlet's action. (We never see Laertes in soliloquy, of course, because he is morally certain of what he must do, and does not explore the subject further.) However, we possibly feel some sympathy with the view that:

> '*blest are those*
> *Whose blood and judgement are so well*
> *commeddled*
> *That they are not a pipe for Fortune's*
> *finger.*'

Ironically, these words, spoken by Hamlet in praise of Horatio, actually describe the former in some respects, and particularly when we see him in comparison with Laertes. After all, whilst his endless reflection might appear to serve, at times, only to exacerbate and rationalize his delay, at least he can only rarely be accused of being rash. Laertes believes that, '*That drop of blood that's calm proclaims me bastard.*' However, this rage, this refusal to reason calmly and to reflect on what has happened, allows the slippery Claudius to manipulate Laertes for his own ends, leading to the treachery which destroys Claudius and Laertes themselves, and Gertrude, as well as Hamlet.

Ultimately, there is a certain nobility to be found in the exchange of forgiveness between Hamlet and Laertes (the final link between these 'parallel' characters), and the latter's assurance that:

   'Mine and my father's death come not upon thee,

   Nor thine on me!'

which is greater than Laertes's revengeful triumph over Hamlet.

This is not to say that Shakespeare's presentation of Laertes serves entirely as an indictment of the process of revenge. Both Hamlet and Laertes speak of the 'honour' of revenge, and we certainly feel, when Hamlet finally does kill Claudius, that he is 'justly served.' However, I feel that considering Laertes' contribution to the theme of revenge is only useful when seen alongside Hamlet's reaction to the same theme, and perhaps this portrayal of a traditional revenger who is rash, manipulative and finally self—destructive, allows us to see Hamlet in a more favourable light when he is unable to assume the same role as traditional revenger.

There are several points to note about this essay.

1 The opening paragraphs clearly set out the general direction the essay will take, in arguing that Laertes's contribution to the theme of revenge is to form a contrast with Hamlet which illuminates the character of Hamlet and extends our response to the problems of revenge. The overview is securely established.

2 The opening paragraphs also touch briefly on the parallels between Hamlet and Laertes but implicitly insist that the real emphasis should be placed on the behaviour of Laertes when he too is placed in the situation of having to respond to the murder of a father.

3 The paragraphs which follow then begin to explore and develop the basic point that Laertes acts as a dramatic foil to Hamlet. Each paragraph takes a key action or quotation

and, pausing to discuss and elaborate each point, moves towards the initial conclusion that Laertes is the 'more effective revenger' precisely because he is not troubled by moral or existential concerns. Fortinbras and Pyrrhus are also mentioned as examples of the active revenger.

4 The essay then begins to challenge and question the impression that Laertes is everything Hamlet should be. The use of 'however' at the beginning of the seventh paragraph signals the change in the direction of the argument and leads to the subtle point that Shakespeare is to a large extent using Laertes as an indictment of the process of revenge.

5 In assessing this essay an examiner would note the depth of knowledge and understanding, the complexity and detail in the argument and the sophistication in expression. At times, the complex argument demands a very ambitious style but control is never lost and the essay sustains the thread of argument to its conclusion.

6 You will notice how quotation is also used skilfully and purposefully in short, apt extracts which are invariably integrated into the developing argument.

OSRIC

ONLY IN ACT 5.

TAKES ON DRAMATIC FUNCTIONS OF POLONIUS.

It COURTIER FOR KING.

5:2 SHAKESPEARE USES OSRIC TO DEMONSTRATE THE WAY
The MISUSE OF LANGUAGE REFLECTS MORAL
DISORGANISATION OF KINGDOM.

Essay questions

1 Horatio describes Hamlet as '*sweet prince*'. How far do you agree with this assessment?

2 Do you think Hamlet is mad?

3 What do the soliloquies reveal about Hamlet and his state of mind?

4 Hamlet says, '*frailty, thy name is woman.*' Consider Ophelia and Gertrude in the light of this comment.

5 Do you think Claudius is a '*mighty opposite*' or '*A king of shreds and patches*'?

6 Why do you think Hamlet finds the task of revenge so difficult?

7 The play has an atmosphere of mystery and uncertainty. How far do you agree with this statement?

8 Consider the dramatic function of the Ghost in Hamlet.

9 Compare and contrast the characters of Hamlet and Laertes.

10 A critic has described Gertrude as 'weak and foolish rather than wicked'. Do you agree?

11 How far would you agree that Hamlet is more concerned about his mother's second marriage than his father's murder?

12 Hamlet describes Polonius as a '*foolish prating knave*'. Do you agree with this assessment?

13 Examine the importance of actors and acting in this play.

14 What exactly is shown to be '*rotten in the state of Denmark*'?

15 Consider the importance of Fortinbras in this play.

16 How does Shakespeare present life at the court of Elsinore?

17 Do you think Gertrude is a changed character after her confrontation with Hamlet in the 'closet' scene?

18 Consider Hamlet's attitudes to death in this play.

19 Do you have any sympathy for Rosencrantz and Guildenstern?

20 Hamlet is capable of violence; his problem is knowing where to direct that violence. How far do you agree with this comment?

Glossary

Alliteration: A figure of speech in which a number of words close to each other in a piece of writing begin with the same sound:
'Here in the cheer and comfort of our eye
Our chiefest courtier, cousin, and our son.'
(Act 1 scene 2 line 116, page 23)
Alliteration helps to draw attention to these words.

Antithesis: A figure of speech in which the writer brings two opposite or contrasting ideas up against each other:
'With an auspicious and a dropping eye,
With mirth in funeral and with dirge in marriage,
In equal scale weighing delight and dole,
Taken to wife;'
(Act 1 scene 2 line 11, page 15)

Apostrophe: When a character suddenly speaks directly to someone or something, which may or may not be present:
'O heat, dry up my brains, tears seven times salt
Burn out the sense and virtue of mine eye.'
(Act 4 scene 5 line 154, page 215)

Aside: A speech which can be long or, more usually, short, made by one of the characters for the ears of the audience alone, or for the benefit of another, named character. As with a soliloquy (see below) we rely on an aside to express the true feelings of the character. Hamlet's first words in the play are an aside, which instantly sets the tone for his relationship with his uncle:
'A little more than kin, and less than kind.'
(Act 1 scene 2 line 65, page 19)

Assonance: The repetition of vowel sounds within words in a line, sometimes for poetic effect or, as here, to reinforce a point:
'With witchcraft of his wits, with traitorous gifts –
O wicked wit and gifts that have the power
So to seduce'
(Act 1 scene 5 line 43, page 51)

Double meaning: see *Pun*

Dramatic irony: A situation in a play when the audience (and possibly some of the characters) knows something that one or more of the characters does not. An example from *Hamlet* is when Hamlet finds Claudius apparently at prayer and assumes that if he killed him now Claudius would go straight to heaven, but we know he is unable to pray:

'*and am I then revenged,*
To take him in the purging of his soul,
When he is fit and seasoned for his passage?
No.'

(Act 3 scene 3 line 84, page 167)

Epilogue: A speech at the end of the play summing it up and commenting on it; also the character who delivers such a speech.

Exeunt: A Latin word meaning 'They go away', used for the departure of characters from a scene.

Exit: A Latin word meaning 'He (or she) goes away', used for the departure of a character from a scene.

Hendiadys: A figure of speech expressed by two nouns joined by 'and' ('*but in our circumstance and course of thought*', Act 3 scene 3 line 83, page 167) rather than by an adjective and a noun ('indirect course of thought').

Hyperbole: Deliberate exaggeration, for dramatic effect.

'*Now could I drink hot blood,*'

(Act 3 scene 2 line 388, page 161)

Irony: When someone says one thing and means another. When Hamlet has killed Polonius, Claudius pretends he is sending him to England for safety's sake. Hamlet has guessed there is a more sinister reason, and indeed Claudius is planning his death:

KING	*and every thing is bent*
	For England.
HAMLET	*For England.*
KING	*Ay Hamlet.*
HAMLET	*Good.*
KING	*So is it if thou knew'st our purposes.*
HAMLET	*I see a cherub that sees them.*

(Act 4 scene 3 line 46, page 197)

There can be irony in actions as well as words. In Act 5 scene 2 the Queen takes and drinks from the poisoned cup. Claudius, who loves her, cannot stop her bringing about her death by drinking the wine he has poisoned.

There can also be unintentional irony, as when Claudius, trying to persuade Hamlet that his father's death is not unique, speaks of '*the first corse*' (Act 1 scene 2 line 105, page 21) and so unwittingly invokes the murder of Abel by Cain, just as he killed his own brother. See also *Dramatic irony*

Metaphor: A figure of speech in which a person, or thing, or idea is described as if it were something else:

(1) '*Your bait of falsehood takes this carp of truth.*'
(Act 2 scene 1 line 62, page 73)

(2) '*The serpent that did sting thy father's life*
    Now wears his crown.'
(Act 1 scene 5 line 39, page 51)

Onomatopoeia: Using words that are chosen because they mimic the sound of what is being described:
'*The graves stood tenantless, and the sheeted dead*
Did squeak and gibber in the Roman streets;'
(Act 1 scene 1 line 114, page 11)

Pastiche: A piece of writing done in imitation of the form and style of another writer or literary period.

Personification: Referring to a thing or an idea as if it were a person:
'*But look the morn in russet mantle clad*
Walks o'er the dew of yon high eastward hill.'
(Act 1 scene 1 line 166, page 15)

Play on words: see *Pun*

Pun: A figure of speech in which the writer uses a word that has more than one meaning. The puns on the word '*tender*' (meaning 'offer', 'look after' and 'present') demonstrate the self-regarding long-windedness of Polonius and at the same time ram his point home:

'*think yourself a baby,*
That you have ta'en these tenders for true pay

Which are not sterling. Tender yourself more dearly;
Or – not to crack the wind of the poor phrase
Running it thus – you'll tender me a fool.'
(Act 1 scene 3 line 105, page 39)

Simile: A comparison between two things which the writer
makes clear by using words such as 'like' or 'as':
'Make thy two eyes like stars start from their spheres,
Thy knotted and combined locks to part,
And each particular hair to stand an end,
Like quills upon the fretful porpentine.'
(Act 1 scene 5 line 18, page 49)

Soliloquy: Spoken apparently to himself or herself when a
character is alone on stage, or separated from the other
characters in some way. In *Hamlet* the soliloquies are
particularly important because, in the atmosphere of spying
and intrigue where Hamlet constantly has to watch what he
says, and in his assumed madness, it is only when he is alone
that we can hope to learn his true feelings.

OPHELIA

PASSIVE, MORE EXTREME VERSION OF GERTRUDE,
"FRAILTY THY NAME IS WOMAN" → MUM & GIRLFRIEND.
BEHAVIOR IS LINKED,
RADICALLY DIFFERENT (JULIET)
PUTS LOVE FOR FATHER FIRST (4)
DOES LITTLE TO DEVELOP HER,
NO POINT OF VIEW (39)
NO ATTEMPT TO COMMUNICATE WITH HAMLET.
PRESENTS HERSELF AS VICTIM
(FOLLOWING NUNNERY EPISODE)
HER INCAPACITY TURNS TO MADNESS.
MADNESS LESS 'REAL' THAN HAMLETS,
IT IS UNPROBLEMATIC
    UNTHREATENING,
INNOCENT VICTIM.
GERTRUDE SAYS SUICIDE IS INVOLUNTARY.

priesthood was widespread. As Ophelia's funeral progresses with the barest ceremony, hard-won from the Church's 'rules' for a presumed suicide, Laertes's resentment against church orthodoxy boils over against the priest himself, and threatens him ('*when thou liest howling*') with hell.

REVENGE TRAGEDY : ← (IS IT TRADITIONAL)

- × LEADING PLOT REVENGE   ✓
- × GHOST - WAITING FOR VENGENCE ·
- × TRAGIC OUTCOME → MULTIPLE DEATHS
- × CENTRAL REVENGE   INNOCENT DEATH
       HERO (HAMLET)   (OPHELIA)
- × DELAY ·
- × MADNESS → FEIGNED / REAL ·
- × SKULLS - COMIC SUB-PLOT
- × POISON → All DENMARK ·
       EXTENSION OF "NORM"
- × SWORD FIGHTS ·
- × IMAGERY OF DISEASE, INFECTION
- × SETTING AN ALIEN (- FOREIGN COUNTRY)

(NO MELODRAMATIC LANGUAGE → NATURAL

STRENGTHS OF ENDING.
276, 283, 275, 278.

NO SOLILOQUY IN ACT V. ABLE TO
NOW EXPRESS HIMSELF TO HORATIO.

MADNESS

"FOR TO DEFINE TRUE MADNESS --- 2:2.

FEIGNED

ANTI-DISPOSITION 1:5.
"CRAFTY MADNESS" TO R+G.
4:1 MOTHER USES TO EXCUSE
    POLONIUS' MURDER.
UNDERSTAND HIS ACTIONS.
USES IT TO GET RID OF HAMLET.
SPEAKING TO OPHELIA 2:1.

REAL.

CONTINUING MOURNING "MIND IMPATIENT."
HORATIO GIVES INFO OF FATHER RECENT DEATH 1:2.
"FATHERS DEATH"
"O'ER HASTY MARRIAGE" 2:2.
HIS "WILD + WHIRLING WORDS".
HAMLET EUPHORIC WHILST HORATIO IS DISTINCTLY COOL.
SOLILOQUIES → CONFUSSED,
        MAD.
NO SOLILOQUY IN V → SHOWS RECENT REASONING.
DISCREPANCY BETWEEN WHAT HE SAYS + SUBSEQUENT
                      BEHAVIOR.

SIGNIFICANCE OF PLAY WITHIN THE PLAY.

CRITICS PUZZLED THAT C + G WERE UNAFFECTED.

C. IS USED TO CONCEALING GUILT.

MAY BE AFFECTED.

G. HAS NO REASON TO BE AFFECTED,

LEARN IN 3:4 SHE DIDN'T KNOW THAT HUBBY WAS
    MURDERED.

PLAYER QUEEN RESPONDS TO POISONERS ADVANCES AFTER
PLAYER KING HAD DIED.

COMMON SENSE SUGGEST C + G WERE LOVERS LONG BEFORE.

MURDER OF GONZAGO.

PLAY IN 2 PARTS.

DIFFERENT FUNCTIONS.

DURING INTERVAL

C ASKED H. WHAT THE PLAY IS CALLED.

"MOUSETRAP".

3:4,184 → MOUSE IS A NICKNAME H. IMAGINES C CALLS G.

OUT TO CATCH MOTHERS CONCIENCE 1st.

FOCUS ON HER BEHAVIOR BEFORE + AFTER HUBBY'S DEATH.

ACT 5 H IS 30.

PLAY MARRIAGE 30 YRS.

INDICTMENT OF G. IN -

ANOTHER VERSION OF NUNNERY EPISODE.

"ALL BUT ONE SHALL LIVE".

CLUMSY WARNING TO C.

HIS LIFE IS IN DANGER.

2ND TIME H. HAS "REVENGE" BELLOWED INTO C. EAR.

PROVOKE C TO ACT

SO HE WON'T HAVE TO.

WHEN C RISES, UNCLEAR IF H. OR PLAY HAS UNSETTLED HIM.

HERE LATER IT'S DUE TO H. RUDENESS.

NOTHING SINISTER.

HAS NOT PROVED C IS GUILTY.

END.

H. EUPHORIA BECOMES FOR A MOMENT LIKE THE MELODRAMATIC
LANGUAGE OF LUCIANUS.

THE NEPHEW ABOUT TO KILL HIS UNCLE (394)

YET HIS NEXT MOVE IS TO VISIT HIS MUM NOT C.